Domain-driven Design with Java

Building scalable and maintainable Java applications with DDD principles

Otavio Santana

bpb

www.bpbonline.com

First Edition 2026

Copyright © BPB Publications, India

ISBN: 978-93-65894-462

LIMITS OF LIABILITY AND DISCLAIMER OF WARRANTY

To View Complete
BPB Publications Catalogue
Scan the QR Code:

Dedicated to

My beloved wife:
Poliana

About the Author

Otavio Santana is an award-winning software engineer and architect who is passionate about empowering other engineers with open-source best practices to build highly scalable and efficient software. He is a renowned contributor to the Java and open-source ecosystems and has received numerous awards and accolades for his work. Otavio's interests include history, the economy, travel, and fluency in multiple languages, all seasoned with a great sense of humor.

About the Reviewer

Karina Varela's career is focused on the technologies that connect and power enterprise software. She has deep knowledge of a large technology stack, patterns, and best practices, especially in the scope of Java enterprise solutions. This background gives her a strong foundation for shaping mission-critical solutions, from the early design stages to architectural definitions and execution on cloud and container infrastructure platforms.

This deep specialization in application platforms, combined with active involvement in open source, is the base of her involvement in critical enterprise solutions for over a decade at Red Hat and IBM.

As a published author and active contributor to many communities (e.g., coordinator of SouJava), her work has always been about building robust technology and empowering developers with open knowledge.

This background was the natural foundation for her most recent work as a co-founder of Aletyx, where she is building the next generation of intelligent automation, grounded in years of hands-on, real-world experience and open-source leadership.

Acknowledgment

I want to express my deepest gratitude to my family, friends, and the Java community for the incredible support in allowing me to dedicate time to creating this book.

I am also grateful to BPB Publications for their guidance and expertise in bringing this book to fruition. It was a long journey of revising this book, with the valuable participation and collaboration of reviewers, technical experts, and editors.

Finally, I would like to thank all the readers who have taken an interest in my book and for their support in making it a reality. Your encouragement has been invaluable.

Preface

For a long time, I have been in several conferences talking about one of my favorite topics: software design and DDD. As usual, I start asking how many have heard about DDD? The answer is unanimous, the vote changes when I go to the second question: How many of you have used DDD properly? The answer usually goes to none of the people or only a few people. So, why do we have a vast number of people knowing DDD, yet only an exception can apply it correctly? To solve this point, I wrote this book to help you.

Many teams struggle to implement DDD effectively in real-world projects. The root of the issue is quite simple: although these patterns are well recognized, their purpose is frequently misunderstood or overlooked. This book aims to bridge that gap, not only by explaining what DDD is but also by guiding how to apply it effectively, starting with the reasoning behind it.

This book begins by exploring the foundational reasons for the existence of DDD. By understanding its strategic principles, developers can avoid common—and often costly— implementation mistakes. Many books on DDD assume that readers are already convinced of its value; this one takes a step back to build that foundational understanding, incorporating insights from other authors and complementing them with practical examples and real-life experiences. This book avoids dogma, combining established theory with modern use cases to help you make better design decisions tailored to your specific context.

To guide you through this journey, the book is structured into three parts. The first part lays the strategic foundations of DDD, emphasizing the importance of comprehending the domain, collaborating with business experts, and organizing systems using concepts like bounded contexts and context maps. This section is intentionally placed at the outset because mastering strategic DDD is essential for preventing misalignment and over-engineering later on.

Once that foundation is established, the second part transitions into the tactical aspects of DDD, where design meets implementation. You will learn how to model aggregates, encapsulate business rules, and apply DDD across various architectural styles, including monoliths, microservices, and distributed systems. This section also features a chapter focused on testing and validation, helping you maintain your model's integrity and expressiveness over time.

The final part of the book synthesizes all the concepts by examining how to integrate DDD into real-world enterprise environments using tools like Jakarta EE, Spring, Eclipse MicroProfile, and Quarkus. It also addresses advanced design practices, including code-level decisions and anti-patterns to avoid. The book concludes with a reflection on domain storytelling—a technique designed to help teams build shared understanding and bridge the gap between business and technology.

Chapter 1: Understanding Domain-driven Design- The journey begins with an introduction to domain-driven design itself—its history, motivation, and the fundamental problem it aims to solve: the disconnect between business needs and software delivery. This chapter lays the groundwork by showing how DDD encourages communication between technical and business teams and how it helps create models that are both expressive and aligned with the core domain.

Chapter 2: Strategic DDD Concepts- This chapter deepens this understanding by exploring strategic DDD concepts. It introduces the most forgotten part and the pitfall of DDD, the strategic level. Indeed, that is usually the biggest mistake on DDD, where we will explore several strategic DDD concepts, such as bounded context, map, and so on. Together, these tools help teams manage complexity and create clearer, more purposeful systems.

Chapter 3: Tactical DDD Implementation- In this chapter, we move into tactical implementation. Here, the building blocks of DDD—entities, value objects, aggregates, services, and repositories—are not just explained but illustrated through practical Java code. This chapter connects the abstract concepts of the previous sections to concrete programming practices, showing how to bring domain logic to life while keeping it decoupled from infrastructure concerns.

Chapter 4: Testing and Validating DDD Applications- This chapter follows naturally by addressing how to validate and protect the domain logic through testing. It goes beyond unit testing to include integration tests and architectural validation using tools like ArchUnit and jMolecules. It also shows how testing in a DDD context reinforces the domain model as living documentation and a source of truth about business behavior.

Chapter 5: DDD in Microservices, Monoliths, and Distributed Systems- DDD is agnostic of Software architecture; indeed, it can apply to several architectural structures, such as the classic and straightforward monolith and distributed system. This chapter covers several architecture choices and explains how to use them on DDD.

Chapter 6: Integrating DDD with Clean Architecture- This chapter explores the synergy between DDD and Clean Architecture. Rather than treating them as separate disciplines, it demonstrates how they complement each other by reinforcing the separation of concerns and ensuring that domain logic remains at the core. You will learn how to structure applications to promote flexibility, maintainability, and clear boundaries between the domain and external systems.

Chapter 7: DDD and Data Modeling - Databases are the heart of any modern application, where we need to consider modeling on SQL and NoSQL databases; furthermore, combining them with DDD. Handling data modeling with the domain is the core component and scope of this chapter, where it examines the impact of work on two different paradigms, one from the database and one from the application.

Chapter 8: Enterprise Java with Jakarta EE- This chapter brings the conversation into enterprise Java, focusing on Jakarta EE. It introduces how recent Jakarta specifications, including Jakarta Data, support DDD-friendly designs.

Chapter 9: Enterprise Java with Spring- This chapter introduces a practical sample of how to use DDD with the Spring platform, focusing on the most popular components, such as Spring Data and Spring Boot, and code structure to apply to DDD.

Chapter 10: Eclipse MicroProfile and Domain-driven Design - This chapter introduces Eclipse MicroProfile and explains how it empowers cloud-native DDD applications. With features like configuration, fault tolerance, and observability, MicroProfile helps developers build systems that are both resilient and centered on business logic. The chapter walks through structuring applications that remain modular and expressive in dynamic environments.

Chapter 11: Quarkus and Domain-driven Design- In this chapter, the spotlight shifts to Quarkus—a modern Java framework designed for high performance and developer productivity. The chapter explains how to use Quarkus extensions, reactive programming, and efficient dependency injection to implement DDD in lightweight, container-friendly applications without sacrificing design quality.

Chapter 12: Code Design and Best Practices for DDD- This chapter focuses on design quality itself. It discusses best practices for maintaining an expressive and sustainable codebase, including how to avoid anemic domain models, when to apply the Builder pattern or fluent APIs, and how to structure code for long-term readability and collaboration. It also offers practical advice for refactoring and evolving your domain model responsibly.

Chapter 13: Final Considerations- This chapter concludes the book and explains how to extract the strategic domain and start to implement it using the most ancient technology: storytelling. This technique brings developers and domain experts into closer alignment by visually modeling processes in a narrative form. By using storytelling, teams can uncover hidden assumptions, clarify terminology, and ensure that the software being built truly represents the business it serves.

Throughout this book, the goal is to demystify DDD and equip you with the tools and mindset to apply it in real-world Java projects. Whether you are designing a system from scratch or refactoring a legacy codebase, each chapter builds toward helping you create software that speaks the language of the domain—and delivers real value.

Code Bundle and Coloured Images

Please follow the link to download the
Code Bundle and the *Coloured Images* of the book:

https://rebrand.ly/c46852

The code bundle for the book is also hosted on GitHub at
https://github.com/bpbpublications/Domain-driven-Design-with-Java.
In case there's an update to the code, it will be updated on the existing GitHub repository.

We have code bundles from our rich catalogue of books and videos available at
https://github.com/bpbpublications. Check them out!

Errata

We take immense pride in our work at BPB Publications and follow best practices to ensure the accuracy of our content to provide with an indulging reading experience to our subscribers. Our readers are our mirrors, and we use their inputs to reflect and improve upon human errors, if any, that may have occurred during the publishing processes involved. To let us maintain the quality and help us reach out to any readers who might be having difficulties due to any unforeseen errors, please write to us at: errata@bpbonline.com

Your support, suggestions and feedbacks are highly appreciated by the BPB Publications' Family.

At www.bpbonline.com, you can also read a collection of free technical articles, sign up for a range of free newsletters, and receive exclusive discounts and offers on BPB books and eBooks. You can check our social media handles below:

Instagram

Facebook

Linkedin

YouTube

Get in touch with us at: business@bpbonline.com for more details.

Piracy

If you come across any illegal copies of our works in any form on the internet, we would be grateful if you would provide us with the location address or website name. Please contact us at business@bpbonline.com with a link to the material.

If you are interested in becoming an author

If there is a topic that you have expertise in, and you are interested in either writing or contributing to a book, please visit www.bpbonline.com. We have worked with thousands of developers and tech professionals, just like you, to help them share their insights with the global tech community. You can make a general application, apply for a specific hot topic that we are recruiting an author for, or submit your own idea.

Reviews

Please leave a review. Once you have read and used this book, why not leave a review on the site that you purchased it from? Potential readers can then see and use your unbiased opinion to make purchase decisions. We at BPB can understand what you think about our products, and our authors can see your feedback on their book. Thank you!

For more information about BPB, please visit www.bpbonline.com.

Join our Discord space

Join our Discord workspace for latest updates, offers, tech happenings around the world, new releases, and sessions with the authors:

https://discord.bpbonline.com

Table of Contents

CHAPTER 1

Understanding Domain-driven Design

Introduction

The need for software became a strategic and integral element of business success, permeating every layer of modern organizations. Companies increasingly depend on technology to enhance efficiency, deliver value, and remain competitive. This growing reliance highlights the importance of development practices that can tightly align software solutions with business objectives. **Domain-driven design (DDD)** emerges as a response to this need, offering a straightforward methodology to bridge the persistent gap between business expectations and technical implementation. It enables teams to deliver software that consistently supports and advances business outcomes with precision and clarity.

As business environments become more dynamic and multifaceted, the challenge of translating domain knowledge into effective software solutions becomes increasingly evident. A frequent issue lies in the misalignment between what stakeholders envision and what software ultimately delivers. Industry observations point to critical failure points in many software projects: excessive focus on planning and design without validation, ambiguous or shifting client expectations, unforeseen complexity during implementation, and weak collaboration between product and engineering teams. These problems often result in technical efforts that diverge significantly from business goals.

The paradox of choice further exacerbates the disconnect in today's tooling landscape. While development teams have access to an unprecedented range of frameworks and technologies, the sheer number of options can lead to decision paralysis, inefficiency, and a loss of focus on what truly matters. In such a context, complexity becomes a liability rather than a strength, making it increasingly difficult to maintain clarity and business alignment throughout the development process.

It is where DDD practices take on their relevance. By grounding development in the business domain and encouraging intentional, collaborative modeling, DDD provides a framework for delivering solutions that reflect the actual needs of stakeholders. Rather than prescribing a specific architecture or stack, DDD promotes clarity, shared understanding, and long-term maintainability, regardless of technical constraints.

This chapter introduces the rationale behind DDD, explaining why it matters and what problems it aims to solve. It lays the groundwork for the deeper technical and strategic topics that follow. Mastery of DDD involves more than learning patterns—it begins with understanding its principles, particularly the strategic and tactical dimensions that guide development from discovery to implementation. This chapter serves as a first step in that journey.

Structure

In this chapter, we will explore the following topics:

- Importance of domain-driven design
- Connecting business goals with technical implementation
- Core concepts and methodologies

Objectives

This chapter establishes the foundation for understanding why DDD is essential in software development, focusing on the challenges that often lead to project failures, such as misalignment between business and technical teams, unclear client expectations, and unnecessary complexity. By exploring the principles of DDD, this chapter demonstrates how it provides a structured approach to bridging the gap between business and technology, fostering collaboration, and ensuring that software solutions align with real-world needs. Rather than diving into implementation details, this chapter introduces the reasoning behind DDD, setting the stage for deeper discussions on its strategic and tactical applications throughout the book.

Importance of domain-driven design

DDD can address common challenges that often derail software projects by:

- **Aligning business and technical teams**: The practices presented by DDD can clarify business needs and ensure the technical implementation delivers on those requirements and expectations.

- **Clarifying client expectations**: Reducing misunderstandings and vague requirements leads to software that truly meets stakeholders' goals.

- **Simplifying the solution's design**: Breaking down the complexity of systems into manageable parts can reduce the complexity that often feels overwhelming, slow down the progress, and make long-term maintenance difficult. With the right set of practices at hand, teams can benefit from simpler designs, therefore, less daunting maintenance of the software.

- **Improving cross-team collaboration**: When business and technical teams do not work closely together, key business insights may be lost in translation. With DDD, everyone can collaborate and start working towards the same objectives.

By grounding software development in the business domain and nurturing an ongoing close collaboration between technical and business teams, DDD practices can lead your teams to have every class, method, and variable properly aligned with the core business needs, finally giving you control over the final product's value and its alignment with stakeholder expectations.

One of DDD's most significant advantages is its ability to manage complexity. In a world where the number of software development tools and frameworks is ever-growing, it is just a matter of time until developers start feeling overwhelmed by choices and lose sight of their business goals. DDD counters this with a structured approach that allows breaking down complex business domains into manageable and focused subdomains. In this way, software becomes easier to understand and maintain while ensuring the development process remains aligned with the overarching business strategy.

Moreover, DDD emphasizes the importance of a shared language, the *Ubiquitous Language,* used consistently between business and technical teams. A common vocabulary can minimize misunderstandings and drive everyone involved in the project to work towards the same goals. The development process is transformed into a collaborative cross-team effort, where business and IT can create and deliver solutions that accurately reflect the business's needs and objectives.

Now, looking into DDD instrumental adoption in real-world scenarios, we can refer to industries where precision and teams' alignment are critical. For example, in the banking industry, where compliance and accuracy are paramount, DDD ensures that loan management systems and trading platforms are designed to meet both regulatory requirements and the specific needs of financial professionals. In the e-commerce space, DDD enables the development of platforms that can quickly adapt to changing market demands while maintaining a seamless customer experience.

Ultimately, DDD's importance lies in its ability to bring clarity and focus to the software development process. By ensuring the software reflects and supports the business's strategic goals, DDD increases the solutions' overall quality and business value. Knowing the value delivered by your work can inspire you to implement DDD effectively in your projects. In the following section, let us explore how DDD helps bridge the gap between business and technical teams, providing you with the foundational knowledge that can improve cross-team collaboration throughout your projects.

Connecting business goals with technical implementation

One of the biggest challenges in software development is the gap between business goals and technical implementation. This gap often leads to misunderstandings, conflicting priorities, and software failing to meet the target. DDD can overcome this challenge by integrating domain experts into the development process.

The core idea of DDD is to have software development closely aligned with the business domain it supports. Instead of relying on a large number of documents that describe requirements, developers can work directly with the business experts (a.k.a. domain experts), where they can learn firsthand about the business's core activities, challenges, and goals. This close collaboration is a critical practice that allows domain experts to provide crucial insights for better, informed, technical decision-making.

A key way to bridge the communication gap is by using a common language, a vocabulary shared by both teams, the Ubiquitous Language. In collaboration, teams define and agree to these terms, which are later used consistently throughout the project phases, from initial discussions to implementation, validation, and final deliveries. It is an approach that minimizes misinterpretation, saving time by reducing errors and incorrect deliveries that do not meet its requirements.

DDD also encourages teams to structure software systems around the business domain by designing the code in a way that mirrors the structure of the business itself. This approach makes the software more intuitive and maintainable, simplifying potential changes in the industry to be reflected in the software.

Empowering organizations to create technically good software closely aligned with corporate strategic goals can be made possible by using DDD practices to bridge the business and technical divide. As a result, more effective, efficient, and valuable software solutions that deliver tangible benefits to the business can be created.

In the next section of this chapter, we will break down the core concepts and methodologies of DDD and provide a better understanding of how to apply the theory in your software projects.

Core concepts and methodologies

Before going into the depths of DDD, we must first break down the main concepts and their meanings.

The **domain** refers to the specific subject matter or knowledge area we aim to translate into code. The size or complexity of a domain is not a problem, as we can apply the *Divide and Conquer*[7] principle to break complex domains down into smaller, more comprehensible subsets.

The following figure illustrates this *divide and conquer* approach in software development. It visually represents how knowledge within software development can be broken down into various domains, such as databases, documentation, and architecture, with further subdivisions into subdomains like SQL and NoSQL. This visual breakdown helps clarify how DDD encourages understanding and managing complexity by focusing on specific business domains.

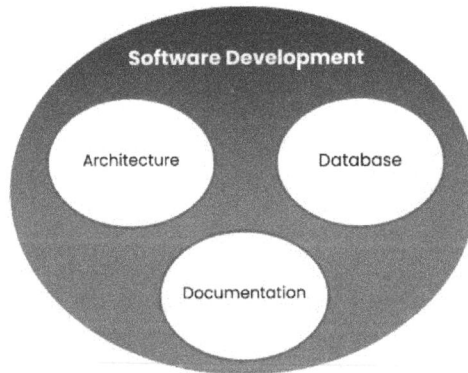

Figure 1.1: *Software development as a domain*

In the context of DDD, the business domain is the company's primary activity area, reflected by its core offering value. For example, *Starbucks* is primarily associated with coffee, while Amazon operates in multiple domains, such as retail and cloud computing. Companies can evolve, changing or expanding their business domains over time.

To manage a domain's complexity, subdivide it into subdomains. These can be further categorized into core, supporting, and generic subdomains.

Given the limited knowledge of software engineers about the client's business, the domain expert plays a crucial role. The domain expert deeply understands the business intricacies, details that naturally become requirements in their software.

Note: **The final term, 'Design', can be tricky to define, often leading to confusion with software architecture. Classic texts like The Fundamentals of Software Architecture[10] describe architecture as the stuff or design that is hard to change, but this is still an abstract concept because what is hard to change can vary. Neal Ford's book, Head First in Software Architecture[11], offers a more nuanced view, defining architecture and design along a spectrum, where design is about making decisions that shape the structure and organization of a software system to manage complexity and create a coherent, maintainable architecture.**

The following figure demonstrates the spectrum of decisions that stem from software architecture to design. It represents the close connection between design and architecture, and how design decisions can either be an easier definition or how they can become intrinsic to the core structure of a software system.

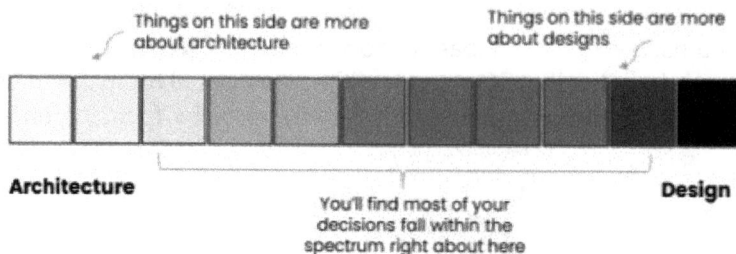

Figure 1.2: The architecture vs design spectrum

Considering this, we can define DDD as making *intentional* decisions about a software system's structure and organization, aiming to extract and translate business knowledge into code.

DDD is language-agnostic and can be adopted for solutions built with any programming language, paradigm, or framework. Although commonly associated with **object-oriented programming (OOP)** and Java, DDD practices also fit any other language chosen based on a project's needs.

TIP: **This book is not intended to replace classic literature on DDD, but rather to complement it with practical guidance. Foundational works like Domain-Driven Design: Tackling Complexity in the Heart of Software by Eric Evans[7] and Implementing Domain-Driven Design by Vaughn Vernon[8] are essential reads, even if they seem challenging.**

DDD has two major components: strategy and tactics. Both are essential to ensuring good technical quality and proper business alignment. Let us explore the differences between these two aspects and how they interact.

Strategic aspect of DDD

DDD serves as the foundation upon which all development efforts are built, with a focus on deepening the understanding of the business, its core domain, and subdomains that altogether make up its operations.

Strategy in DDD is about looking at the big picture, identifying the most critical areas of the business that should be prioritized and reflected in the software. This requires not only collaboration but a partnership with domain experts, who can convey the complexities that need to be captured in the system. A strategic approach is what enables every decision during the development process to be backed by a solid, thorough understanding of the business context. It guides the overall software project's structure and direction.

Tactical aspect of DDD

The tactical aspect of DDD involves the practical application of strategic insights into the code.

Once the business domains and subdomains are clearly defined, and the Ubiquitous Language (the domain's terminology and key concepts) is established, the tactical side of DDD comes into play. It includes implementing specific design patterns and coding practices that can bring the strategic vision to life through the software. Tactics ensure that the software architecture aligns with the business model, as the domain's abstract concepts are translated into concrete, functional system components. Standard definitions of the DDD strategy are accurately represented through actionable tasks, such as creating entities, value objects, aggregates, and repositories.

When combined, strategy and tactics in DDD create a cohesive approach to software development. This approach is not just a choice but a necessity in DDD. Strategy provides the overarching vision and ensures that the software aligns with the business's needs, while tactics handle the practicalities of translating that vision into a working system. Both are essential; without a solid strategic foundation, the software may not adequately address the business's core challenges; without effective tactics, even the best strategic plans can fail in execution. By integrating both aspects, DDD enables the creation of software that is both technically robust and highly relevant to the business.

Tip: **As explained in A Philosophy of Software Design[12], a strategic software engineer understands that software development goes beyond writing code. In contrast, focusing solely on tactics can lead to more harm than good, earning the moniker of a Tactical Tornado.**

While it is easy for software engineers to get excited about the tactical side of DDD, it is important to remember that an effective implementation must begin with the strategy. DDD aims to extract and encode business knowledge into software, making strategy the crucial first step. Throughout the book, we will explore the core strategy and tactics knowledge that can bring your DDD practices to the next level.

Conclusion

This chapter tackled the essential challenge of ensuring software development meets client and stakeholder expectations. By exploring the core principles of DDD, we showed how this approach aligns software with business goals. We highlighted the crucial role of understanding the domain, making intentional design decisions, and the strategic foundation necessary for successful DDD implementation. The key points from this chapter include how DDD ensures alignment between development and business needs, the role of domain and design in translating business knowledge into software, and the importance of collaboration between business and technical teams.

The next chapter will dive into *strategic DDD*, exploring how to effectively identify and categorize domains and subdomains. This strategic insight will provide the tools to make informed, business-aligned decisions, ensuring that your DDD efforts deliver real value to the client.

Points to remember

- **DDD focuses on business alignment**: The primary goal of DDD is to ensure that software development aligns with business objectives and delivers real value.

- **Common project failures stem from misalignment**: Issues such as unclear client expectations, poor collaboration, and overcomplicated designs often result in software that does not meet business needs.

- **The business domain is at the core of DDD**: Software should be structured around the actual business domain, using concepts and language that reflect real-world operations.

- **Collaboration is key**: Effective communication between business and technical teams, facilitated by a shared *Ubiquitous Language*, reduces misunderstandings and improves software outcomes.

- **DDD is strategic and tactical**: The strategic side focuses on understanding domains and subdomains, while the tactical side involves implementing patterns and structures that reflect business needs.

- **Complexity should be managed, not increased**: DDD helps break down complex systems into manageable parts, ensuring that software remains adaptable, maintainable, and aligned with evolving business needs.

- **This chapter sets the foundation for DDD**: Rather than covering every detail, it introduces the reasoning behind DDD, preparing you for a deeper exploration of its strategic and tactical applications.

Multiple choice questions

1. **What is the primary challenge that DDD aims to address?**

    a. Reducing the cost of software development

    b. Aligning software development with business goals

    c. Improving the speed of software delivery

    d. Increasing the technical complexity of software projects

    e. Enhancing the aesthetic design of software interfaces

2. **Which of the following is not a key focus of DDD discussed in this chapter?**

   a. Domain

   b. Design

   c. Tactical implementation

   d. Strategic foundation

   e. Aesthetic user interface design

3. **Why is having a strategic foundation in DDD essential?**

   a. It helps reduce the cost of software tools.

   b. It ensures the software architecture is complex to change.

   c. It aligns software solutions closely with business objectives.

   d. It focuses solely on technical aspects of development.

   e. It eliminates the need for domain experts.

4. **In DDD, why is collaboration between business and technical teams crucial?**

   a. To increase the complexity of the project

   b. To ensure that the software is delivered on time

   c. To foster a shared understanding and language, reduce unnecessary complexity, and ensure that the software delivers what the business truly needs

   d. To reduce the number of technical resources required and deliver what the business truly needs without the extra complexity

   e. To allow technical teams to make all decisions independently

5. **What is one of the main roles of the domain expert in DDD?**

   a. To write the code for the software

   b. To provide deep business knowledge that informs the development process

   c. To manage the technical resources of the project

   d. To design the user interface of the software

   e. To create detailed software architecture diagrams

Answers

Question number	Answer option letter
1.	b.
2.	e.

3.	c.
4.	d.
5.	b.

References

1. *Sinek, Simon. Start with Why: How Great Leaders Inspire Everyone to Take Action, 2009.*

2. *McAfee, Andrew. Now Every Company Is A Software Company, Forbes Techonomy, 2011.*

3. *Quidgest. Every Business Is a Software Business, Quidgest Articles, n.d.*

4. *Forbes Technology Council. 16 Obstacles To A Successful Software Project (And How To Avoid Them), Forbes, 2022.*

5. *Schwartz, Barry. The Paradox of Choice: Why More Is Less, 2004.*

6. *Krill, Paul. Complexity Is Killing Software Developers, InfoWorld, 2012.*

7. *Evans, Eric. Domain-Driven Design: Tackling Complexity in the Heart of Software, 2003.*

8. *Vernon, Vaughn. Implementing Domain-Driven Design, 2013.*

9. *Richards, Mark & Ford, Neal. Fundamentals of Software Architecture: An Engineering Approach, 2020.*

10. *Ford, Neal. Software Architecture: The Hard Parts, 2021.*

11. *Ousterhout, John. A Philosophy of Software Design, 2018.*

Join our Discord space

Join our Discord workspace for latest updates, offers, tech happenings around the world, new releases, and sessions with the authors:

https://discord.bpbonline.com

CHAPTER 2
Strategic DDD Concepts

Introduction

It is common for developers to concentrate predominantly on technical implementation, even when adopting **domain-driven design** (**DDD**). While essential, this focus can lead to overlooking foundational strategic elements and, as a consequence, result in misaligned and flawed software design. Skipping the initial critical steps can set the entire development process toward failure, as the design may require extra effort to align with the core business requirements and domain complexities.

This chapter explores the often overlooked yet essential aspect of DDD: strategic design. We will explore core concepts, such as bounded contexts, context mapping, and domain events, laying the groundwork for an effective DDD implementation.

Structure

In this chapter, we will explore the following topics:

- Domains and subdomains
- Understanding bounded contexts
- Context mapping techniques
- Aligning business strategy with software design

Objectives

This chapter aims to provide a strategic understanding of DDD by exploring how to structure complex systems using bounded contexts and context-mapping techniques. By defining clear boundaries within a domain and establishing effective relationships between contexts, developers can create scalable and maintainable architectures that align with business goals. This chapter will help readers grasp how strategic DDD principles shape both system design and team collaboration, laying the foundation for a more cohesive and adaptable software architecture.

Domains and subdomains

Developers who claim to embrace DDD often misapply its principles given a misunderstanding of fundamental goals and processes.

A comprehensive view of the problem domain is non-negotiable; it is the cornerstone of successful development. This initial strategic effort of understanding the domain and its subdomains is where DDD truly begins. It is not about jumping into code or choosing technical patterns—it is about aligning everyone involved around a shared comprehension of the business. This includes identifying the core domain, where the company's unique value lies, the supporting subdomains that enable core operations, and the generic subdomains that are necessary but not differentiators. Mapping these areas requires input from domain experts who have a deep understanding of the business, product stakeholders who define the vision, and engineers who will translate that knowledge into software. When this collaborative exploration is skipped or done in isolation, the resulting system may be technically well-built but disconnected from the organization's actual needs and goals.

The steps to understanding the business domains and their subdomains are as follows:

- The business domain encompasses a company's core operations, divided into specific subdomains.

- The core subdomain distinctly sets the company apart from its competitors, while generic subdomains are common across industries and do not offer any competitive advantage.

- Supporting subdomains enhances the main business activities but does not provide a direct edge.

The following table compares the three types of subdomains—core, supporting, and generic—using practical examples to illustrate their distinct roles. Each subdomain can be treated as a strategic sector within the organization, contributing in different ways to drive the company forward. The comparison highlights two key dimensions: the complexity of the business logic and the level of business differentiation, which refers to the extent to which a subdomain contributes to the company's unique value proposition and competitive advantage in the market. In this view, business differentiation is not about how different one subdomain is from another internally, but how critical it is to what makes the company stand out externally. Although not all subdomains carry the same strategic weight, each plays a vital role in enabling the organization to operate effectively and achieve its objectives.

Subdomain type	Role	Business differentiation	Complexity of business logic	Example
Core subdomain	Unique to the company, defining its identity and competitive advantage	High	High	A bank's risk assessment engine
Generic subdomain	Can be common across other companies, standard business activities	Low	High	Payroll processing system
Supporting subdomain	Supports core business activities without providing a direct competitive advantage	Medium	Varies	Customer service management tools

Table 2.1: Types of subdomains

This table visually represents the differences between these subdomain types, clarifying how each contributes to the overall architecture. The intersection between supporting and generic subdomains represents a grey area where the roles may overlap, depending on the specific context.

The following figure represents the interplay between the three types of subdomains regarding business differentiation and the complexity of business logic:

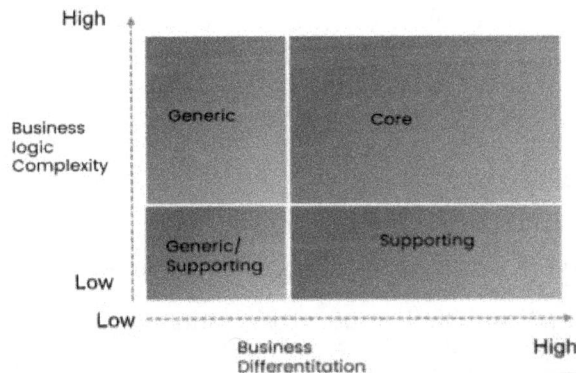

Figure 2.1: The domains and the business logic vs. business differentiation

Understanding the differences between types of domains is essential for correctly applying strategic DDD principles to manage business complexity.

Example scenario with EcoTrack Logistics

Before presenting the details of EcoTrack, readers are encouraged to exercise their analytical skills by abstracting domain insights from the business context. The objective is to identify the core domain, supporting subdomains, and generic subdomains based on the information provided in the business overview. This exercise reinforces the ability to recognize domain boundaries and understand their respective roles within a realistic scenario. The identified subdomains will be presented immediately following the overview for comparison.

Consider a fictitious organization called *EcoTrack Logistics*, founded to transform the logistics industry through sustainable operations. EcoTrack emerged from the growing need for greener transportation solutions, aiming to deliver eco-friendly logistics services that meet and exceed industry standards for sustainability.

At the heart of EcoTrack's operations is the eco-friendly route optimization system. This advanced algorithm, designed to minimize carbon emissions and fuel consumption by analyzing real-time data like traffic conditions and weather patterns, distinguishes EcoTrack in a competitive market. This innovation has positioned EcoTrack as a leader in green logistics, demonstrated by a 25% reduction in delivery-related emissions for a significant e-commerce partner within just one year.

EcoTrack efficiently manages its fleet under the *standard fleet management* subdomain, supporting this core innovation. This subdomain handles essential yet routine tasks such as vehicle maintenance scheduling, GPS tracking, and driver management. While these operations are standard across the industry, EcoTrack's dedication to executing them efficiently ensures a consistently high level of service, reinforcing the company's operational excellence.

In addition to its logistical prowess, EcoTrack emphasizes building strong customer relationships, which are managed through the **customer relationship management (CRM)** subdomain. The CRM system enhances client satisfaction by offering real-time shipment tracking, personalized updates, and responsive support. Although this subdomain does not directly drive logistical innovations, it is crucial in maintaining customer loyalty and sustaining overall business success.

EcoTrack focuses on delivering precision and efficiency in sustainable logistics solutions by structuring its operations into these distinct subdomains.

The following are the identified domain and subdomain types:

- **Core subdomain**: Eco-friendly route optimization.
- **Generic subdomain**: Standard fleet management.
- **Supporting subdomain**: CRM.

The following figure illustrates this structure to support the understanding of the domains:

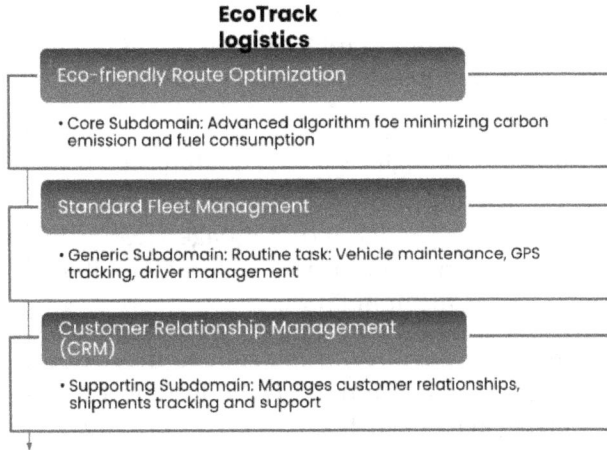

EcoTrack logistics

Eco-friendly Route Optimization

• Core Subdomain: Advanced algorithm foe minimizing carbon emission and fuel consumption

Standard Fleet Managment

• Generic Subdomain: Routine task: Vehicle maintenance, GPS tracking, driver management

Customer Relationship Management (CRM)

• Supporting Subdomain: Manages customer relationships, shipments tracking and support

Figure 2.2: The eco-friendly domains representation

This fictional company offers a practical example for better understanding and applying the concepts of domains and their types. As we continue, our next step will be to explore the idea of bounded contexts, which will build upon our understanding of domains and subdomains and provide further clarity on managing different parts of the domain model effectively. Understanding the connection between bounded context, language, and domains can enable you to structure and manage complexities effectively through clearly defined boundaries.

Understanding bounded contexts

In DDD, the term *domain* refers to the *problem domain,* which encompasses the specific issues the software addresses. *Vaughn Vernon,* a veteran software craftsman and thought leader in simplifying software design and implementation, distinguishes the *problem space,* where business challenges are identified, from the *solution space.*

Bounded context derives from the complexities associated with communication. Effective communication is non-negotiable when translating domain knowledge into software. A Ubiquitous Language must be established to ensure that all team members, developers, domain experts, and stakeholders thoroughly understand the domain. This shared language evolves as new insights are gained through collaboration with domain experts.

Tip: **To check if you are on the right path when determining the project's Ubiquitous Language, the team's guidepost, try articulating a business concept: If you can communicate it clearly, you are on the right track. If you cannot clearly explain a concept commonly used in the domain, it is a sign that you should revisit your domain model in collaboration with the experts.**

Just as in natural language, where a single word can have multiple meanings depending on the context, the same applies to the Ubiquitous Language in a domain. For instance, the word *Ajax* could refer to a sports team, a cleaning product, or a web development technique, depending on the context. Similarly, in a domain, a term might have different meanings in different contexts, or other terms might describe the same concept. This complexity leads us to the concept of bounded contexts.

A **bounded context** is a distinct domain segment within which a particular subset of the Ubiquitous Language is consistently used. It is a way of dividing the domain into smaller, manageable sections, each with its model and language clearly defined by its boundaries. Each bounded context has its name and is part of the Ubiquitous Language, simplifying management and reasoning about the domain.

Bounded contexts do not need to be entirely independent; they often have relationships with other contexts. These relationships can influence the technical solution (how systems will interact) and the development phase (how teams will collaborate).

One of the simplest ways to identify relationships between bounded contexts is to classify them as upstream or downstream contexts. Imagine contexts as cities along a river: Upstream cities influence what flows downstream. Some of what flows downstream is valuable, and downstream cities must retrieve it. This analogy helps in understanding how changes or information flow between contexts.

The relationships between contexts can be represented graphically using a dependency diagram, where arrows point from downstream contexts to upstream contexts or denote their roles with **upstream (U)** and **downstream (D)**:

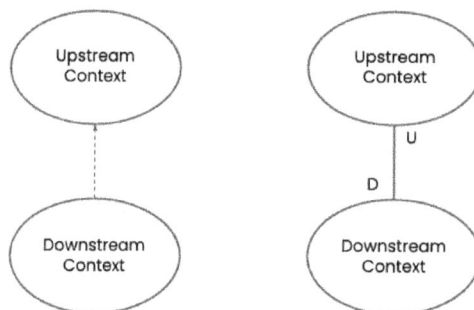

Figure 2.3: Bounded context diagram sample

Once the contexts and their relationships are identified, the next step is to decide how to integrate them. This involves answering the following key questions:

- How will technical communication happen between contexts?
- How can we map the language between the contexts' domain models (i.e., translate from one Ubiquitous Language to another)?
- How can we avoid issues related to unwanted or breaking changes occurring upstream?
- How can we avoid problems caused in downstream contexts?

The answers to these questions are compiled into a context map, as shown in *Figure 2.4*. The context map visually represents how different bounded contexts interact and the strategies used to manage these interactions.

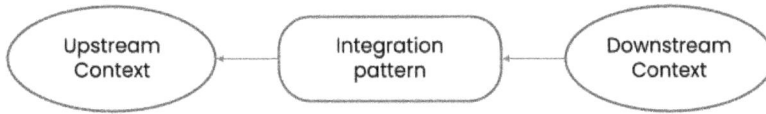

Figure 2.4: Context map sample

The next section will explore several techniques for creating effective context maps, including shared kernel, customer-supplier, conformist, anticorruption layer, published language, separate ways, and open host service. These techniques can serve as tools to navigate the complexities of integrating and managing multiple bounded contexts.

Context mapping techniques

Having established the importance of bounded contexts, we will now focus on the techniques used to manage the interactions and relationships between contexts. This process, known as **context mapping**, is a critical component of DDD as it ensures well-defined and manageable boundaries and connections between different parts of your system.

Context mapping visually represents how different bounded contexts relate to each other within a system. This map identifies where context boundaries lie and provides insights into how these contexts should communicate and integrate. A well-crafted context map makes the relationships between different system parts explicit, helping teams avoid misunderstandings and misalignments. See the main patterns and techniques used in context mapping as follows:

- **Shared kernel pattern**: It occurs when two teams or contexts need to share a small part of their domain models. This shared part, the kernel, is usually a minimal, well-defined subset of the domain that both teams agree to co-develop and maintain. The Shared kernel pattern is handy when tight integration is necessary between contexts, but due to the shared responsibility, care must be taken to avoid it becoming a bottleneck.

- **Customer-supplier pattern**: One context (the supplier) provides services or functionality that another context (the customer) consumes. The customer has specific needs and expectations, and the supplier must ensure that its services meet these requirements. This relationship often requires close collaboration to ensure that changes in the supplier context do not negatively impact the customer context.

- **Conformist pattern**: Arises when a downstream context (the conformist) is forced to adhere to the model and decisions of an upstream context, even if it would prefer a different approach. This pattern typically occurs when the downstream context has little or no influence over the upstream context and must conform to whatever the upstream context dictates.

- **Anti-corruption layer (ACL) pattern**: Is a defensive strategy used when a context must interact with another context with a different or poorly designed model. The ACL acts as a protective layer that translates between the two models, preventing the *corruption* of the downstream context by isolating it from the complexities or inadequacies of the upstream context. This pattern is essential when integrating legacy systems or external services that cannot be changed.

- **Published language pattern**: Involves creating a shared language or protocol for communication between contexts. This language is typically standardized and documented, allowing different contexts to interact consistently and predictably. Published language is beneficial in situations where multiple contexts need to exchange data or commands in a loosely coupled manner.

- **Separate ways pattern**: This is employed when two contexts do not need integration. The contexts are developed and maintained independently, with no shared models or communication requirements. This pattern is often used when the cost of integrating two contexts outweighs the benefits, allowing each to evolve independently.

- **Open host service pattern**: Provides a standardized, public interface that other contexts can use to interact with a particular context. This pattern is proper when a context needs to offer its services to multiple other contexts in a consistent and controlled manner. By exposing a well-defined interface, the open host service pattern ensures that different contexts can interact with it without needing to understand its internal complexities.

Each pattern serves a specific purpose and provides a way to manage the complexities of integrating multiple bounded contexts within a system. The choice of pattern depends on the nature of the relationships between contexts, the degree of coupling required, and the overall goals of the system architecture.

These context-mapping techniques bridge strategic planning and actual implementation, shaping how different parts of the application will interact. Each technique directly influences the system's integration behavior, guiding how contexts communicate, share data, and handle dependencies. These mappings are not static; they can evolve alongside the organization and its needs, adapting when existing interactions no longer serve the application's goals. Use context mapping as a practical blueprint that informs and adjusts the application's architecture to align with the organization's structure and desired outcomes.

Mastering context mapping techniques is crucial for developing scalable and maintainable software systems. These methods enable various components to evolve independently while functioning effectively together. In this chapter, we will assertively explore essential concepts in DDD, such as bounded contexts and context mapping techniques, illustrating how these principles drive software architectures that directly align with business objectives. The subsequent section will focus on *aligning business strategy with software design* to further solidify this alignment.

Aligning business strategy with software design

One of the core principles of DDD is ensuring that the software architecture is closely aligned with the overall business strategy. This alignment is essential because software is not just a technical tool but a direct enabler of business goals and outcomes. When software design reflects the business's strategic objectives, it can adapt quickly to market changes, streamline operations, and offer competitive advantages.

The first step in aligning software design with business strategy is understanding the domain. It involves deeply understanding the business's leading processes, challenges, and objectives. By identifying the organization's core, supporting, and generic subdomains, developers can prioritize areas where innovation and competitive differentiation are most needed. Focusing efforts on the core subdomain ensures the software reflects the business's unique value proposition. Handling generic subdomains with standardized solutions allows for more efficient resource allocation.

Furthermore, communication between business stakeholders and developers is vital. Creating a shared vocabulary—a Ubiquitous Language—between domain experts and developers is essential to aligning both teams with business objectives. This common language reduces misinterpretation and keeps development focused on delivering value.

To be effective, this language should be explicitly documented as a living glossary and included in user stories, model names, API definitions, and visual aids, such as diagrams. These resources help ensure clarity and consistent use throughout the project.

Ultimately, by aligning business strategy with software design, organizations can create systems that support their current operations and evolve as their business and market demands grow. This approach creates a symbiotic relationship between the software and the business, where each drives and supports the success of the other.

Conclusion

In this chapter, we covered the fundamental concepts of DDD, concentrating on the strategic elements that help to manage complexity and align software architecture with business objectives. We began by discussing domains and subdomains, followed by a detailed exploration of bounded contexts and the importance of a shared language. The chapter also introduced context mapping techniques, essential for managing the relationships between different system parts and ensuring that each context can evolve independently while maintaining coherence across the system.

In the next chapter, we will shift our focus from strategic to tactical DDD. We will explore the tactical implementation of DDD, provide practical examples and code to illustrate how these concepts are applied in software development, and equip you with the tools to apply DDD principles effectively in your projects.

Points to remember

- **Domain in DDD refers to the problem space**: It represents the business challenges that the software is designed to solve. *Vaughn Vernon* defines it as consisting of a problem space and a solution space.

- **Bounded context defines clear boundaries**: It ensures that different parts of the system use consistent terminology and models without interference from other contexts.

- **Ubiquitous Language is key to alignment**: A shared language between developers and domain experts ensures clarity and consistency in communication and implementation.

- **Context mapping helps manage integration**: It defines how different bounded contexts interact, guiding how data flows and dependencies are handled between them.

- **Context mapping techniques reflect system behavior**: These techniques shape how applications communicate and evolve based on business needs and organizational structures.

- **Bounded context relationships impact design decisions**: Identifying upstream and downstream dependencies helps define ownership, responsibilities, and potential integration challenges.

- **Context boundaries are flexible when necessary**: While initially defined, they can evolve as the system and organization change to better fit business needs.

Multiple choice questions

1. **What is the primary purpose of a bounded context in DDD?**

    a. To define the physical boundaries of the system.

    b. To separate the database from the application logic.

    c. To split the domain model into smaller, manageable models with consistent terminology.

    d. To ensure that all developers use the same programming language.

    e. To manage network communications between microservices.

2. **What does the Ubiquitous Language in DDD help achieve?**

    a. It enforces strict coding standards across the team.

    b. It ensures that all team members and domain experts share a common understanding of the domain.

    c.   It replaces the need for technical documentation.

    d.   It standardizes the user interface design.

    e.   It defines the structure of the database schema.

3. **In context mapping, what is the role of an anticorruption layer?**

    a.   To prevent unauthorized access to the database.

    b.   To isolate a context from external systems with differing models.

    c.   To synchronize data between two bounded contexts.

    d.   To standardize communication protocols within a bounded context.

    e.   To manage version control across teams.

4. **Which context mapping pattern involves creating a small, shared subset of a domain model?**

    a.   Open host service

    b.   Conformist

    c.   Shared kernel

    d.   Separate ways

    e.   Customer-supplier

5. **What should you do if you struggle to explain a business concept using the Ubiquitous Language?**

    a.   Abandon the concept as unnecessary.

    b.   Ignore the issue and proceed with the implementation.

    c.   Simplify the concept by removing details.

    d.   Collaborate with a domain expert to refine the language and model.

    e.   Replace the term with technical jargon.

Answers

Question number	Answer option letter
1.	a.
2.	b.
3.	b.
4.	c.
5.	d.

References

1. *Forbes Technology Council. 16 Obstacles To A Successful Software Project (And How To Avoid Them),* 2022. **https://www.forbes.com/councils/forbestechcouncil/2022/06/21/16-obstacles-to-a-successful-software-project-and-how-to-avoid-them/**

2. *Richards, Mark & Ford, Neal. Software Architecture: The Hard Parts, 2021.*

3. *Vernon, Vaughn. Implementing Domain-Driven Design, 2013.*

Join our Discord space

Join our Discord workspace for latest updates, offers, tech happenings around the world, new releases, and sessions with the authors:

https://discord.bpbonline.com

CHAPTER 3

Tactical DDD Implementation

Introduction

This chapter focuses on the practical side of **domain-driven design** (**DDD**), exploring the specific patterns that bring DDD to life in your code. After laying the groundwork in earlier chapters, we are ready to see how these concepts are implemented in real-world projects, giving you the confidence to apply them in your work.

This chapter is essential for developers who want to connect theory with practical application. We will explore the effective use of tactical DDD through Java patterns, such as entities, value objects, services, aggregates, and repositories. The detailed code samples demonstrate how software development can reflect the business domain while managing complexity effectively.

Structure

In this chapter, we will explore:

- Entities and value objects
- Aggregates and aggregate roots
- Services and their roles
- Implementing repositories

Technical requirements

To follow along with the code examples and exercises in this chapter, ensure you have the following tools and setup in place:

- Java 21
- Git
- Maven
- Any preferred IDE

For more information on the library configuration, please refer to the GitHub repository for this chapter.

Objectives

This chapter aims to provide a practical understanding of tactical DDD by exploring key patterns such as entities, value objects, aggregates, services, and repositories. By the end of this chapter, you will be able to structure your domain model, ensuring clear boundaries and responsibilities, and apply best practices aimed at the implementation of business logic that is clean and maintainable. Through hands-on examples and implementation guidance, you will learn how to translate DDD principles into code while avoiding common pitfalls.

Entities and value objects

When starting tactical DDD, the concept to look at is the entity. The starting point for domain modeling is the core of the implementation within your code, in other words, the entities.

> **Tip:** While entities are essential in tactical DDD, it is important to remember that their design should always be guided by the strategic DDD decisions made earlier in the process.

Entities serve as a representation of the information stored in database systems and are the foundation for implementing design patterns and business or domain definitions.

The core characteristics of an entity are continuity (often referred to as its lifecycle) and identity, as outlined in the book *Domain-Driven Design*[1]:

> *Many objects are not fundamentally defined by their attributes, but rather by a thread of continuity and identity.*

> *-Eric Evans*

Identity is a unique and unchanging characteristic that distinctly sets an entity apart from others, regardless of changes to its attributes. It guarantees continuity and traceability over time, typically represented by a unique identifier such as an ID or code.

In DDD, identity is imperative for consistently recognizing an entity, even as its other attributes evolve. For example, in a university enrolment system, a student's identity is firmly defined by a unique student ID, which remains constant despite any changes to their name or address. This concept is vital for effective entity design, ensuring they unequivocally represent the same object throughout their lifecycle.

An entity is defined by its identity, which uniquely distinguishes it from others, rather than by its attributes. This identity allows the entity to remain recognizable over time, even as its attributes change. For instance, in a university enrolment system, a student is identified by their constant student ID, regardless of changes to their name or email. This consistent identity ensures continuity throughout the entity's lifecycle.

When implementing an entity, ask this domain-specific question: *As time goes by, what determines that this object is still the same as it was before?* This understanding shapes how the identity is defined as an entity code. As Evans points out:

> **Be alert to requirements that call for matching objects by attributes.**

> *-Eric Evans*

Sometimes, an object perceived as an entity can be of a different object type (such as a value object, concept explored later in the chapter). One way to test this is to examine whether the requirements imply that two objects should be treated as the same when compared, meaning they are considered equal and have matching attributes. Understanding this distinction is critical when designing your domain model. Let us start by exploring some pitfalls.

Entities pitfalls

When building our first entity based on adopting tactical DDD practices, a typical pitfall can be avoided, especially when combining Java entities with the **Plain Old Java Object** (**POJO**) model.

One of the most common mistakes is creating anemic entities: objects that hold data but contain no domain logic or encapsulation[4]. The following code demonstrates this issue with a simple **Traveller** entity where the passport number acts as the ID:

```
public class Traveller {
    private String passportNumber;
    private String name;
    private Set<String> countries;
}
```

At first glance, this design may appear sufficient, as it allows us to set all fields and initialize an instance, like in the following example:

```
@Test
void shouldCreateTraveller() {
    Traveller traveller = new Traveller();
    traveller.setPassportNumber("123456");
    traveller.setName("John Doe");
    traveller.setCountries(Set.of("USA", "UK"));

    Assertions.assertThat(traveller.getPassportNumber()).isEqualTo("123456");
    Assertions.assertThat(traveller.getName()).isEqualTo("John Doe");
    Assertions.assertThat(traveller.getCountries()).contains("USA", "UK");
}
```

However, this approach has a glaring flaw: Where is the domain logic in this POJO entity? Does it make sense for a **Traveller** to exist without a valid passport number or name? This structure has code that lacks proper encapsulation.

Using public getters and setters for every field offers no difference from directly exposing public fields.

Moreover, this API design is prone to errors that can easily break data consistency and business rules' integrity. For example, the following code demonstrates how the **Traveller** entity can be left in an inconsistent state, which could cause a **NullPointerException**:

```
@Test
void breakingApiContract() {
    Traveller traveller = new Traveller();
    traveller.setPassportNumber("123456");
    traveller.setName("John Doe");
    traveller.setCountries(Set.of("USA", "UK"));
    traveller.setCountries(null);

    Assertions.assertThatThrownBy(() -> traveller.getCountries().
contains("USA"))
            .isInstanceOf(NullPointerException.class);
}
```

Allowing the **countries** field to be set to null is not just an inconvenience; this practice compromises the integrity of the API and poses security risks. From the perspective of the **confidentiality, integrity, and availability (CIA)** triad[5], this approach undermines the application's integrity by allowing unrestricted changes to critical fields. This lack of protection can result in unintended consequences, even if the issue is introduced accidentally.

This type of design, often referred to as an **anemic domain model**, is considered an anti-pattern in DDD. In his article, *Martin Fowler* elaborates on the shortcomings of anemic models and encourages the use of rich models instead[6]. A rich domain model embraces encapsulation and ensures that business logic and data integrity are tightly coupled within the entity itself.

Robert C. Martin also critiques the anemic model in *Clean Code*[7], explaining that this mistake stems from a misunderstanding of object-oriented paradigms. He emphasizes that the fundamental principle of objects is not merely to group data but to expose behavior and hide the underlying data. When entities only consist of getters and setters without encapsulating behavior, they fail to be true objects. Martin highlights that an anemic model is closer to procedural programming than to object-oriented design, as it treats objects like data structures rather than encapsulating behavior as proper objects should. This means that anemic models are not considered fully object-oriented and break from the core philosophy of **object-oriented (OO)** design.

To address this issue, the **Traveller** entity is refactored to enforce domain logic through constructors and methods, avoiding mutable state. Make it into a more robust *Tourist* entity that avoids setters and ensures domain logic is enforced through constructors and methods. This version follows item 15 from *Effective Java*[4] and aligns with the principles laid out in *Clean Code* by focusing on encapsulating behavior. For example, it does not make sense for a **Tourist** to exist without a valid passport number, so we enforce this through the constructor as follows:

```java
public class Tourist {
    private String passportNumber;
    private String name;
    private Set<String> countries = new HashSet<>();
    public Tourist(String passportNumber, String name) {
        Objects.requireNonNull(passportNumber, "Passport number cannot be null");
        Objects.requireNonNull(name, "Name cannot be null");
        this.passportNumber = passportNumber;
        this.name = name;
    }
    public String getPassportNumber() {
        return passportNumber;
    }
    public String getName() {
        return name;
    }
    public Set<String> getCountries() {
        return Collections.unmodifiableSet(countries);
    }
    public void addCountry(String country) {
```

```
            Objects.requireNonNull(country, "Country cannot be null");
            countries.add(country);
    }
}
```

This refactored **Tourist** entity now encapsulates the data and ensures its integrity by preventing null values and uncontrolled modifications. The constructor guarantees that a **Tourist** always has a valid passport number and name, and the **addCountry** method ensures that countries cannot be null. Additionally, the **getCountries** method returns an unmodifiable set, preventing external modifications to the internal state.

By designing entities with a rich model, we improve our application's integrity and security while aligning with the core principles of tactical DDD. This approach makes the API more robust and ensures that the domain logic remains central to the design, avoiding the pitfalls of anemic models.

Another common mistake in DDD is related to naming conventions for classes and fields. In *Clean Code[7]*, *Robert C. Martin* emphasizes the importance of using meaningful names and avoiding redundancy. This principle applies to field names such as string **nameString**, where the extra **string** suffix adds no value. Instead, the **name** should be a string name, which is more natural and concise. Similarly, redundant class names like **PersonEntity** or **CardEntity** should be avoided. Using clear, concise names that align with the Ubiquitous Language of the domain makes your code easier to read, more relatable, and easier to maintain for both developers and stakeholders.

The same principle applies to class names. There is often no need to append **Entity** to class names. Instead, simply name the class based on the domain terminology, such as **Person**, **Card**, or **Team**. This practice improves code readability and ensures that your code remains closely tied to the business language, making it more intuitive. The goal of strategic DDD is to ensure the language of your code reflects the language of the business domain, which includes class, property, and method names. This approach strengthens the connection between the code and the business rules, helping developers and domain experts understand and communicate more effectively.

In some projects, the **Entity** suffix is part of a convention to help identify domain objects easily. While this can serve as a quick search aid, it also indicates a fear-driven design that can lead to architecture becoming too rigid as a consequence of governance rules. It is essential to remember that naming conventions should enhance clarity, not detract from it.

It is important to avoid weak models and unnecessary naming to build strong and effective models. This allows us to concentrate on creating comprehensive models that accurately represent behavior. For example, let us consider a scenario using the **Team** entity to represent a soccer team. In this case, the team is identified by a unique FIFA code that adheres to specific rules, such as having a maximum of 23 players and ensuring each player is unique.

```
public class Team {
    private final String fifaCode;
    private final String name;
    private final List<Player> players;
    private Team(String name, String fifaCode) {
        this.name = name;
        this.fifaCode = fifaCode;
        this.players = new ArrayList<>();
    }
    public String getFifaCode() {
        return fifaCode;
    }
    public String getName() {
        return name;
    }
    public List<Player> getPlayers() {
        return Collections.unmodifiableList(players);
    }
    public void add(Player player) {
        Objects.requireNonNull(player, "Player is required");
        if (players.contains(player)) {
            throw new IllegalArgumentException("Player already exists");
        } else if (players.size() >= 23) {
            throw new IllegalArgumentException("Team is full");
        }
        players.add(player);
    }
    public static Team create(String name, String fifaCode) {
        Objects.requireNonNull(name, "Name is required");
        Objects.requireNonNull(fifaCode, "FIFA code is required");
        return new Team(name, fifaCode);
    }
}
```

This implementation decisively harnesses key principles from Effective Java, such as adopting static factory methods instead of constructors and minimizing mutability. By designing the **Team** class to be primarily immutable, except for the ability to add players, we significantly reduce the risk of bugs in our domain model.

Certain Java frameworks, like *JPA*, fail to support immutable entities due to their requirement for a default constructor. The clear solution is to separate the domain model from the persistence model, which allows us to maintain a robust domain model while effectively addressing persistence needs.

When it comes to entities' mutability, this decision must be grounded in the specific business context, as emphasized in *Eric Evans'* DDD book. In cases where entities do not change frequently, such as books, immutability is not just appropriate; it is preferable, as new editions should be created rather than modifying existing ones.

An effective strategy to bring immutability characteristics is the usage of Java's record feature:

```
public record Book(String isbn, String name, String author, int edition, Year
year) {
    public Book newEdition(String isbn, Year year) {
        return new Book(isbn, name, author, edition + 1, year);
    }
}
```

In this example, notice that instead of *class*, this is an object of type **record**, which is a type designed to be immutable. This **Book** entity, being a record, is now immutable, meaning that changes result in the creation of new books (e.g., new edition) rather than modifying the existing one. This behavior aligns with the natural evolution of certain domains, such as publishing, where a new edition represents a significant update rather than a minor modification.

Builders and domain-specific language

After discussing the entity structure, it is time to move into entity creation, particularly for more complex cases. Using a dedicated class to ensure a proper creation of new instances might be the best approach when dealing with such entities, as entity creation often involves business rules. Isolating the entity construction logic breaks this process into separate components and helps maintain SOLID[8] principles, particularly the single responsibility principle.

The two common approaches to creating complex objects are the Builder pattern and the fluent API (or **domain-specific language (DSL)**). While both patterns allow you to define rules and run validations during object creation, the fluent API offers closer alignment with the domain's Ubiquitous Language.

The Builder pattern is well-known and broadly adopted by developers. However, while implementation is simpler, it can lack semantic clarity. Key aspects of the Builder pattern to have in mind are:

- Easier to implement.

- Unclear visibility of which methods are required for object construction.

- Most issues are only caught at runtime.

- Builders can be automatically generated by some tools and frameworks.

- Requires strong validation in the **build()** method to ensure all required fields are set.

On the other hand, the fluent API, a concept introduced by *Martin Fowler* in 2005, aims to improve code readability by creating a DSL[13].

With fluent API, there is no need to memorize the sequence of method calls to invoke when creating a new instance. It enables a natural, intuitive coding flow by facilitating the visualization of the steps required to build an object.

When designing a fluent API, the following principles are to be considered:

- Each method should validate inputs for fast failure on invalid parameters.

- The method chain should return a valid object for completeness.

Let us consider an example with a **Player** entity to understand this better:

```
public class Player {
    private String name;
    private Year start;
    private Year end;
    private String email;
    private Position position;
    private int goal = 0;
}
```

This entity contains fields like **name**, **start** and **end** years of the contract, **position**, and the number of goals scored. There are some business rules involved as follows:

- The player's name and position are required.

- The number of goals cannot be negative.

- The contract must have valid start and end dates.

To enforce these rules, we can use either a builder or a fluent API. Each has the following trade-offs:

- **Builder pattern**: Allows us to build the object step-by-step, but we need to ensure that we do not miss any required fields. Validation typically happens in the **build()** method, which might cause problems at runtime if required fields are missing. The following is an example:

```
Player player = Player.builder()
        .name("Ronaldo")
        .start(Year.of(2003))
        .end(Year.of(2020))
        .position(Position.FORWARD)
```

```
          .email("ronaldo@bahia.com")
          .build();
```

While this is easy to implement, it does not explicitly guide the developer toward the required fields. If the **name** method were accidentally skipped, the error would only surface at runtime.

- **Fluent API**: Provides a more intuitive and guided approach to building complex entities. Each step in the API leads naturally to the next, enforcing business rules along the way. This makes the process more readable and domain-specific, aligning better with the DDD terminology.

```
Player player = Player.name("Ronaldo")
          .start(Year.of(2003))
          .end(Year.of(2020))
          .position(Position.FORWARD)
          .email("ronaldo@bahia.com");
```

Here, the API ensures that the developer specifies the player's name, position, and valid contract period. Each method can validate inputs immediately, ensuring invalid parameters, such as a negative goal count or a missing position, are handled at the point of entry rather than at runtime. This approach gives more clarity and confidence in object creation.

While both approaches have their place in software design, the fluent API can provide better alignment with the domain model, offering semantic clarity and reducing the risk of runtime errors. In more complex cases, the fluent API offers an intuitive and domain-specific development experience, which is especially important in DDD, where terminology and behavior closely reflect the business domain.

In the player, we are using email as a string, which means the user can put **banana** without any validation; one way to solve this is to use the value object, which is covered in the following section.

Value object

A value object is an immutable construct in software design, central to DDD, that encapsulates specific values without any unique identity. The primary function of a value object is to represent the concept of distinct elements in the problem domain. Once created, a value object cannot be altered. This characteristic reduces complexity and ensures reliability by minimizing the risks associated with a mutable state. By centralizing a particular value or set of values, value objects simplify business logic and give developers a greater sense of control and higher expressiveness in the domain model.

Value objects offer several advantages in software design. Their immutability guarantees greater reliability, as they are less likely to introduce bugs related to state changes. Furthermore, their modular nature allows for easy reuse across multiple system parts. This reusability makes the software more resourceful and maintains consistency across business logic. This reusability enhances the modularity of the system and promotes consistency in the business logic, making the software easier to maintain and extend. Additionally, value objects enhance the domain model by explicitly representing business concepts, thereby improving the readability and clarity of the code. Observe the following example of the pattern present in Java libraries, in this case, the money API:

```
CurrencyUnit usd = Monetary.getCurrency("USD");
Money money = Money.of(12, usd);
```

Java's date and time API also demonstrates how value objects can improve semantics and align with the Ubiquitous Language of the domain. Instead of using the generic **getInstance()** method from the older calendar API, the new API provides meaningful methods like **now()** as follows:

```
LocalDate localDate = LocalDate.now();
```

This API improvement mirrors domain thinking, where **now** more clearly reflects the business context of time than a generic factory method.

Let us put this concept into practice using our **Player** entity and creating an **Email** value object that guarantees consistency and validity. The following example demonstrates an **Email** value object that ensures that every new instance of **Email** is valid. As a value object, it is immutable, and validation is enforced at the moment of creation, ensuring that only valid email addresses are accepted.

NOTE: **This class does a basic email validation pattern (local@domain) and checks the structure and top-level domain.**

```
public final class Email implements Supplier<String> {
    private static final String EMAIL_PATTERN =
            "^[_A-Za-z0-9-\\+]+(\\.[_A-Za-z0-9-]+)*@"
                    + "[A-Za-z0-9-]+(\\.[A-Za-z0-9]+)*(\\.[A-Za-z]{2,})$";
    private static final Pattern PATTERN = Pattern.compile(EMAIL_PATTERN);
    private final String value;
    @Override
    public String get() {
        return value;
    }
    private Email(String value) {
        this.value = value;
    }
    @Override
    public boolean equals(Object o) {
        if (this == o) {
```

```
                return true;
            }
            if (o == null || getClass() != o.getClass()) {
                return false;
            }
            Email email = (Email) o;
            return Objects.equals(value, email.value);
        }
        @Override
        public int hashCode() {
            return Objects.hashCode(value);
        }
        @Override
        public String toString() {
            return value;
        }
        public static Email of(String value) {
            Objects.requireNonNull(value, "email is required");
            if (!PATTERN.matcher(value).matches()) {
                throw new IllegalArgumentException("Invalid email: " + value);
            }
            return new Email(value);
        }
    }
}
```

The following points can be observed from the preceding code:

- In this **Email** class, the email address is stored as an immutable value once validated, not allowing further changes after creation.

- The **Email.of()** factory method guarantees that a valid email is created by throwing an exception if the provided value does not match the required format.

- The format is validated using a **regular expression** (**regex**) that checks for valid email patterns.

- The class implements **Supplier<String>**, allowing it to provide the email string value when needed, thus encapsulating the validation logic and keeping it separate from the rest of the system.

By using this approach, you ensure that whenever an email is used within the domain, it is guaranteed to be valid, which minimizes the risk of bugs or inconsistencies later in the code.

In addition to immutable value objects, enums can play an important role when modeling constant values that are intrinsic to your domain. Enums provide a fixed set of constants, ensuring that only predefined values are used. In *Effective Java*[4], *Joshua Bloch* highlights the use of enums as a powerful alternative to traditional constant fields.

For example, in our **Player** entity, we could add a **Color** enum to represent the player's jersey color. This enhances the domain model by providing clear, unchangeable values tied directly to the domain, with minimal risk of error.

```java
import java.util.function.Supplier;
public enum Colors implements Supplier<String> {
    BLUE("#00FFFF"), WHITE("#FFFFFF"),
    BLACK("#000000"), GREEN("#008000");
    private final String value;
    Colors(String value) {
        this.value = value;
    }
    @Override
    public String get() {
        return value;
    }
}
```

For enums, such as the **Colors** enum in the example, the predefined color values are represented as hexadecimal codes, providing an immutable set of constant values that can be easily referenced. The enum also implements **Supplier<String>**, which allows it to return the color value when needed. By defining colors in this way, we ensure consistency and reduce the risk of errors if colors are represented as free-form strings throughout the codebase. This approach simplifies the logic and enforces uniformity, ensuring that domain values are always valid and consistent across the application.

Enums and value objects serve the same purpose of encapsulating and validating domain logic while ensuring immutability. Together, they make the domain model more expressive, readable, and aligned with business needs.

As we move forward, we will explore the concepts of *aggregate and aggregate root*, DDD constructs that govern your domain model's consistency by defining boundaries and enforcing business rules across related entities.

Aggregates and aggregate roots

After discussing the core of tactical DDD, entities, and value objects, it is time to dive into one of the most misunderstood yet essential concepts: aggregates and aggregate roots. Aggregates play a crucial role in structuring the domain model by defining boundaries and ensuring consistency within those boundaries.

To clarify, an aggregate is not:

- Just a collection of entities.

- Simply a behavior-rich object.

- Or, a group of entities you can store in your database.

As *Martin Fowler* explains[14]:

> *Aggregates are the basic elements of data storage and transfer; you request to load or save whole aggregates. Transactions should not cross aggregate boundaries.*

-Martin Fowler

The first tactical elements DDD introduces are entities and value objects, each with the following distinct characteristics:

- Value objects lack identity, are immutable, and are always valid. They encapsulate specific values in the domain model.

- Entities possess identity, and their validity depends on their state. Entities can contain value objects as part of their structure.

When we combine entities and value objects, we get an aggregate. *Eric Evans* defines an aggregate as a *cluster of associated objects that we treat as a unit for data changes*. Aggregates ensure consistency within their boundaries, often encapsulating one or more entities and value objects that are closely related in the domain.

An aggregate has a single aggregate root, which is the entry point for interacting with it. The aggregate root controls access to the other entities within the aggregate and ensures that all changes to the aggregate happen consistently. A key feature of aggregates is well-defined transactional boundaries, meaning that changes within an aggregate must either completely succeed or fail. It ensures data consistency and integrity across the system.

Let us consider an example of a **Team** aggregate in a soccer management application. The **Team** is the aggregate root, controlling access to its **Player** entities. Each **Team** can have a list of players, but operations on the **Team**, such as adding or removing players, must follow specific rules, such as maintaining a maximum roster size of 23 players.

The following is an example of a **Team** aggregate:

```java
public class Team {

    private final String fifaCode;
    private final String name;
    private final List<Player> players = new ArrayList<>();
```

```java
    private static final int MAX_PLAYERS = 23;

    public Team(String fifaCode, String name) {
        Objects.requireNonNull(fifaCode, "FIFA code is required");
        Objects.requireNonNull(name, "Team name is required");
        this.fifaCode = fifaCode;
        this.name = name;
    }

    public String getFifaCode() {
        return fifaCode;
    }

    public String getName() {
        return name;
    }

    public List<Player> getPlayers() {
        return Collections.unmodifiableList(players);
    }

    public void addPlayer(Player player) {
        Objects.requireNonNull(player, "Player is required");
        if (players.size() >= MAX_PLAYERS) {
            throw new IllegalArgumentException("Cannot add more than " + MAX_
PLAYERS + " players");
        }
        players.add(player);
    }

    public void removePlayer(Player player) {
        Objects.requireNonNull(player, "Player is required");
        players.remove(player);
    }
}
```

In this example, the **Team** is the aggregate root, responsible for managing its internal state and enforcing rules on its **Player** entities. You can only add or remove players through the **Team** aggregate root, which ensures that the team never exceeds the maximum number of players and that all business rules are enforced consistently.

The aggregate ensures that any modification to its internal state occurs through the root and that all changes follow the necessary validation rules. This approach provides data integrity within the aggregate.

One of the most critical aspects of an aggregate is its transactional boundary. Any changes within the aggregate, whether adding a player or updating a team's name, must occur as part of a single transaction. Either all changes within the aggregate are applied successfully, or none are. It keeps the aggregate in a consistent state.

Aggregates help control complexity by defining clear boundaries, limiting how other parts of the system can interact with the internal details of the aggregate. Other components in the system should only interact with the aggregate root and should not directly modify the entities inside the aggregate.

As we have seen, aggregates and aggregate roots define clear transactional boundaries and help enforce business rules within those boundaries. However, some responsibilities go beyond what aggregates can handle independently, especially when dealing with interactions across multiple aggregates. It is where services come into play. Services encapsulate domain logic that does not naturally belong within an aggregate or entity.

In the next section, we will explore services and their roles, discussing how they complement aggregates by managing interactions across aggregate boundaries. Understanding services in conjunction with aggregates is critical to building a robust domain model.

Services and their roles

Defining *Service* in software development can be challenging, as this word has been largely adopted across architectural concepts, such as **service-oriented architecture** (**SOA**) and microservices. However, within DDD, the word *service* has a well-defined meaning, as well described by *Eric Evans* in his DDD book:

> *When a significant process or transformation in the domain is not a natural responsibility of an ENTITY or VALUE OBJECT, add an operation to the model as a standalone interface declared as a SERVICE. Define the interface in terms of the language of the model and make sure the operation name is part of the Ubiquitous Language. Make the SERVICE stateless.*

-Eric Evans

Note: **To facilitate a clearer exploration of the topic, the readers are advised to assume that the term service refers to the concept as defined in DDD throughout this section.**

A service acts as a critical component when domain logic does not naturally belong to an entity or value object. It orchestrates the interaction between different components, such as entities, value objects, and repositories. Services are essential for handling complex business processes and interactions across these components. Services can be classified into three types as follows:

- **Application services**: act as the entry point to the domain layer and coordinate domain objects like entities and value objects to fulfill specific use cases. They do not usually contain business logic but orchestrate domain behavior and manage the application flow.

- **Domain services**: hold business logic that does not naturally belong to any specific entity or value object. They represent operations that involve multiple entities or abstract domain logic that does not fit cleanly within a particular entity.

- **Infrastructure services**: manage technical concerns like file handling, sending emails, and interacting with external systems or databases. They focus on infrastructure-related tasks, often supporting domain or application services but remaining outside the domain logic.

The following table shows the different types of services. It is important to note that services working together can bring huge benefits to your organization and project. In general, avoid having a single service handling the whole type of responsibility, as it is hard to maintain, and it is super difficult to read and understand the business on it.

Service type	Description	Purpose	Example
Application services	Coordinate domain interactions and manage application flow	Orchestrate domain objects to fulfill use cases	Hiring a player by coordinating the **Player**, **Team**, and **Finance** entities
Domain services	Encapsulate domain logic not belonging to a specific entity	Represent business logic that spans multiple entities	Currency conversion for player salaries based on their country of residence
Infrastructure services	Handle technical concerns and external system interactions	Provide technical support (file I/O, email, database interactions)	Sending an email notification when a player is hired

Table 3.1: The different types of services in DDD

Let us explore these concepts using our soccer team example to better understand how services work.

We will create a **HiringService** to handle the hiring process, interacting with domain objects (**Player**, **Team**) and other services (**FinanceService**, **EmailService**). This service represents an *application service* since it coordinates domain logic across multiple entities and services to fulfill a business use case.

The following code shows how the **HiringService** works as an orchestrator, being a bridge between services such as **Team**, **Player**, **Finance**, and **Notification**:

```java
public class HiringService {

    private final FinanceService financeService;
    private final EmailService emailService;

    public HiringService(FinanceService financeService, EmailService emailService)
{
        this.financeService = financeService;
        this.emailService = emailService;
    }

    public void hirePlayer(Team team, Player player, MonetaryAmount salary) {
        if (!team.canAdd()) {
            throw new IllegalStateException("Team already has maximum players");
        }

        financeService.processSalary(player, salary);
        team.add(player);

        emailService.sendHiringNotification(player, team);

        System.out.println("Player " + player.getName() + " hired for team " +
team.getName());
    }
}
```

The **HiringService** coordinates interactions between the **Team** and **Player** objects, working as application services. It ensures that the team can add the player, process the player's salary through the **FinanceService**, and send a hiring notification using the **EmailService**.

The **FinanceService** handles salary-related business logic that does not naturally belong to any specific entity, making it a clear example of a domain service in our sample:

```java
public class FinanceService {

    public void processSalary(Player player, MonetaryAmount salary) {
        // Process salary payment logic here
        System.out.println("Processing salary of " + salary + " for player " +
player.getName());
    }
}
```

Finally, our infrastructure service, the **EmailService**, is responsible for sending an email notification when a player is hired, representing an infrastructure service that handles communication-related technical tasks:

```
public class EmailService {

    public void sendHiringNotification(Player player, Team team) {
        // Email sending logic here
        System.out.println("Email sent: Player " + player.getName() + " hired
by team " + team.getName());
    }
}
```

Services are potent tools for orchestrating domain logic and managing complex business processes. However, eventually, we need to store this information, which means that, with any database engine, they rely on repositories to interact with the persistence layer and manage data access. In the next section, we will explore how to build repositories that enable services to persist and retrieve entities and value objects effectively. Repositories are critical in abstracting database interactions and ensuring clean, maintainable code.

Implementing repositories

We often need to handle data persistence when developing software using a relational database or a NoSQL solution. The Repository pattern, central to DDD, focuses on abstracting the details of persistence and storage, allowing the business logic to remain clean and concentrate on domain concerns. The repository provides a domain-centric interface to interact with data without exposing the technical details of how that data is stored. As *Eric Evans* writes in *Domain-Driven Design*:

> *A repository maps the data retrieved from the database into a structure and provides an interface to access domain objects.*

> *-Eric Evans*

The Repository pattern allows developers to work with the Ubiquitous Language of the domain while abstracting infrastructure details. This way, the business logic does not need to concern itself with database-specific queries, updates, or data operations. A common mistake is the misuse of terminology in repositories. For instance, in a domain focused on cars or books, it is better to name repositories in line with the domain's Ubiquitous Language, like **Garage** for cars or **Library** for books, rather than using technical terms such as **CarRepository** or **BookRepository**. While adding **Repository** as a suffix makes the class easier to identify, it detracts from the domain focus.

The following is an example of a **Library** interface acting as a repository for managing a collection of books. The operations provided are domain-centric, focusing on registering, finding, and unregistering a book while abstracting the underlying storage mechanism.

```
import java.util.Optional;

public interface Library {

    Book register(Book book);//to insert into the collection

    Optional<Book> findByTitle(String title);

    void unregister(Book book); //to remove
}
```

In contrast, the **Data Access Object (DAO)** pattern exposes database-related operations such as inserting, updating, or deleting records. A DAO provides a lower level of abstraction and directly interacts with the database, in contrast to the Repository pattern, which focuses on domain logic, as shown in the following code:

```
public interface BookDAO {
    Optional<Book> findById(String id);
    void insert(Book book);
    void update(Book book);
    void deleteByTitle(String title);
}
```

The following table is a comparison between the DAO and Repository patterns, highlighting their differences in focus, abstraction, and role within the application:

Aspect	DAO	Repository
Focus	Technical, database-related operations	Domain-centric, focused on business logic
Abstraction level	Low-level (database queries, operations)	High-level (abstract data storage details)
Terminology	Often technical (insert, update, delete)	Ubiquitous Language (register, find, etc.)
Direct data handling	Explicit database interaction	Hides database interaction from the domain
Usage	Handles CRUD operations explicitly	Manages domain objects and state changes
Example	`insert(Book book)`	`register(Book book)`

Table 3.2: The differences between DAO and Repository pattern

The Repository pattern plays a pivotal role in DDD by abstracting storage and persistence details, allowing the business logic to remain focused on the domain. Unlike DAOs, which are more technically oriented and expose database operations directly, repositories offer a higher-level interface aligned with the domain's Ubiquitous Language. This abstraction ensures that domain logic is not polluted by infrastructure concerns, promoting clean and maintainable code. As we move forward, repositories will serve as the bridge between the domain and persistence layers.

Conclusion

In this chapter, we explored tactical aspects of DDD, focusing on implementing key patterns such as entities, value objects, aggregates, services, and repositories. Through these components, we demonstrated how to bring DDD principles into your code, making your application reflect the business domain and robust, maintainable, and capable of handling complexity. From understanding the pitfalls of anemic models and enhancing entities with rich domain logic to leveraging value objects and services for a more precise separation of concerns, we emphasized the importance of designing software that is deeply aligned with the business domain.

As you apply DDD, validating and testing these tactical patterns is crucial to ensure they work correctly within your system. In the next chapter, we will explore how to test DDD components, focusing on validating domain logic, enforcing business rules, and ensuring data consistency across your aggregates and services. Testing these elements will provide confidence that the DDD implementation meets the business needs and remains flexible as requirements evolve.

Points to remember

- **Entities are defined by identity, not attributes**: An entity maintains its identity over time, even if its attributes change. Identity ensures continuity and traceability within the domain.

- **Value objects are immutable and lack identity**: They represent concepts fully defined by their attributes and should not be modified after creation. Instead, a new instance should be created when changes are needed.

- **Anemic models are an anti-pattern**: Avoid POJOs with only getters and setters. Instead, encapsulate domain logic within entities to ensure consistency and maintainability.

- **Aggregates enforce consistency within boundaries**: Aggregates group related entities and value objects, ensuring that changes within them occur as a single transactional unit.

- **The aggregate root controls access**: Only the aggregate root should manage updates to its internal entities, preventing direct modifications from external components.

- **Services encapsulate domain logic that does not belong to an entity**: Use domain services for business operations that span multiple entities and application services for coordinating workflows.

- **Repositories abstract data persistence**: A repository provides access to domain objects using *Ubiquitous Language*, ensuring the domain model is not polluted with database logic.

- **DAOs focus on database operations, while repositories are domain-centric**: DAOs explicitly manage CRUD operations, whereas repositories provide a higher-level abstraction focused on business logic.

- **Use builders or fluent APIs for complex object creation**: These patterns ensure proper validation and enforce required attributes when constructing entities.

- **Naming should align with the Ubiquitous Language**: Avoid redundant or technical names, choose names that reflect the business domain to improve clarity and maintainability.

Multiple choice questions

1. **What is a key characteristic of an entity in DDD?**
   a. It is always immutable
   b. It has a unique identity
   c. It is defined by its attributes only
   d. It can be replaced by value objects

2. **What is a common pitfall when designing entities in DDD?**
   a. Using immutable objects
   b. Creating rich models with domain logic
   c. Using an anemic model
   d. Using value objects instead of entities

3. **Which statement best describes a value object in DDD?**
   a. A mutable object defined by its attributes
   b. An object that has identity and a lifecycle
   c. An immutable object without identity
   d. A database object containing business rules

4. **What is the main role of a repository in DDD?**
   a. To manage low-level database queries and CRUD operations
   b. To abstract storage and provide access to domain objects
   c. To handle the validation of domain logic
   d. To manage technical concerns like file I/O

5. **Which of the following is not a type of service in DDD?**
   a. Application service
   b. Infrastructure service
   c. Utility service
   d. Domain service

6. **What is the main difference between a repository and a DAO?**
    a. A repository is domain-centric, while a DAO focuses on technical CRUD operations
    b. A repository handles infrastructure, while a DAO handles business logic
    c. A repository works with low-level queries, while a DAO abstracts the database
    d. A repository is for NoSQL, while a DAO is for relational databases

7. **What is an aggregate in DDD?**
    a. A collection of unrelated objects
    b. A group of associated objects treated as a unit
    c. A behavior-rich object without any identity
    d. A cluster of entities without any transactional boundaries

8. **Which of the following patterns is used to simplify object creation when complex business rules exist?**
    a. Singleton pattern
    b. Prototype pattern
    c. Builder pattern
    d. Factory pattern

9. **When should you use a domain service?**
    a. When an operation spans multiple entities or does not naturally belong to a specific entity
    b. When you need to manage application flow
    c. When managing infrastructure concerns like sending emails
    d. When validating user input

10. **Which of the following ensures that changes within an aggregate either completely succeed or fail?**
    a. Transactional boundaries
    b. Eventual consistency
    c. Application services
    d. Repository pattern

Answers

Question number	Answer option letter
1.	b.
2.	c.

3.	c.
4.	b.
5.	c.
6.	a.
7.	b.
8.	c.
9.	a.
10.	a.

References

1. *Evans, Eric (2003). Domain-Driven Design: Tackling Complexity in the Heart of Software.*

2. *Apache Maven (n.d.). Introduction to Archetypes.* **https://maven.apache.org/guides/introduction/introduction-to-archetypes.html**

3. *Apache Maven (n.d.). Maven Archetype Quickstart.* **https://maven.apache.org/archetypes/maven-archetype-quickstart/**

4. *Bloch, Joshua (2018). Effective Java (3rd Edition).*

5. *TechTarget (n.d.). Confidentiality, Integrity, and Availability (CIA).* **https://www.techtarget.com/whatis/definition/Confidentiality-integrity-and-availability-CIA**

6. *Fowler, Martin (2003). Anemic Domain Model.* **https://martinfowler.com/bliki/AnemicDomainModel.html**

7. *Martin, Robert C. (2008). Clean Code: A Handbook of Agile Software Craftsmanship.*

8. *Martin, Robert C. (2002). Principles and Patterns (Archived Article). Object Mentor.* **Archived link**

9. *Fowler, Martin (2006). When to Make a Type. IEEE Software.* **https://www.martinfowler.com/ieeeSoftware/whenType.pdf**

10. *Baeldung (n.d.). Java Money and Currency.* **https://www.baeldung.com/java-money-and-currency**

11. *Baeldung (n.d.). Java 8 Date and Time Intro.* **https://www.baeldung.com/java-8-date-time-intro**

12. *Fowler, Martin (2009). DDD Aggregate.* **https://www.martinfowler.com/bliki/DDD_Aggregate.html**

13. *Fowler, M. (2005). FluentInterface. MartinFowler.com. Retrieved from:* **https://martinfowler.com/bliki/FluentInterface.html**

CHAPTER 4
Testing and Validating DDD Applications

Introduction

The arduous task of assuring a practical implementation of complex rules and requirements is also challenging for applications designed using **domain-driven design** (**DDD**). The practice of automating tests is a way to ensure the code reflects a desired outcome. Unfortunately, when developers overly focus on testing the functionality's behavior, the result may be a test that lacks the crucial validation of the expected business logic, and that cannot ensure the core domain model reflects the desired design. Over time, such gaps may lead to a drift from DDD principles. Having a structured approach is the best way to ensure the integrity of the deliverables' domain logic and overall architecture.

Mastering effective testing strategies is how you can clear the way and focus on the domain model, not only catching defects but also reinforcing DDD principles throughout your application. Unit testing, in particular, plays a crucial role in safeguarding business logic within key components, such as aggregates and entities. Technologies, such as ArchUnit, are available to support in ensuring the alignment between the architecture and the DDD best practices. By leveraging techniques for test automation, integration, and code validation, you can empower your team to create and evolve complex DDD applications confidently.

Structure

In this chapter, we will explore the following topics:

- Introduction to testing in DDD
- Unit testing DDD components
- Using ArchUnit for architectural validation

Technical requirements

The examples in this chapter cover testing and will rely on Java 21+, Maven, and library dependencies such as JUnit 5 and AssertJ.

The following is the list of technical requirements:

- Java 21
- Git
- Maven
- IDE of choice

Refer to the GitHub repository of the chapter for more information on library configuration.

Objectives

This chapter aims to provide a comprehensive understanding of how to test and validate DDD applications to ensure architectural integrity, domain consistency, and maintainable code. By exploring unit testing, integration testing, architectural validation with ArchUnit, and automated code validation tools like *Checkstyle* and *pattern matcher for design (PMD)*, we demonstrate how to safeguard DDD principles throughout the development lifecycle. Additionally, we introduce jMolecules to enhance domain modeling clarity and enforce DDD compliance. By the end of this chapter, you will have the knowledge and tools to test, validate, and maintain a DDD-compliant codebase effectively.

Introduction to testing in DDD

While some developers may view testing as a burden, its value in DDD goes beyond just catching bugs and extends across several aspects of development. A solid test suite, for example, serves as a safety net as the codebase and domain model change. It allows confident delivery of changing business requirements, preventing impacts on both the codebase and associated business rules.

The power of testing in DDD lies in its ability to support tactical and strategic design elements. At the tactical level, unit tests verify the behavior of the domain's building blocks, such as aggregates, entities, and value objects, ensuring the domain's behavior reflects the desired outcomes. These tests can also serve as a living version of the documentation, as a Ubiquitous Language can be used to name or describe tests with domain-specific terms. On the strategic side, tests validate the limits and interactions between bounded contexts, delivering high integrity of boundaries' definition, management, and cross-communication.

The following section presents practical techniques to unit-test DDD components, such as aggregates and entities, and learn how to structure tests that reflect your domain's business logic.

Unit testing DDD components

An ability counted as one of the most significant yet challenging for developers is to be able to comprehend and translate business requirements into working software. With a practical example, we will explore the power of building a foundation with structured domain components and how it simplifies maintainability and improves domain integrity in an application. As we go through the implementation of a *customer loyalty program*, we will rely on a simplified project to learn core DDD components such as value objects, entities, and aggregates. For starters, a simple domain model for a customer loyalty program is introduced to illustrate loyalty point accumulation and status progression, where customers can earn loyalty points through purchases and get upgrades through different loyalty categories (bronze, silver, gold, and platinum). Each category offers progressively better perks, such as discounts.

The following table provides an overview of the components of the domain model that we will explore in detail. Among these components, value objects are critical in expressing concepts without identity, focusing purely on their attributes. In the implementation, particular emphasis is placed on their immutable nature, which ensures clarity and predictability for the domain model by preventing unintended side effects. Another key characteristic is that equality checks are based on the set of attribute values, meaning that two instances are considered equal if all their attributes are equal. This behavior aligns with the principle that value objects represent descriptive aspects of the domain and not tracked entities.

Component	DDD pattern	Type	Attributes
LoyaltyPoints	Value object	record	int points
Customer	Value object	record	String name String email
CustomerCategory	Value object	enum	int pointsThreshold int discountPercentage

Component	DDD pattern	Type	Attributes
LoyaltyCard	Aggregate root	class	String id Customer customer LoyaltyPoints loyaltyPoints boolean isPremium CustomerCategory category
LoyaltyCardRegistration		class	String id Customer customer LocalDate registrationDate CardStatus status

Table 4.1: Components at unit test

Now, let us look at each model's implementation aspects, starting with the value objects.

Defining the domain components

First, examine the domain model for **LoyaltyPoints**, a value object that represents the number of accumulated points of a customer, as shown in the following code:

Note: LoyaltyPoints is an immutable object. It cannot be modified once created. The only possible way to add new points is by creating a new instance of LoyaltyPoints.

```
// Value Object that represents points accumulated
public record LoyaltyPoints(int points) {

    public LoyaltyPoints addPoints(int additionalPoints){
        return new LoyaltyPoints(this.points + additionalPoints);
    }

    public boolean canUpgradeToPremium() {
        return this.points >= 1000;
    }
}
```

Next, we have the **Customer** model, which is also a value object.

```
// Value Object holding customer information
public record Customer(String name, String email) {}
```

Note: **The customer's identity number (e.g., document number) is irrelevant to the loyalty program itself. Instead of the identity number, this class's unique identifier is the combination of name and email.**

The next value object we will look into is the **CustomerCategory**. This Enum encapsulates the loyalty tiers (bronze, silver, gold, and platinum), associated thresholds, and respective discount percentages. The reason why Enum is the perfect fit for this component is the match between the need to predefine these values and also offer them in an immutable manner. Following the same pattern, the **CustomerCategory** value object equality is based solely on its attributes, point thresholds, and discount percentages.

```java
// Value Object with loyalty tiers, thresholds and discounts
public enum CustomerCategory {
    BRONZE(0, 0),
    SILVER(1000, 5),
    GOLD(5000, 10),
    PLATINUM(10_000, 15);

...

    private final int pointsThreshold;
    private final int discountPercentage;
...


    public static CustomerCategory getCategoryByPoints(int points) {
        if (points >= PLATINUM.pointsThreshold) {
            return PLATINUM;
        } else if (points >= GOLD.pointsThreshold) {
            return GOLD;
        } else if (points >= SILVER.pointsThreshold) {
            return SILVER;
        } else {
            return BRONZE;
        }
    }
}

}
```

The following code examines the aggregate root of the loyalty program, the **LoyaltyCard**:

```java
public class LoyaltyCard {
    private final String id;
    private final Customer customer;
```

```
    private LoyaltyPoints loyaltyPoints;
    private boolean isPremium;
    private CustomerCategory category;
...
}
```

Note: Different from the value objects, the `LoyaltyCard` is an entity, uniquely identified (e.g., by a card ID) and with a state that evolves as customers make purchases, accumulate points, and advance through different loyalty categories. The `LoyaltyCard` encapsulates business rules such as adding points, determining if a customer qualifies for a premium status, and upgrading their category. As the aggregate root, the `LoyaltyCard` ensures consistency across the related components within the aggregate.

Lastly, **`LoyaltyCardRegistration`** is an aggregate root and serves as an entity focused on the lifecycle of the loyalty card itself. It tracks metadata like the registration date and the status of the card (active, inactive, suspended). While it does not manage points or categories directly, it plays an important role in defining the customer's engagement with the program.

```
public class LoyaltyCardRegistration {
    private final String id;
    private final Customer customer;
    private final LocalDate registrationDate;
    private CardStatus status;
...
}
```

By modeling these components carefully, we established a clean domain model that reflects the business rules of a loyalty program. Each component plays a clear role in the system, with value objects encapsulating immutable domain values and the **`LoyaltyCard`** acting as the aggregate root to enforce business consistency across related components.

Using tests to validate expected behavior

After creating the classes, the next logical step is to define how to validate the behavior and ensure that the domain works as intended. We will start by introducing test libraries with powerful mechanisms to structure tests:

- JUnit 5 (Jupiter) brings advanced capabilities for writing, organizing, and running unit tests, supporting a set of annotations and customizations, parameterized tests, test lifecycle management, and more.

- AssertJ is a fluent API that increases the readability and expressiveness of tests. AssertJ can also be used as a Jupiter combination, allowing for a natural flow in testing.

To test the **CustomerCategory**, we can start shaping the test class by following a test naming convention[7]: a test method starts with the prefix **should** and describes the expected behavior. Additionally, the **@DisplayName** annotation provides the domain context in a human-readable format, ensuring that tests verify and document the business rules. Let us also leverage a Jupiter feature known as **parameterized tests** to use **data-driven testing** (DDT).

DDT is a methodology known for designing tests with a clear separation between the test's logic and data. An advantage is to be able to use different inputs to test the same logic, a behavior that derives from the ability to use data from external data sources (such as spreadsheets, databases, and CSV files) or as inline parameters. This practice makes tests more flexible and reusable, ensuring comprehensive coverage of multiple scenarios.

Observe the following code, the usage of the **@ParameterizedTest**, and notice how it allows data injection directly as parameters on the **@ValueSource** annotation. The data injected by parameters will be used to validate the tests.

```java
import org.junit.jupiter.api.DisplayName;
import org.junit.jupiter.params.ParameterizedTest;
import org.junit.jupiter.params.provider.ValueSource;

import static org.assertj.core.api.AssertionsForClassTypes.assertThat;


public class CustomerCategoryTest {

    @ParameterizedTest
    @ValueSource(ints = {-20, -10, 0, 500, 999}) // inline data parameters
    @DisplayName("should return Bronze category for points less than 1000")
    void shouldReturnBronzeCategoryForPointsBelow1000(int points) {
        CustomerCategory category = CustomerCategory.
getCategoryByPoints(points);

        assertThat(category).isEqualTo(CustomerCategory.BRONZE);
    }

    @ParameterizedTest
    @ValueSource(ints = {1000, 2000, 4999})  // inline data parameters
    @DisplayName("should return Silver category for points between 1000 and
4999")
    void shouldReturnSilverCategoryForPointsBetween1000And4999(int points) {
        CustomerCategory category = CustomerCategory.
getCategoryByPoints(points);
```

```java
        assertThat(category).isEqualTo(CustomerCategory.SILVER);
    }

    @ParameterizedTest
    @ValueSource(ints = {5000, 6000, 9999})  // inline data parameters
    @DisplayName("should return Gold category for points between 5000 and
9999")
    void shouldReturnGoldCategoryForPointsBetween5000And9999(int points) {
        CustomerCategory category = CustomerCategory.
getCategoryByPoints(points);

        assertThat(category).isEqualTo(CustomerCategory.GOLD);
    }

    @ParameterizedTest
    @ValueSource(ints = {10000, 15000})  // inline data parameters
    @DisplayName("should return Platinum category for points 10000 or more")
    void shouldReturnPlatinumCategoryForPoints10000OrMore(int points) {
        CustomerCategory category = CustomerCategory.
getCategoryByPoints(points);

        assertThat(category).isEqualTo(CustomerCategory.PLATINUM);
    }

    @ParameterizedTest
    @ValueSource(ints = {5})  // inline data parameters
    @DisplayName("should return correct discount percentage for Silver
category")
    void shouldReturnCorrectDiscountForSilverCategory(int expectedDiscount) {
        CustomerCategory category = CustomerCategory.SILVER;

        assertThat(category.discountPercentage()).isEqualTo(expectedDiscount);
    }

    @ParameterizedTest
    @ValueSource(ints = {5000})  // inline data parameters
    @DisplayName("should return correct points threshold for Gold category")
    void shouldReturnCorrectPointsThresholdForGoldCategory(int
```

```
expectedThreshold) {
    CustomerCategory category = CustomerCategory.GOLD;

    assertThat(category.pointsThreshold()).isEqualTo(expectedThreshold);
    }
}
```

The preceding test has various test definitions to validate the **CustomerCategory** Enum and its multiple loyalty point thresholds and discounts. Observe how the tests are being used not to validate that the *enum works*, but instead, to ensure that the business logic behind each category correctly reflects the needs of multiple business scenarios.

Moving forward, let us apply a similar approach to test the **LoyaltyPoints** entity, where immutability and accuracy on loyalty points management are indispensable:

```java
import org.junit.jupiter.api.DisplayName;
import org.junit.jupiter.params.ParameterizedTest;
import org.junit.jupiter.params.provider.ValueSource;

import static org.assertj.core.api.AssertionsForClassTypes.assertThat;

public class LoyaltyPointsTest {

    @ParameterizedTest
    @ValueSource(ints = {100, 200, 300})
    @DisplayName("should add points correctly")
    void shouldAddPointsCorrectly(int additionalPoints) {
        LoyaltyPoints points = new LoyaltyPoints(100);
        LoyaltyPoints updatedPoints = points.addPoints(additionalPoints);

        assertThat(updatedPoints.points()).isEqualTo(100 + additionalPoints);
    }

    @ParameterizedTest
    @ValueSource(ints = {1000, 1500, 2000})
    @DisplayName("should return true if points are enough for premium")
    void shouldReturnTrueForPremiumEligibility(int points) {
        LoyaltyPoints loyaltyPoints = new LoyaltyPoints(points);

        assertThat(loyaltyPoints.canUpgradeToPremium()).isTrue();
    }
```

```
@ParameterizedTest
@ValueSource(ints = {999, 500, 0})
@DisplayName("should return false if points are not enough for premium")
void shouldReturnFalseForPremiumEligibility(int points) {
    LoyaltyPoints loyaltyPoints = new LoyaltyPoints(points);

    assertThat(loyaltyPoints.canUpgradeToPremium()).isFalse();
}

}
```

Here, the **LoyaltyPointsTest** ensures that point addition works as expected and that the premium eligibility is correctly determined. Finally, testing the **LoyaltyCard**, the aggregate root, gives us a broader view of how the system handles customers' loyalty status and premium upgrades:

```
import org.junit.jupiter.api.DisplayName;
import org.junit.jupiter.params.ParameterizedTest;
import org.junit.jupiter.params.provider.CsvSource;

import static org.assertj.core.api.Assertions.assertThat;

public class LoyaltyCardTest {

    @ParameterizedTest
    @CsvSource({
            "0, BRONZE",
            "999, BRONZE",
            "1000, SILVER",
            "1500, SILVER",
            "5000, GOLD",
            "7000, GOLD",
            "10000, PLATINUM",
            "15000, PLATINUM"
    })
    @DisplayName("should return the correct category based on points")
    void shouldReturnCorrectCategoryBasedOnPoints(int points, String
expectedCategory) {
        Customer customer = new Customer("John Doe", "john.doe@example.com");
```

```
        LoyaltyCard card = new LoyaltyCard("1", customer);
        card.addPoints(points);

        assertThat(card.getCategory().toString()).isEqualTo(expectedCategory);
    }

    @ParameterizedTest
    @CsvSource({
            "999, false",
            "1000, true",
            "1500, true",
            "5000, true"
    })
    @DisplayName("should determine if premium status is reached")
    void shouldCorrectlyDeterminePremiumStatus(int points, boolean
expectedIsPremium) {
        Customer customer = new Customer("Jane Doe", "jane.doe@example.com");
        LoyaltyCard card = new LoyaltyCard("1", customer);
        card.addPoints(points);

        assertThat(card.isPremium()).isEqualTo(expectedIsPremium);
    }
}
```

This approach ties together the core principles of DDD with practical testing methodologies. By maintaining consistent test naming and a domain-aligned structure, the tests serve as validation and living documentation for your business logic.

Enhancing your tests

Writing effective tests and designing them is crucial, particularly when working with DDD. Understanding the domain's semantics and exploring the correct terminology is central to achieving success. This section will explore six essential steps to enhance testing methodologies and guide you in writing practical tests as follows:

1. **Testing guidelines**: A well-established testing guideline acts as a compass, ensuring that project contributors follow a unified approach to testing. These guidelines help create consistency in how tests are written and maintained, ultimately fostering a commitment to quality.

The guidelines typically include the following:

a. **Tools to use**: Defined sets of testing tools to streamline testing processes and ensure uniformity across contributions.

b. **Naming conventions**: Consistent naming conventions for test classes and methods enhance test readability and maintainability.

c. **Specific test creation approach**: Guidelines on test creation approaches, such as soft assertions and extensive assertions, ensure comprehensive validation of code behavior.

d. **Coverage extension**: Techniques such as mutation testing help uncover hidden bugs and improve overall code quality.

As an example, the documentation in *Jakarta Data*[3] outlines the frameworks to be utilized, naming conventions, and test structure, setting the standard for testing practices within the project. Tools like JUnit 5, combined with AssertJ, provide a powerful testing framework. Following clear naming conventions, like **should + action + expected result,** also ensures that tests are both descriptive and domain-aligned. The following code shows a sample structure code:

```java
public class LoyaltyCardTest {

    @Test
    @DisplayName("Should correctly create LoyaltyCard with default
category")
    void shouldCreateLoyaltyCardWithDefaultCategory() {
        Customer customer = new Customer("John Doe", "john.doe@example.
com");

        LoyaltyCard card = new LoyaltyCard("1", customer);
        assertThat(card.getCategory()).isEqualTo(CustomerCategory.
BRONZE);
    }
}
```

A soft assertion allows multiple assertions within a single test without stopping at the first failure. Unlike regular assertions, which immediately terminate the test if one assertion fails, soft assertions continue running, capturing all assertion failures. This is particularly useful when validating multiple conditions in a test and getting a complete view of all the issues. For instance, if a test method contains ten assertions, using **SoftAssertions** from the AssertJ library lets you see precisely how many of those assertions failed in one run, rather than stopping at the first failure and rerunning the test until all validations pass. This approach provides more comprehensive feedback in each test execution and can save time when diagnosing multiple issues as follows:

```
assertSoftly(softly -> {
    softly.assertThat(pageable.size()).isEqualTo(20);
    softly.assertThat(pageable.page()).isEqualTo(1L);
    softly.assertThat(pageable.cursor().size()).isEqualTo(3);
});
```

2. **Modern testing libraries**: Selecting modern tools is critical for writing effective tests. Migrating to JUnit 5 (JUnit Jupiter) brings features that make testing more efficient, such as improved test descriptions, environment-specific conditions, and data-driven testing capabilities. JUnit 5 simplifies complex testing needs, for example, with Jupiter assertions and parameterized parameters, while libraries like **AssertJ** enhance readability by providing a fluent API, allowing for clean and intuitive assertions.

3. **Data-driven approach**: A data-driven approach to testing involves running the same test logic with multiple sets of data, which improves test coverage and maintainability by validating how code behaves under various conditions. In JUnit Jupiter, the **@ ParameterizedTest** annotation facilitates this approach by allowing dynamic data injection into test cases. This enables tests to be executed with various inputs, ensuring they account for diverse scenarios and edge cases. For instance, in the **shouldAssignCorrectCategoryBasedOnPoints** test, points and their corresponding expected categories are injected as parameters, systematically verifying each possible outcome without requiring multiple test methods.

The **arrange, act, assert** (**AAA**) pattern is a clear and practical approach for writing unit tests. In the **Arrange** step, you set up the necessary objects and configurations. In the **Act** step, you execute the action to be tested, like calling a method. Finally, in the **Assert** step, you check that the outcome matches the expected result using assertions. This pattern enhances readability and defines each test's setup, execution, and expected outcome.

```
@ParameterizedTest
@CsvSource({
    "0, BRONZE",
    "1000, SILVER",
    "5000, GOLD",
    "10000, PLATINUM"
})
@DisplayName("Should assign correct category based on points")
void shouldAssignCorrectCategoryBasedOnPoints(int points, String
expectedCategory) {
    // Arrange
    Customer customer = new Customer("Jane Doe", "jane.doe@example.
com");
```

```
        LoyaltyCard card = new LoyaltyCard("3", customer);

        // Act
        card.addPoints(points);

        // Assert
        assertThat(card.getCategory().toString()).
    isEqualTo(expectedCategory);
    }
```

This flexibility allows seamless integration with external data sources, providing a mechanism to explore edge cases and ensure robustness.

4. **Coverage extension**: To track and ensure thorough test coverage, tools like **PITest**, **JaCoCo**, and **Cobertura** are invaluable. **PITest**, in particular, helps evaluate the strength of your tests through mutation testing, uncovering latent bugs by introducing mutations in the codebase and checking if tests catch these faults [6]. Finally, using containers for testing has revolutionized integration tests. With **TestContainers**[8], developers can spin up Docker containers for databases or other services during testing, ensuring isolated, consistent environments. The following is an example of the usage of **TestContainers** for PostgreSQL:

```
@Testcontainers
public class LoyaltyCardRepositoryTest {
    @Container
    public PostgreSQLContainer<?> postgresContainer = new
PostgreSQLContainer<>("postgres:13")
                .withDatabaseName("testdb")
                .withUsername("test")
                .withPassword("test");

    @Test
    void shouldSaveAndRetrieveLoyaltyCard() {
        // Test implementation
    }
}
```

This approach allows for comprehensive testing of database interactions within real environments, ensuring that tests are reliable and easy to replicate. Consider *Effective Software Testing: A Developer's Guide*[7]. This book provides valuable insights into test-driven development, testing strategies, and best practices for writing reliable tests in software projects. By embracing these six steps: guidelines, modern libraries, data-driven testing, coverage extension, and containers, you can elevate the quality of your testing practices, ensuring that your Java projects are robust, maintainable, and aligned with DDD principles.

In the next section, we will explore *using ArchUnit for architectural validation*, where you will learn how to ensure your application's architecture remains compliant with DDD principles.

Using ArchUnit for architectural validation

A guarantee that an application's architecture is based on DDD principles is critical for long-term maintainability and business alignment. However, enforcing architectural rules can be challenging as the codebase evolves, mainly when we need to identify manually or something to memorize; the basic rule for us is: everything that we must remember, we will forget. That is when ArchUnit comes into the scene.

ArchUnit is a powerful tool that lets you write tests to enforce architectural constraints, helping to ensure your application remains aligned with DDD principles over time. By specifying architectural rules, ArchUnit validates that the structure of your application adheres to defined boundaries, preventing unwanted dependencies and interactions. For instance, you can create tests to verify that specific packages do not depend on others or that only certain layers can interact with particular components. This proactive approach reinforces architectural integrity and keeps the codebase consistent with DDD standards as it evolves.

In DDD, maintaining the integrity of bounded contexts, aggregates, and other core domain elements is essential for keeping your domain model clean. ArchUnit helps validate that these architectural patterns are respected across the codebase.

Let us look at how we can use ArchUnit to validate architectural rules in our loyalty program context. For instance, we might want to enforce that all classes in the **domain** package should not depend on classes from the application layer. The following test ensures the domain model does not rely on the application layer:

```java
import com.tngtech.archunit.core.domain.JavaClasses;
import com.tngtech.archunit.core.importer.ClassFileImporter;
import com.tngtech.archunit.lang.syntax.ArchRuleDefinition;
import org.junit.jupiter.api.Test;

class ArchitectureTest {

@Test
    void domainClassesShouldNotDependOnApplicationLayer() {
        String packageName = CardStatus.class.getPackageName();
        JavaClasses importedClasses = new ClassFileImporter().
importPackages(packageName);
```

```
        ArchRuleDefinition.noClasses()
                .that().resideInAPackage(packageName)
                .should().dependOnClassesThat().resideInAPackage(".."
application..")
                .check(importedClasses);
    }
}
```

While ArchUnit focuses on architectural validation, jMolecules introduces a set of DDD-specific annotations and building blocks, making it easier to express domain concepts directly in your code. jMolecules provides annotations like **@AggregateRoot**, **@ValueObject**, and **@Entity** that make the domain model more explicit and enforce DDD principles.

Using jMolecules, we can annotate our loyalty program domain classes to improve clarity and alignment with DDD. These annotations help tools like *ArchUnit* identify core domain components, enabling more precise architectural validation.

Let us now rewrite the loyalty card domain model, using jMolecules annotations to enforce clarity in DDD concepts as follows:

```
@ValueObject
public enum CardStatus {
...
}

@AggregateRoot
public class LoyaltyCard {
...
}

@Entity
public class LoyaltyCardRegistration {
...
}
```

By including jMolecules annotations, you can validate that your design attaches to the intended layers and applies these annotations correctly. jMolecules provides several integration options, including tools like jQAssistant and ArchUnit, which can be used together to enforce architecture rules.

For instance, the following code sample demonstrates using ArchUnit with jMolecules to validate DDD-specific rules. In this example, we check layer integration, which we will cover in greater detail in *Chapter 5, DDD in Microservices, Monoliths, and Distributed Systems*, and the DDD rules. Those rules on DDD ensure that entities conform to DDD principles, such as having an identifier field appropriately annotated. The following code introduces validation rules provided by jMolecules, where we are checking the layers and also the DDD validation rules based on the annotations that we offered in our classes:

```java
import com.tngtech.archunit.core.domain.JavaClasses;
import com.tngtech.archunit.core.importer.ClassFileImporter;
import org.jmolecules.archunit.JMoleculesArchitectureRules;
import org.jmolecules.archunit.JMoleculesDddRules;
import org.junit.jupiter.api.Test;

public class JMoleculesDddUnitTest {

    @Test
    void shouldCheckTheLayerIntegration() {
        String packageName = CardStatus.class.getPackageName();
        JavaClasses classes = new ClassFileImporter().
importPackages(packageName);
        JMoleculesArchitectureRules.ensureLayering().check(classes);
    }

    @Test
    void shouldCheckDDDIntegration() {
        String packageName = CardStatus.class.getPackageName();
        JavaClasses classes = new ClassFileImporter().
importPackages(packageName);
        JMoleculesDddRules.all().check(classes);
    }
}
```

This section introduces ArchUnit for architectural validation and jMolecules to improve domain modeling and enforce DDD principles. Combining these tools provides a robust framework for maintaining architectural consistency throughout a project's lifecycle. In the next section, we will continue to explore architecture governance, microservices, monoliths, and distributed systems with DDD.

Conclusion

Throughout this chapter, we have gone into various techniques for ensuring that DDD implementation maintains architectural integrity, domain clarity, and high code quality. From testing strategies that validate the domain model to leveraging tools like *ArchUnit, jMolecules, Checkstyle, and PMD,* we have seen how automated checks can help safeguard your project from technical drift and ensure it stays aligned with the business needs. These practices reduce bugs and inefficiencies and allow teams to focus on the core domain, fostering long-term sustainability.

As we continue this journey into DDD, the next chapter will expand on how DDD adapts to different architectural paradigms. Whether you are building a microservices-based architecture or working with a monolithic or distributed system, we will explore applying DDD principles effectively in these diverse environments and maintaining the balance between business logic and system structure.

Points to remember

- **Testing is essential for maintaining a DDD-compliant application**: Properly structured tests validate domain logic, prevent regressions, and ensure that business rules are enforced correctly.

- **The AAA pattern improves test clarity**: This pattern structures tests in a way that makes them easier to read, maintain, and debug.

- **Data-driven testing enhances test coverage**: Using JUnit Jupiter's `@ParameterizedTest` allows for testing multiple scenarios efficiently without duplicating test logic.

- **Integration testing is more accessible than ever**: With modern frameworks like *Spring, Quarkus, Payara, Open Liberty,* and *Helidon,* and tools like `Testcontainers`, integration tests can be automated and executed efficiently.

- **ArchUnit enforces architectural constraints in code**: Writing architecture validation tests helps maintain proper DDD layering and prevents unintended dependencies.

- **jMolecules simplifies expressing DDD concepts in code**: Using annotations like `@AggregateRoot`, `@ValueObject`, and `@Entity` clarifies the role of domain objects and aids in validation.

- **Checkstyle and PMD prevent code quality degradation**: These tools enforce coding standards and detect potential issues before they impact the domain model.

- **Mutation testing improves test effectiveness**: Tools like `PITest` verify how well tests catch real-world changes by introducing controlled faults into the code.

- **Software erosion can be mitigated through continuous validation**: Automating architecture and code quality checks ensures that the domain model remains aligned with business requirements.

- **DDD principles must be validated across different architectures**: Whether in a monolith, microservices, or distributed system, applying testing and validation strategies ensures long-term maintainability and scalability.

Multiple choice questions

1. **What is the main purpose of code validation tools in DDD?**

    a. To write more complex code

    b. To automate deployment processes

    c. To ensure the code adheres to DDD principles and maintains code quality

    d. To improve database performance

    e. To bypass manual testing procedures

2. **Why is it important to enforce coding standards, particularly in a DDD project?**

    a. To make the code harder to read for new developers

    b. To ensure the domain language is consistently applied across the codebase

    c. To make the build process slower

    d. To create more complex architecture

    e. To increase the number of tests needed

3. **Which of the following is an example of a rule that could be enforced by Checkstyle in a DDD project?**

    a. Maximum number of microservices allowed in the architecture

    b. Ensuring aggregates are saved only in specific repositories

    c. Enforcing proper naming conventions for domain entities

    d. Validating correct use of API endpoints

    e. Limiting the size of test data sets used

4. **How do Checkstyle and PMD contribute to DDD compliance?**

    a. By automatically generating domain models

    b. By enforcing architectural rules and detecting code issues that could compromise domain integrity

    c. By reducing the need for testing

    d. By managing microservices communication

    e. By writing test cases automatically

5. **Why is software erosion a concern in DDD?**

    a. It leads to slower application performance

    b. It causes a disconnect between the domain model and the actual implementation

    c. It increases the number of microservices needed

    d. It enhances code readability

    e. It simplifies testing

6. **Which of the following is a key benefit of unit testing in a DDD project?**

    a. It automates the creation of domain events

    b. It ensures that each domain component behaves as expected and aligns with business rules

    c. It reduces the need for code validation tools

    d. It minimizes the number of aggregates in the domain model

    e. It increases the number of microservices

7. **How does data-driven testing enhance testing effectiveness in a DDD project?**

    a. It increases the performance of the domain model

    b. It generates new domain entities automatically

    c. It allows the exploration of different scenarios and edge cases by running the same test logic with varying input data

    d. It validates code style consistency

    e. It reduces the need for testing domain aggregates

Answers

Question number	Answer option letter
1.	c.
2.	b.
3.	c.
4.	b.
5.	b.
6.	b.
7.	c.

References

1. *Martin Fowler. (2012). The Practical Test Pyramid.* **https://martinfowler.com/articles/ practical-test-pyramid.html**

2. *Alex Garcia. (2021). Rethinking the Testing Pyramid: The Balance Between Fast and Slow Tests.* **https://www.infoq.com/articles/testing-pyramid-slow-fast-tests/**

3. *Eclipse Foundation. Jakarta Data - Testing Guideline.* **https://github.com/jakartaee/data/blob/main/TESTING-GUIDELINE.adoc**

4. *Eclipse Foundation. ValueWriterDecoratorTest Example – Eclipse JNoSQL.* **https://github.com/eclipse/jnosql/blob/main/jnosql-communication/jnosql-communication-core/src/test/java/org/eclipse/jnosql/communication/writer/ValueWriterDecoratorTest.java**

5. *Datafaker Project. Datafaker.* **https://www.datafaker.net/**

6. *Henry Coles et al. PITest – Mutation Testing for Java.* **https://pitest.org/**

7. *Effective Software Testing: A Developer's Guide.*

8. *Testcontainers Team. Testcontainers: Lightweight, Throwaway Instances for Testing.* **https://testcontainers.com/**

9. *Elias Nogueira. Base Test Class Testing Pattern – Why and How to Use.* **https://eliasnogueira.com/base-test-class-testing-pattern-why-and-how-to-use/**

10. *Testcontainers Documentation. Manual Lifecycle Control with JUnit 5.* **https://java.testcontainers.org/test_framework_integration/manual_lifecycle_control/**

Join our Discord space

Join our Discord workspace for latest updates, offers, tech happenings around the world, new releases, and sessions with the authors:

https://discord.bpbonline.com

CHAPTER 5

DDD in Microservices, Monoliths, and Distributed Systems

Introduction

Consider a scenario where a development team must modernize a legacy application that has been in production and actively used within the organization for several years. The chances of coming across a large, tangled codebase are not only high, but it also generates that feeling of breaking features not even associated with the change you may need to make in a particular section of the code. This is where DDD plays a special supporting role to developers and architects who aim to design systems that can evolve and scale. Software architecture serves as the guide for how a system may grow, adapt, and meet business needs. **Domain-driven design** (**DDD**) offers a structured approach to addressing these challenges, especially when dealing with intricate domains. Understanding the business requirements is as critical as the technology itself.

This chapter examines how DDD can serve as a strategic approach to managing complexity in software systems that reflect intricate business domains. It explores the application of DDD across various architectural styles, including monolithic applications, microservices, and other distributed system models, to support the development of functional, maintainable, and scalable solutions. Through practical scenarios, the chapter highlights how DDD helps drive informed architectural decisions, such as evaluating whether a system should remain a monolith or transition to a microservices architecture.

Additionally, it addresses how DDD principles can be applied when refactoring legacy systems, offering guidance for aligning existing codebases with business-driven models while preserving operational continuity. By the end of the chapter, readers will gain a clear understanding of how and when to apply DDD effectively across different architectural contexts, enabling more deliberate and business-aligned software design choices.

Structure

In this chapter, we will explore the following topics:

- DDD in monolithic architecture
- DDD in microservices architecture
- Need for microservices
- Applying DDD in distributed systems
- Refactoring legacy code to align with DDD principles

Technical requirements

In this chapter, we will explore these approaches using Java SE along with the jMolecules framework. We aim to keep the code as framework-agnostic as possible, so we will avoid relying on any specific Java frameworks for now:

- Java 21
- Git
- Maven
- Any preferred IDE

Objectives

This chapter aims to explore how DDD applies across different architectural styles, from monolithic applications to distributed systems, including microservices, event-driven design, and cloud-native architectures. It aims to provide a structured approach to evaluating when to use each architecture, how to refactor legacy systems while maintaining business continuity, and how to enforce architectural governance to prevent recurring issues. By the end of this chapter, readers will understand the trade-offs involved in these decisions and how to apply DDD principles effectively in both new and existing systems.

DDD in monolithic architecture

Software architecture and design present an ongoing battle for achieving simplicity, for creating easily adaptable software while simultaneously being cautious and avoiding software erosion (which can lead to code that becomes increasingly harder to maintain as time goes by).

As *George Fairbanks* explained in *Just Enough Software Architecture*, the solution lies in partitioning, knowledge, and abstraction, where the latter is the key to breaking down bigger problems into smaller pieces. This strategy of divide-and-conquer has been used in engineering's history since we were faced with the need to solve complex problems. As an example, we can refer to the design of prominent buildings and the creation of intricate engines, such as those in steam-powered boats. In the software industry, this strategy is often applied through the concept of layered architectures.

Software layers are like *stacks* within a system, each responsible for a specific function. As you move deeper through the stacks, the functions and responsibilities become more granular and detailed. A typical example is the MVC architecture, which divides the application into three parts: model, view, and controller. This separation, represented in the following figure, reduces the impacts of one layer on the others and helps improve the overall maintenance of the solution:

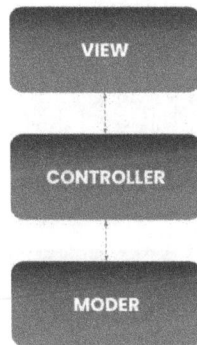

Figure 5.1: The MVC representation

To expand on this concept, DDD brings the idea of four distinct layers[2], where the recommendation is to split systems into four layers, each responsible for a specific block:

- **Presentation layer**: Responsible for presenting the system to the users and handling their interactions. It could be a web page, mobile app, desktop application, or any other user interface form. The user interface layer should be thin and simple, delegating most logic and functionality to the application layer.

- **Application layer**: Coordinates the system's actions and workflows. It mediates between the user interface and the domain layers, orchestrating the use cases and scenarios that the system supports. This layer should be kept thin and stateless, holding only the logic specific to the application.

- **Domain layer**: Is the system's core, implementing the essential business logic and rules. It houses the domain model, encapsulating entities, value objects, aggregates, services, and other domain-centric components. The domain layer is where DDD shines, as it focuses on the core of the business problem, allowing the model to evolve naturally as the business needs to grow.

- **Infrastructure layer**: Provides technical services and external components required by the system, such as databases, message brokers, and APIs. This layer should be generic and adaptable, offering support to the higher layers without becoming tightly coupled to them.

Note: **The domain layer is isolated from the presentation layer, and the infrastructure layer is also isolated. Even though this separation allows components to be replaced or upgraded independently, it is important to know that, in practice, it might be compromised in scenarios where, for instance, domain entities get annotated with infrastructure-specific details (e.g., JPA annotations). Although it is ideal to follow the book's recommendations, architecture involves trade-offs based on context.**

Figure 5.2 is a representation of how these layers work together:

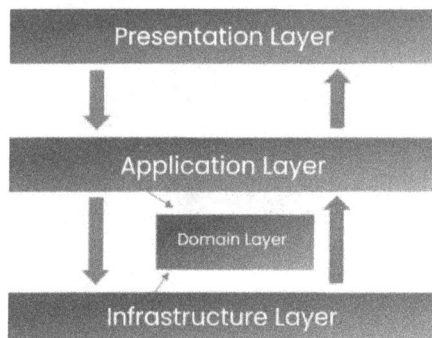

Figure 5.2: *The DDD layer's representation*

When organizing these layers, a common choice is a monolithic application, a single unified software application, self-contained and independent of others. Monolithic architecture is often chosen for its simplicity, handling everything in a single component reduces complexity in terms of deployment, **continuous integration/continuous delivery or deployment (CI/CD)** pipelines, logging, and more. However, scalability in monolithic architectures, particularly team scalability, can become challenging. For example, having thousands of developers working on a single repository can lead to bottlenecks in code reviews, merges, and rebasing, making collaboration inefficient.

Nevertheless, a monolith is not a deprecated architectural choice. When designed well, monolithic architectures can be scalable and maintainable. There are even variations, such as distributed monoliths and modular monoliths. The key is to organize your layers and modules within the application to prevent the common pitfall known as the *big ball of mud*, where code becomes tangled and difficult to manage.

The following figure illustrates two modular monolithic approaches, where internal boundaries within the monolith help maintain order and prevent code erosion. A layered monolith organizes the application into distinct layers, such as presentation, application, domain, and infrastructure, with each layer responsible for a specific aspect of the system. This structure allows for a clear separation of concerns, making the system easier to understand and maintain. In contrast, a modular monolith takes this further by introducing internal boundaries within the monolith, grouping related functionality into modules that can evolve independently while still residing in the same codebase. This modular approach allows teams to work more efficiently while reducing the risks of code entanglement.

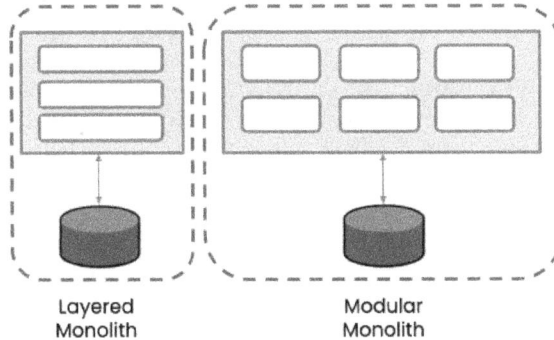

Layered
Monolith

Modular
Monolith

Figure 5.3: The architecture representation of the layered and modular monolith

To demonstrate this approach in action, we will use layers to create a hotel management system as a monolithic application, employing DDD principles to handle hotel room reservations. Our first step is identifying the strategic part of the domain, which revolves around room availability and reservations. Throughout this book, we will also touch on extracting domain knowledge from experts using storytelling techniques, which we will expand on in later chapters. For now, it is essential to understand a few key points that will shape our approach as follows:

- The core of the hotel domain centers around the rooms and their availability.

- A guest can only check in if the room is available.

- Room availability is directly tied to payment.

- Upon checkout, the room must be cleaned and available for the next guest.

We aim to keep the Java SE application as simple and agnostic as possible. We will not implement every feature or integrate external services. However, we will explain clearly how this system could fit into more complex environments like Spring and Jakarta EE, particularly within the Jakarta and MicroProfile ecosystems, using providers like Quarkus and Helidon. This approach will give you a strong understanding of how to apply DDD principles effectively in various Java contexts.

We will also integrate jMolecules to clearly define the DDD layers and components within the architecture, ensuring that the different aspects of the design, like entities and value objects, are explicitly represented. Additionally, we will utilize MapStruct for conversion between the domain and other layers, which we will cover in more detail later.

Creating the domain layer and organizing packages

When structuring a Java project, discussions often arise around package organization, specifically the debate between *package by layer* and *package by feature*. Since we are applying DDD, it is highly recommended that packages be structured by feature. This aligns the codebase with the domain model and makes it easier to extract parts of the domain into separate components or microservices later, a topic we will explore in future sections.

Our first practical step in layering the application is to create a **package-info.java** file. This file will serve as metadata for the package, providing important contextual information. Additionally, we will apply the **@DomainLayer** annotation from jMolecules to denote this package as part of the domain layer as follows:

```
/**
* This package contains the classes that represent the domain model of the
hotel
* booking bounded context.
*/
@DomainLayer
package expert.os.books.ddd.chapter04.hotels;


import org.jmolecules.architecture.layered.DomainLayer;
```

At the core of our domain lies the concept of the **Room**. For simplicity in this chapter, we will represent a guest as a value object, as the focus is not on the guest's details once payment is completed. This minimalistic approach allows us to stay focused on the room's lifecycle within the hotel, without overcomplicating the design. The following code defines the **Room** entity and the **Guest** value object. In this example, only the **Room** possesses an identity, represented by its room number, which naturally serves as a unique identifier in a hotel system.

```
import org.jmolecules.ddd.annotation.ValueObject;
import org.jmolecules.ddd.annotation.Entity;

@ValueObject
public record Guest(String documentNumber, String name) {
}

@Entity
public class Room {

    static final Guest EMPTY_GUEST = new Guest("0", "EMPTY");

    @Identity
```

```
        private int number;

        private Guest guest;

        public int getNumber() {
            return number;
        }

        public Guest getGuest() {
            return guest;
        }

        public void setGuest(Guest guest) {
            this.guest = guest;
        }

        public void cleanRoom() {
            this.guest = EMPTY_GUEST;
        }

        public Room(int number, Guest guest) {
            this.number = number;
            this.guest = guest;
        }
    }
}
```

Here, the **Room** class serves as an entity with a unique identifier, its **number**, while the **Guest** class is a value object that contains basic guest information like **documentNumber** and **name**. The **Room** entity maintains the state of the room and its current guest. After a guest checks out, the **cleanRoom()** method is invoked, resetting the room's state and marking it as available by assigning the **EMPTY_GUEST** value object. This method provides a simple mechanism for managing room availability, a core concept in our domain.

This layered approach not only organizes the code around the domain's core elements but also adheres to DDD best practices, ensuring that the business logic remains clean, isolated, and extensible as we build more system components.

As the next step, we will cover the repository, which, as mentioned in the previous chapter about DDD tactics, represents a collection and handles storage interaction in a domain-centric manner. The vital difference between the **Data Access Object** (**DAO**) and the DDD repository is their focus. While a DAO is more data-centric, focusing on **Create, Read, Update, and**

Delete (CRUD) operations, a repository in DDD is domain-centric, leveraging the Ubiquitous Language of the domain to provide a more natural and business-oriented interface for storage operations.

One of the easiest ways to determine whether your project uses a DAO or a DDD Repository pattern is to examine the method names. DAO methods typically revolve around database operations like **insert**, **update**, and **delete**. In contrast, a repository in DDD will have methods that align with the business domain. For example, in a car rental system, instead of **insert** or **delete**, a repository might have methods like **park** or **unpark**. This terminology shift reflects the domain's language and shows if the repository is being used as part of the domain layer rather than just a technical data access layer.

Our hotel management system implements the repository as a **Hotel** interface. We could also have named it **RoomRepository**, which is common in many Java projects. Still, the semantic choice of **Hotel** focuses on the domain and its business logic rather than the underlying data storage operations. This distinction is important, as the domain should drive the terminology used throughout the system. As the following code shows:

```java
import org.jmolecules.ddd.annotation.Repository;
import java.util.Optional;

@Repository
public interface Hotel {

    Room checkIn(Room room);

    void checkOut(Room room);

    Optional<Room> reservation(String number);

    Long countBy();

    Optional<Room> findEmptyRoom();
}
```

In this repository interface, we see domain-centric methods such as **checkIn**, **checkOut**, and **reservation**. These methods align with the hotel business, abstracting away the technical details of data manipulation and instead focusing on the hotel's actions in the real world. For example, **checkIn** represents assigning a guest to a room, and **reservation** allows us to reserve a specific room by its number.

The next class we will explore is the **HotelService**, which orchestrates the interactions between the repository and other services. It adheres to SOLID principles, particularly the single responsibility principle. By keeping certain logic out of the entity, the service class handles complex workflows such as checking availability, processing payments, and ensuring that rooms are properly cleaned upon checkout.

The **HotelService** handles the key processes of checking guests in and out, ensuring that payments are made before a guest can check in, and interacting with the payment service to complete transactions. The service methods encapsulate business logic that the **Room** entity should not be responsible for, maintaining a clean separation of concerns. It is important to note that the hotel services also act as an application layer once they orchestrate tasks, but do not define business rules themselves. It coordinates interactions between domain objects and external services. The following is a simple example, and in this case, it does make sense to have a mix of those layers, but you can isolate layers where the project gets bigger:

```java
@Service
public class HotelService {

    private final Hotel hotel;
    private final PaymentService paymentService;

    public HotelService(Hotel hotel, PaymentService paymentService) {
        this.hotel = hotel;
        this.paymentService = paymentService;
    }

    public Room checkIn(Guest guest) {
        if (hotel.countBy() >= 100) {
            throw new IllegalStateException("Hotel is full");
        }

        var emptyRoom = hotel.findEmptyRoom().orElseThrow(() -> new
IllegalStateException("No empty room"));
        paymentService.pay(guest);
        emptyRoom.setGuest(guest);
        return hotel.checkIn(emptyRoom);
    }

    public void checkOut(Room room) {
        Objects.requireNonNull(room, "Room is required");
        room.cleanRoom();
        hotel.checkOut(room);
    }
```

```
    public Optional<Room> reservation(String number) {
        return hotel.reservation(number);
    }
}
```

In this **HotelService** class, the **checkIn** method verifies whether there are available rooms and interacts with the **PaymentService** to process the guest's payment before completing the check-in. The **checkOut** method ensures the room is cleaned and returned to its available state after a guest checks out. These actions are orchestrated in the service layer to keep the domain entities focused solely on the core business rules.

Finally, we define the **PaymentService** interface, which handles the interaction with the payment process as follows:

```
@Service
public interface PaymentService {
    void pay(Guest guest);
}
```

The **PaymentService** abstracts away how payments are processed, ensuring that the **HotelService** can focus on the check-in and check-out processes without becoming bogged down with payment logic. This keeps the system modular and easier to maintain, as different services can evolve independently.

This structure demonstrates how to implement a clean and modular domain model, with repositories handling the persistence logic, and services coordinating complex business processes while adhering to DDD principles.

Creating the application layer

After completing the domain layer, the next step is the application layer, which coordinates the execution of business flows without embedding the business rules themselves. Instead, it utilizes the domain layer to achieve its goals. The application layer is responsible for orchestrating workflows, potentially spanning multiple systems or bounded contexts, and can track the progress of these workflows.

As mentioned earlier, the **HotelService** class plays this coordinating role, exposing the domain logic to the presentation layer. In some cases, it might be necessary to split the responsibilities further, creating one class for handling domain logic and another for interfacing with the presentation layer, such as use cases. This split is a concept from Clean Architecture, which we will cover later. Splitting responsibilities like this helps prevent classes from taking on too many roles, improves testability, and adheres to the single responsibility principle. However, premature separation may overcomplicate the code structure, so it is important to find a balance based on the project's complexity.

The next layer is the user interface (presentation) layer, which handles external requests from users or other systems. In a web application, for example, the controller's primary role is to manage incoming HTTP requests and transform them into commands or queries that the application layer can process. This layer should be designed to isolate the domain from user interactions, ensuring that no domain rules are accidentally violated.

A good strategy to achieve this isolation is to use **Data Transfer Objects** (**DTOs**), which act as intermediaries between the user interface and the domain. The DTOs encapsulate data and guarantee that domain entities are not directly exposed to the outside world. The DTO terminology can vary depending on the architecture, with names like **RoomRequest** and **RoomResponse** in REST APIs or **RoomBean** in **Jakarta Server Faces** (**JSF**). Using DTOs also allows us to handle sensitive information securely by excluding fields that should not be exposed. For example, a `GuestDTO` might omit sensitive data such as a password, and you do not need to have this field, keeping it only on the entity.

In our project, we adopted immutable DTOs by utilizing Java records, which makes our DTOs simple and clean while ensuring immutability. The following is an example of our `GuestDTO` and **RoomDTO**:

```
public record GuestDTO(String documentNumber, String name) {
}
public record RoomDTO(int number, GuestDTO guest) {
}
```

Creating the controller layer

The next part is the controller, which acts as a bridge between the presentation and application layers. It ensures that the domain does not interact directly with DTOs and vice versa, applying this translation layer to maintain the isolation between the two layers. The controller might be implemented as a REST resource or any other user interface gateway, and its main purpose is to expose application services while keeping the domain logic decoupled from presentation concerns. Refer to the following code:

```
// Controller or resource to expose application services
public class HotelController {

    private final HotelService hotelService;
    private final HotelMapper hotelMapper;

    public HotelController(HotelService hotelService, HotelMapper hotelMapper)
{
        this.hotelService = hotelService;
        this.hotelMapper = hotelMapper;
    }
```

```
    public RoomDTO checkInRoom(GuestDTO guestDTO) {
        var guest = hotelMapper.toEntity(guestDTO);
        Room room = hotelService.checkIn(guest);
        return hotelMapper.toDTO(room);
    }

    public void checkOutRoom(RoomDTO roomDTO) {
        var room = hotelMapper.toEntity(roomDTO);
        hotelService.checkOut(room);
    }
}
```

The controller uses a **HotelMapper** class to convert between DTOs and domain entities. While it is possible to handle this conversion manually, using a framework like MapStruct is highly recommended. MapStruct avoids the overhead of Java reflection by leveraging annotation processing, which ensures that the communication between layers is as fast as manually written code. MapStruct automatically generates the mapper implementations at compile time, offering a clean and efficient way to handle conversions.

It is important to note that even when using a mapping framework like MapStruct, renaming a field in the domain or DTO could silently break the mapper. Therefore, writing tests for this layer is crucial to ensure that refactoring does not introduce issues. The following is the **HotelMapper** interface, implemented with MapStruct. While this is a simple Java SE implementation, it could easily be defined as a Spring or **Contexts and Dependency Injection** (**CDI**) component, allowing it to integrate smoothly with platforms like Spring and Jakarta EE.

```
@Mapper
public interface HotelMapper {

    HotelMapper INSTANCE = Mappers.getMapper(HotelMapper.class);

    RoomDTO toDTO(Room room);

    Room toEntity(RoomDTO roomDTO);

    GuestDTO toDTO(Guest guest);

    Guest toEntity(GuestDTO guestDTO);
}
```

Although the **HotelMapper** class could be classified as a support component, in this context, we treat it as part of the application layer since it facilitates interaction between the presentation and domain layers.

Creating the infrastructure layer

The final layer we will discuss here is the infrastructure layer, which provides technical support to all other layers, such as persistence, message handling, or security. This layer offers the technical capabilities needed to implement the application's business logic and facilitate its interactions.

In addition to the **HotelMapper**, another example of infrastructure support is the implementation of the **PaymentService**, which processes payments using a **CreditCard** class. The infrastructure layer may also implement the **Hotel** repository for storing or retrieving room data. The following is a simple example of the **CreditCard** class and a memory-based **Hotel** repository:

```
public class CreditCard implements PaymentService {

    private static final Logger LOGGER = Logger.getLogger(CreditCard.class.
getName());

    @Override
    public void pay(Guest guest) {
        LOGGER.info("Payment with credit card: " + guest);
    }
}

public class MemoryHotel implements Hotel {
    // the implementation class is not within the book's scope
}
```

The **CreditCard** class simulates a payment process by logging a payment with the guest's details, demonstrating how the infrastructure layer can interact with the domain to support business operations. The **MemoryHotel** class provides a simple in-memory implementation of the **Hotel** repository for demonstration purposes. However, in a real-world application, it would likely interact with a database or external system.

With this structure, we have completed a foundational look at building a layered, domain-driven system with a clear separation of concerns between the domain, application, presentation, and infrastructure layers. Each layer serves a distinct purpose, and the isolation between them ensures the system's maintainability, scalability, and testability as it evolves.

We have our project done. Building a monolithic application using DDD ensures a well-organized and maintainable structure where each layer has a clear responsibility. This approach simplifies the development of complex systems by isolating the domain logic from the application's technical concerns. Now that we have explored how DDD works within a monolithic architecture, we will focus on applying these principles in a microservices architecture, where additional challenges like distributed systems and service boundaries come into play.

DDD in microservices architecture

When considering software architecture, monolithic systems remain a valid and effective solution in many cases. However, every architectural decision involves trade-offs, particularly in scalability. One of the main challenges with monolithic architectures is team scalability. Coordinating thousands of developers in a single repository can lead to significant overhead, as time is often spent managing merges, rebases, and resolving conflicts. Additionally, as the project grows, the startup time of monolithic applications increases, especially in Java-based reflection frameworks, where larger codebases require more time to scan and initialize.

This is where microservices come into play. Microservices architecture breaks down the application into smaller, self-contained services, enabling teams to work independently on different system parts. This *divide and conquer* approach aligns well with DDD, as DDD helps to define clear domain boundaries that naturally lend themselves to being separated into microservices. With microservices, you can isolate the most critical parts of the system, such as the core business logic, and allocate resources more efficiently, providing flexibility in scaling specific services independently. Refer to the following table for a detailed analysis of the same:

Aspect	Monolithic architecture	Microservices architecture
Team scalability	Difficult to scale across large teams due to shared codebase	Easier to scale teams, as each service can be owned by smaller teams
Startup time	Slower as the application grows due to reflection and class scanning	Faster as services are smaller and independent
Deployment	Single deployment unit, slower to deploy large systems	Independent deployment of services, enabling faster updates
System complexity	Lower initial complexity, but it can grow into a big ball of mud	Higher initial complexity due to the distributed nature
Communication	Direct method calls between components within the same process	Requires network communication (e.g., HTTP, gRPC), introducing latency
Scaling	Whole system scaling, even if only one part needs more resources	Individual services can be scaled independently

Table 5.1: Challenges facing microservices and monoliths

As software systems grow in complexity, managing business domains becomes increasingly challenging, especially in large-scale distributed architectures. DDD provides a strategic approach to modeling business domains, which naturally complements the microservices architecture. Organizations can break down complex systems into smaller, more manageable components by aligning DDD principles with microservices, allowing for independent development and deployment.

The synergy between DDD and microservices creates a flexible, scalable structure that mirrors the business. The DDD and microservices can fit naturally for several reasons as follows:

- **Bounded contexts**: In DDD, each bounded context defines a clear boundary for a specific part of the business logic. These contexts can be implemented as independent microservices, ensuring each service focuses on a specific domain.

- **Autonomy**: Microservices allow each part of the system to evolve independently, making it easier to adapt to changing business requirements without impacting the entire system.

- **Decoupled teams**: DDD encourages autonomous teams that can focus on specific domains. Microservices align with this by allowing teams to work on independent services without needing to coordinate changes across the entire application.

- **Scaling business logic**: By isolating domains, you can allocate more powerful resources to the core business services that require high performance, such as payment processing, without affecting the rest of the system.

When combined with microservices architecture, DDD offers several key advantages that help streamline the development process and improve system scalability. The combination of clear domain boundaries and independent services allows teams to focus on specific business areas while maintaining a cohesive system. The natural decoupling of microservices, driven by DDD, makes evolving the system easier, allocating resources efficiently, and ensuring each service can scale based on its unique demands.

The following are some of the key advantages of combining DDD with a microservices architecture:

- **Clear separation of concerns**: Each microservice is responsible for a specific part of the domain, reducing the complexity within individual services and improving maintainability.

- **Independent evolution**: Each microservice can evolve at its own pace, allowing different parts of the system to be updated or replaced without impacting other services.

- **Better resource allocation**: Resources can be allocated efficiently, focusing on the most critical parts of the system without scaling the entire monolith.

For example, in our case, consider a **`PaymentService`** that initially handles credit card payments but later expands to support third-party providers like Stripe, PayPal, and others. By splitting this functionality into a dedicated microservice, we can scale it independently and add new payment providers without impacting the rest of the system.

While microservices offer clear benefits when used with DDD, they also have inherent challenges that can complicate system design and operations. Managing multiple independent services introduces distributed complexity, making it more challenging to maintain data consistency and handle inter-service communication. Operational overhead increases as each service requires monitoring, logging, and maintenance. Recognizing and addressing these challenges is crucial to ensuring that the transition to microservices does not introduce more problems than it solves. Despite its advantages, microservices come with their own set of challenges as follows:

- **Distributed complexity**: Microservices introduce a new level of complexity by distributing the system across multiple services. This can lead to issues like network latency, service discovery, and communication failures.

- **Data consistency**: Ensuring data consistency across multiple services is harder than in a monolithic system. Distributed transactions and eventual consistency models can introduce complexity.

- **Operational overhead**: Managing multiple services increases the operational overhead, as each service requires independent monitoring, logging, and maintenance.

- **Inter-service communication**: Unlike monoliths, where components communicate via in-process method calls, microservices require network-based communication (HTTP, gRPC), which introduces latency, complexity, and potential failures.

When talking about microservices, we can explore that this architecture capability is a natural choice for an evolutionary architecture. Even though a monolith is still valid in some situations, sometimes it makes sense to move it as a microservice. One of the key strengths of DDD is its focus on organizing software around the domain itself. When exploring DDD, the classes are organized mostly on the package-by-feature structure, where each feature behaves as a domain, and teams naturally create boundaries that align with the business, making the transition to microservices more seamless when the time comes.

```
com.example.hotel.domain
|
├── reservation
|   ├── model
|   |   ├── Guest.java              // Value Object
|   |   ├── Room.java               // Entity
|   |   └── ReservationStatus.java  // Enum or status value
|   ├── service
|   |   └── ReservationService.java // Domain service
|   ├── event
|   |   └── RoomReservedEvent.java  // Domain event
|   └── repository
```

```
|        └── Hotel.java              // DDD Repository interface
|
├── payment
|   ├── model
|   |   └── PaymentMethod.java       // Value Object
|   ├── service
|   |   └── PaymentService.java      // Domain service interface
|   ├── event
|   |   └── PaymentConfirmedEvent.java
|   └── exception
|       └── PaymentDeclinedException.java
|
└── shared
    ├── exception
    |   └── BusinessException.java
    ├── event
    |   └── DomainEvent.java         // Marker or base class/interface
    └── util
        └── RoomNumberValidator.java
```

A practical progression begins with a traditional monolith, which then gradually evolves into a modular monolith. In this stage, different features or subdomains are isolated into distinct modules. This intermediate structure helps clarify responsibilities, define integration points, and solidify the team's understanding of the domain. Once the boundaries between modules are stable and there is a business or technical need for greater independence, such as for scaling, team autonomy, or deployment flexibility, these modules can be transformed into separate microservices.

This shift often leads to the discovery and realization of distinct, bounded contexts, with each microservice encapsulating a specific subdomain of the business. For example, consider a hotel system; a clear division may arise between the reservation and payment subdomains. Each of these can further develop into its bounded context, capable of being separately developed and deployed as a microservice. This enhances the relationship between business goals and technical architecture, improving the system's scalability relative to the organization.

Thus, microservices offer several advantages, especially when aligned with DDD, but they also introduce complexity and operational challenges. Therefore, it is essential to carefully evaluate whether a system truly benefits from microservices before making the shift. In the next section, we will explore the *need for microservices* and help assess whether this architecture fits a project.

Need for microservices

Microservices have gained massive popularity recently, often touted as the go-to solution for building scalable, maintainable systems. However, as with any architectural choice, microservices come with trade-offs. While they can provide clear benefits, they are not a one-size-fits-all solution, and it is essential to carefully evaluate whether they are the right fit for your project.

Sam Newman, a well-known author on microservices, shares this perspective in his books *Building Microservices: Designing Fine-Grained Systems* and *Monolith to Microservices: Evolutionary Patterns to Transform Your Monolith*. Newman emphasizes[1] that microservices are not necessarily the best starting point for an application or a startup business. Instead, beginning with a monolith can be a more practical choice, allowing for simplicity in the early stages of a project. Microservices require a solid infrastructure, automation, and observability processes, which can introduce significant complexity early on.

For example, microservices can become cumbersome if you do not yet have automated deployment pipelines, as each service needs its own deployment process. Similarly, observability is crucial in a microservices architecture. Identifying issues across distributed services can be time-consuming and error-prone without proper logging and tracing, especially when debugging a request that touches multiple services. It may require logging into several machines and manually tracking the flow of a request, a task that becomes a nightmare when under time pressure.

Before jumping into microservices, it is okay to start with a monolithic architecture and only break it apart into microservices when the complexity and size of your system genuinely demand it. This evolutionary approach allows your system to grow while keeping things manageable in the early stages, as shown in the following table:

Scenario	When to use a monolith	When to use microservices
Team size	Small teams that can easily collaborate	Large teams that need to work on independent parts of the system
System complexity	Low complexity with simple business requirements	High complexity where different domains need to evolve independently
Deployment automation	No automation or minimal CI/CD processes	Fully automated CI/CD pipelines in place
Scalability needs	System-wide scaling is sufficient	Specific services require independent scaling
Observability	Minimal need for distributed logging and tracing	Strong need for logging, tracing, and observability
Time to market	Need to deliver quickly without the overhead of managing multiple services	Can afford to invest in the setup and management of multiple services early on

Table 5.2: When to use microservices and when a monolith

Microservices can be an excellent architectural choice, but only if used in the right context. If your team is small, your business domain is simple, or you do not yet have robust automation and monitoring tools, it may be better to stick with a monolith until your system requires the flexibility and scalability that microservices offer.

There is much more to explore regarding software architecture beyond the simple dichotomy of monolith versus microservices. Distributed systems encompass many patterns, challenges, and technologies far beyond these two approaches. In the next section, we will dive into *applying DDD in distributed systems*, exploring how DDD principles can guide the architecture of complex, distributed systems, and what additional considerations come into play in this broader context.

Applying DDD in distributed systems

When thinking about distributed systems, DDD plays an essential role in monolithic or microservices architectures and across various other system architectures. Distributed systems go beyond the traditional dichotomy of monoliths versus microservices, and DDD offers valuable tools to organize complex domains within these more modern and distributed patterns.

In event-driven architecture, such as systems built with message brokers like *Kafka* or *RabbitMQ*, the design focuses on the idea that events trigger business processes and enable services to communicate asynchronously. This approach is particularly valuable in distributed systems, where decoupling is crucial for scalability and resilience.

DDD also emphasizes the use of domain events within systems, even in monolithic or modular monolithic architectures. These events represent significant occurrences in the business and facilitate communication between components without tight coupling, promoting better separation of concerns.

Whether events are sent to external systems or managed internally, emphasizing domain events helps capture the essential actions and reactions relevant to the domain. By clearly defining which events are important and how they propagate through bounded contexts or modules, DDD ensures that business logic remains coherent, even in complex, distributed architectures.

A similar alignment happens with serverless architectures, where the system is broken down into small, stateless functions triggered by specific events. Serverless is perfect for situations that require dynamic scalability (with systems scaling down to zero when not being used), cost-efficiency. Serverless is a great fit for services that serve seasonal types of use cases, as it can handle operations even at increasing user demand, and adapt as it lowers, by decreasing the number of active services. DDD helps keep the focus on the domain by ensuring that each function is tied to a specific domain action. Instead of thinking of functions as technical code units, DDD encourages thinking of them as business operations. Each function performs a single, meaningful task within the domain context. DDD's clarity in this model ensures that the system remains focused on business logic even as infrastructure concerns like scalability and infrastructure management fade into the background.

In cloud-native architectures, the ability to scale and manage resilience is paramount. These applications are designed to be modular, running on containerized platforms that can handle fluctuating demand. Here, DDD provides a powerful way to keep the core business logic intact as infrastructure evolves and scales. DDD's focus on bounded contexts, distinct parts of the system representing specific business areas, ensures that each cloud-native service has a clear responsibility and can evolve independently without impacting the overall system. Even as the infrastructure changes dynamically to meet performance requirements, the domain logic remains steady, allowing businesses to focus on delivering value rather than managing the complexity of scaling distributed services.

It is important to differentiate between architectural styles, which describe the overall structure of distributed systems, and architectural patterns, which guide the internal structure of individual applications. Examples of styles include event-driven architecture, **service-oriented architecture** (**SOA**), and serverless design. These styles dictate how multiple services or applications interact, communicate, and scale within a broader solution. They influence the overall system's composition and deployment across various environments, often involving asynchronous communication, orchestration, or infrastructure-level considerations.

In contrast, architectural patterns, such as monolith, microservices, and hexagonal architecture (also known as ports and adapters), focus on the internal structure of a single application. For instance, hexagonal architecture emphasizes the separation of concerns between the business domain and external interfaces, such as databases, messaging systems, or web controllers. In this pattern, the domain is at the core and is kept isolated from technical details, allowing for independent evolution. DDD aligns well with this structure, as it stresses the importance of separating business logic and clearly defining domain boundaries. This separation is particularly valuable in distributed systems, as it helps maintain a consistent domain model even when technologies and interfaces change.

Lastly, many modern systems adopt hybrid architectures, combining different approaches to fit specific needs. For example, a system might use microservices for the core business domains but rely on serverless functions for auxiliary services or event-driven patterns to facilitate communication between components. DDD ensures the domain model remains consistent, even when the technical implementation involves multiple architectural patterns. Bounded contexts help define which part of the system handles which responsibilities, ensuring that the domain logic is clear, no matter how the underlying infrastructure is structured.

Although distributed and diverse, these architectures greatly benefit from applying DDD principles to maintain clarity and consistency throughout the system. While domain modeling is essential, the actual value of DDD lies in how it influences team structures, communication pathways, and system boundaries. By clearly defining bounded contexts, DDD helps align software components with the organization's business capabilities, enabling teams to fully own specific domains. This alignment simplifies coordination, reduces dependencies across teams, and fosters more autonomous and effective groups, each focused on a well-defined area of the business.

DDD also plays a strategic role in determining when and how new microservices should be developed. Rather than prematurely extracting services based on technical boundaries, teams can make these decisions based on well-understood domain boundaries and their interaction patterns. When communication between services is necessary, DDD promotes the use of meaningful, domain-driven API contracts that reflect a shared Ubiquitous Language while respecting the local language of each subdomain. This clarity enhances cross-team collaboration, improves governance across service boundaries, and provides a solid foundation for distributed coordination patterns, such as the Saga pattern. In fact, in distributed environments where data consistency must be achieved through asynchronous processes and careful orchestration, clear domain ownership and a common language become not just beneficial, but essential.

As we wrap up the exploration of applying DDD to distributed systems, it is essential to remember that as systems evolve, you may encounter legacy code that does not align with DDD principles. Refactoring these systems to suit a DDD approach is often necessary to keep your architecture maintainable and future-proof. In the next section, we will explore how to refactor legacy code to align with DDD principles and modernize the systems without losing sight of the core business goals.

Refactoring legacy code to align with DDD principles

In an ideal world, we would always start with a clean slate, designing our systems with the latest best practices and architectural principles in mind. However, most of us work with existing systems, often profoundly embedded legacy code. This is especially true for a business's core systems, which have been around for years and may not reflect the latest thinking in software architecture. DDD offers a way to modernize these systems, but it requires a thoughtful and deliberate approach to refactoring.

One of the most critical elements of this process is the necessity of a robust legacy modernization strategy. Refactoring is not just about improving the codebase; it is about keeping the system operational while improving its maintainability, scalability, and alignment with business goals. This balance is essential because, in most cases, you must continue the business to perform a massive overhaul. The code must continue functioning while you slowly and carefully transform it to reflect the domain and DDD principles better.

While refactoring, it is vital to consider the human aspect. Developers who have worked with the system for years may have become comfortable with the existing codebase, no matter how tangled or inefficient it might be. A significant refactor can disrupt workflows and affect team morale. Some developers might resist the changes, especially if they have mastered the current system. One way to overcome this challenge is to introduce the concept of an **architecture**

decision record (ADR), a document that helps communicate the reasons behind architectural changes, outlining the proposed refactor's benefits and impact. Presenting the rationale behind refactoring, backed by data and a clear path forward, can help win the support of the development team by making the advantages clear and showing the team that their concerns are being considered.

Once you have aligned the team around the need for refactoring, the next step is communicating with stakeholders. Refactoring takes time, and stakeholders may be focused on immediate deliverables or new features. Negotiating time and space to address technical debt is crucial. By explaining the long-term benefits, such as increased agility, fewer bugs, and improved scalability, you can help stakeholders see the value of this investment. It is essential to agree on a schedule or frequency for tackling technical debt so that it becomes part of the project's ongoing process rather than a one-time effort.

Technically, the first and most crucial step when refactoring legacy code is ensuring that any changes made will not alter the existing behavior of the system, especially in terms of the business logic. This means that we need to guarantee the safety of the changes by establishing tests that provide confidence that the behavior remains unchanged. Refactoring is about altering the structure of the code without affecting its functionality, and testing is the key to maintaining this balance.

Legacy systems often have inadequate test coverage, so building a solid suite of tests is critical before starting any significant refactoring. Once the code is well-covered with tests, you can begin refactoring in small, incremental steps, taking *baby steps* to ensure that if something goes wrong, it is easy to identify the issue and roll back to a previous version.

Introducing many changes at once can make tracing bugs back to their source incredibly difficult. By working incrementally, you can ensure that any issues are contained within a specific version or change set, minimizing the risk of creating new problems while refactoring. This slow, methodical approach is critical when dealing with mission-critical code.

The next essential step in refactoring legacy systems is ensuring that the problems you are fixing will not return. There is little point in cleaning up a messy codebase if it is allowed to become messy again. This is where software architecture governance comes into play. By establishing rules and constraints, you can prevent future developers from inadvertently reintroducing the very issues you are trying to resolve. Tools like *ArchUnit, PMD*, and *Checkstyle* are invaluable in this context. They allow you to enforce architectural rules, coding standards, and best practices across the project. For instance, if part of your refactor involves separating domain logic from infrastructure, you can use ArchUnit to ensure that developers do not accidentally introduce infrastructure dependencies into the domain layer in the future.

Ultimately, refactoring legacy code to align with DDD principles requires more than technical effort; it demands a thoughtful strategy that includes human and technical factors. Modernizing a system involves the people who build and maintain it as much as the code itself. It is essential to take the time to build consensus among your development team, communicate clearly with stakeholders, and create a sustainable approach to technical debt. Only after addressing these human factors can you move on to the technical challenges of refactoring.

More than just cleaning up technical debt, refactoring is about crafting a long-term legacy modernization strategy that aligns your codebase with your business's current needs. Doing so creates a foundation that allows the system to evolve as the industry evolves. This means paying attention to not only the code but also the culture of the team, the expectations of the stakeholders, and the governance that will keep a system clean moving forward.

As we look ahead, applying DDD principles in legacy systems often requires gradual refactoring, and it goes beyond just the technical side. Now that we have explored how to refactor legacy systems, the next step is to consider how to apply these principles across the entire system.

Conclusion

In this chapter, we explored the application of DDD across various architectural styles, from monolithic to distributed systems. We discussed how DDD principles can guide effective software development. We examined the strategic decisions involved in adopting microservices and how to approach legacy system refactoring in a careful, structured way, ensuring the system's continued operation while aligning it with DDD principles. By addressing the technical and human aspects of refactoring, we laid the foundation for modernizing legacy systems with a focus on domain-centric design.

As we move forward, we must consider how DDD can be integrated with other architectural patterns. In the next chapter, we will explore how combining DDD and Clean Architecture can create a robust framework for building maintainable, scalable systems, ensuring that your software remains adaptable as your business evolves.

Points to remember

- **DDD is applicable beyond microservices and monolithic architectures**: It provides value in event-driven, serverless, cloud-native, and hybrid architectures by ensuring clarity in business logic.

- **Monolithic architectures remain a valid choice**: They simplify development and deployment, especially when automation and scalability requirements are minimal.

- **Microservices introduce complexity**: They require strong infrastructure, deployment automation, and observability to be effective.

- **Refactoring legacy systems requires a strategy**: It is essential to ensure business continuity, involve the team in decision-making, and gradually introduce changes to avoid disruption.

- **The human factor matters in refactoring**: Developers may resist change, and stakeholders need to see the long-term benefits before committing to modernization efforts.

- **Small, incremental refactoring steps prevent risk**: Changing too much at once increases the chance of introducing hard-to-trace bugs.

- **Architectural governance prevents recurring issues**: Tools like ArchUnit, PMD, and Checkstyle help enforce best practices and prevent technical debt from resurfacing.

- **Bounded contexts help manage distributed complexity**: They define clear service boundaries in microservices and event-driven architectures, ensuring domain alignment.

- **Observability is crucial for distributed systems**: Without centralized logging and tracing, debugging becomes difficult and time-consuming.

- **Modernizing with DDD is more than a technical change**: It is a continuous process that requires balancing business needs, technical improvements, and team alignment.

Multiple choice questions

1. **What is one key advantage of using DDD in a monolithic architecture?**

   a. It simplifies communication between microservices.

   b. It helps maintain focus on business logic while organizing layers.

   c. It increases the number of external dependencies.

   d. It reduces the need for a database.

2. **Which of the following best explains why microservices are not always the best choice to start with?**

   a. Microservices reduce the flexibility of the architecture.

   b. Microservices make the system harder to scale.

   c. Microservices require significant infrastructure and automation to manage effectively.

   d. Microservices limit the team's ability to add new features.

3. **When considering team scalability in a monolithic architecture, what is a major challenge?**

   a. The need for more databases.

   b. Handling code merges and rebases with large teams.

   c. The complexity of creating domain events.

   d. Deploying the system across multiple cloud providers.

4. **What is a recommended tool to enforce architectural constraints and prevent reintroducing mistakes in a refactored legacy system?**

   a. Gradle

   b. ArchUnit

   c. Maven

   d. Jenkins

5. **Why is it important to take small, incremental steps when refactoring legacy code?**

   a. To avoid upsetting the development team.

   b. To ensure that the code behavior does not change, and bugs can be easily identified.

   c. To minimize the amount of code committed at once.

   d. To simplify database migrations.

6. **How does DDD benefit event-driven architectures in distributed systems?**

   a. By simplifying database transactions.

   b. By defining domain events that capture meaningful business actions and keeping the focus on the domain logic.

   c. By eliminating the need for infrastructure code.

   d. By increasing system complexity for better control.

7. **What is the purpose of using an ADR in a refactoring process?**

   a. To document decisions about the user interface.

   b. To help communicate architectural changes to the team and justify the rationale behind them.

   c. To track deployment processes.

   d. To reduce the number of classes in a system.

8. **What is the key difference between a DAO and a DDD repository?**

   a. A DAO is part of the domain layer, while a repository is part of the infrastructure layer.

   b. A DAO is focused on database operations, while a DDD repository uses business-centric language and focuses on the domain.

   c. A DAO manages domain events, while a repository handles security concerns.

   d. A DAO is only used in monolithic architectures, while a repository is used only in microservices.

9. **What is the primary focus of refactoring legacy code to align with DDD principles?**
   a. Changing the core functionality of the system.
   b. Improving the performance of the system.
   c. Transforming the structure of the code while keeping its behavior the same.
   d. Rewriting the entire system to match the latest technology trends.

10. **What human aspect is crucial when refactoring legacy code?**
    a. Convincing developers to adopt new technology.
    b. Managing team expectations and communicating the reasons for change, often using tools like ADR.
    c. Avoiding any changes to the system's architecture.
    d. Ensuring stakeholders have no involvement in the process.

Answers

Question number	Answer option letter
1.	b.
2.	c.
3.	b.
4.	b.
5.	b.
6.	b.
7.	b.
8.	b.
9.	c.
10.	b.

References

1. *Newman, Sam. (2020). Should I Use Microservices?*
2. *Evans, Eric. (2003). Domain-Driven Design: Tackling Complexity in the Heart of Software.*

CHAPTER 6

Integrating DDD with Clean Architecture

Introduction

Sustainable systems are designed with clarity and adaptability in mind. Additionally, the complexity can be managed by the combination of both **domain-driven design (DDD)** and Clean Architecture, where DDD drives design driven by business logic, and Clean Architecture supports the separation of concerns. Together, they help developers in the creation of flexible and scalable solutions.

This section explores how DDD and Clean Architecture can work together, and how the integration between domain modeling and architectural practices can support the design of well-defined layer boundaries and the benefits that come with it. This exploration will help readers understand how to use both approaches to design software that can evolve gracefully and revolutionize their work.

Structure

In this chapter, we will explore more about the following topics:

- Overview of Clean Architecture
- Combining DDD with Clean Architecture
- Structuring code for maintainability

Technical requirements

The following are the tools for this chapter, where we will use Java 21 or higher and any IDE:

- Java 21
- Git
- Maven
- Any preferred IDE

Objectives

This chapter aims to clarify how Clean Architecture and DDD complement each other to create maintainable, scalable, and adaptable software systems. By the end of this chapter, readers will grasp the principles of Clean Architecture, the importance of the dependency rule, and how to structure software with a clear separation between domain logic and infrastructure concerns. Additionally, they will learn how DDD's domain modeling fits within Clean Architecture's layered approach, ensuring that core business rules remain isolated from external dependencies, ultimately leading to more resilient and testable applications.

Overview of Clean Architecture

Clean Architecture is a software design philosophy that keeps a system's core business logic independent from any external frameworks or infrastructure. It became well-known through *Robert C. Martin's* book *Clean Architecture*[1] and aligned closely with *Alistair Cockburn's Hexagonal Architecture*, also known as *Ports and Adapters*[2]. These approaches focus on creating systems that are easy to understand, test, and maintain over time by enforcing a strict separation of concerns through layered design, thereby enlightening developers about the advantages of this approach.

At the heart of Clean Architecture is the idea of dependency direction; dependencies always flow inward toward the business logic, ensuring that the inner layers, which contain high-level policies, are not affected by changes in the outer layers, which are more concrete. The inner layers are isolated from implementation details like databases or user interfaces, placed in the outermost layers.

This design creates a flexible system where changes in the outermost parts, such as frameworks or UI libraries, do not ripple into the core business logic.

Clean Architecture typically divides a system into four concentric layers, each serving a distinct role:

- **Entities**: These contain enterprise-wide business rules and are the most abstract part of the system. You can think of them as domain entities that encapsulate core business logic independent of specific applications.

- **Use cases**: This layer houses application-specific business rules. Use cases implement your application's actions and should focus on a single responsibility, closely aligning with what DDD calls *application services*.

- **Interface adapters**: This layer translates data between the use case layer and the external systems. It contains things like **Model-View-Controller (MVC)** components, or gateway implementations to interact with external services, ensuring the business logic remains untouched by infrastructure-specific details.

- **Frameworks and drivers**: The outermost layer, which contains tools like databases, UI frameworks, or external APIs. This layer is where you will implement communication with external services or infrastructure, separating it from the core business logic.

The following figure shows the ring architecture:

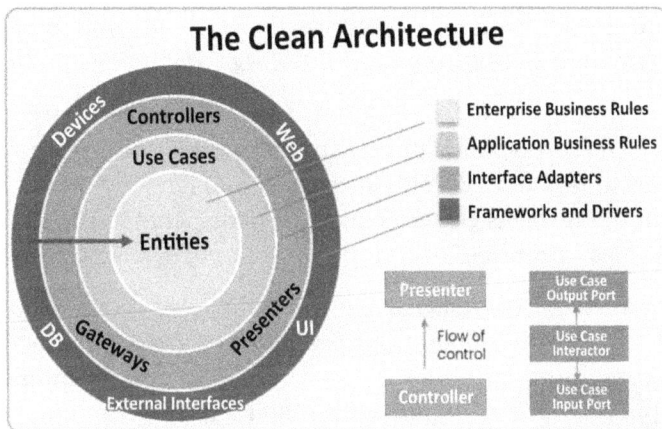

Figure 6.1: The clean architectural illustration

The dependency rule is the cornerstone of this architecture: source code dependencies must always point inward (considering the ring circles as a reference). This rule is not just a guideline but a fundamental principle that ensures the integrity of the architecture. Inner layers should never be aware of the outer layers. Function calls and data formats, data structures, or formats generated by outer layers (like database schema or API response formats) should not be shared with inner layers.

Adhering to this rule ensures a clear separation between high-level policies and low-level details, making adapting to new technologies or evolving business needs easier without significant rewrites.

While the concentric circles are a proper schematic, Clean Architecture is not rigid. Depending on your project's complexity, you might need more or fewer layers. This flexibility empowers you to tailor the architecture to your specific needs, always ensuring that the dependency rule is followed and protecting the core business logic from unnecessary coupling to the outer layers.

Now that we have explored the structure and guiding principles of Clean Architecture, we can explore how DDD fits into this layered approach. In the next section, we will see how combining DDD's rich modeling capabilities with Clean Architecture's separation of concerns leads to highly expressive software systems that are resilient to change.

Combining DDD with Clean Architecture

When examining hexagonal architecture and DDD, it becomes evident that they integrate naturally, forming a robust and maintainable design framework. Hexagonal architecture, also known as **ports and adapters,** emphasizes the separation of the core application from external systems, a principle that aligns closely with DDD's layering. Specifically, DDD's Domain Layer corresponds to the core domain model in the center of the hexagon. At the same time, the Application Layer aligns with the use cases or application services that orchestrate domain behavior. This structural correspondence enforces the clean separation of concerns, ensuring that business rules remain isolated from user interfaces, databases, and other infrastructure components.

The domain layer in DDD corresponds directly to the entities and aggregates of the hexagonal model. These represent the system's core business logic and remain untouched by infrastructure or framework-specific details. This clean separation ensures that the domain remains pure and focused on business rules, regardless of changes in external systems.

Similarly, the application layer in DDD is a natural fit for use cases in hexagonal architecture. Use cases represent the system's operations, orchestrating the business logic, but without containing it. They act as intermediaries between the domain model and the external systems, handling input/output, validation, and invoking the appropriate domain services.

Creating well-defined boundaries with Clean Architecture and DDD

To illustrate this combination, we will continue with the hotel management context from the previous chapter. This example will be converted into a hexagonal model while incorporating the jMolecules framework, particularly the **jmolecules-hexagonal-architecture** module. By leveraging this module, we ensure that the architecture adheres to clean boundaries while remaining Java-agnostic, allowing for flexible integration into any Java-based framework you choose.

We will retain the **Room** as an entity, **Guest** as a value object, and **Hotel** as the repository for managing room reservations and check-ins/check-outs. However, we will significantly change the **HotelService**.

In the previous chapter, the **HotelService** encapsulated both domain logic and application logic. While this approach works, it conflates responsibilities and can lead to a violation of the single responsibility principle. Clean Architecture advocates breaking down such services into use cases, where each class encapsulates the business logic for a specific task that the system must perform. This separation not only improves maintainability but also enhances testability and reuse.

Instead of a single **HotelService**, we now have two distinct use cases: one for check-in and another for check-out. Each of these use cases encapsulates a single, focused task, making the code easier to maintain and ensuring that business rules are applied consistently.

The **CheckOutUseCase** handles checking a guest out of the hotel. By isolating this behavior in a dedicated use case, we ensure the logic is reusable and can be tested independently.

```java
import org.jmolecules.architecture.hexagonal.Application;

@Application
public class CheckOutUseCase {

    private final Hotel hotel;

    public CheckOutUseCase(Hotel hotel) {
        this.hotel = hotel;
    }

    public void checkOut(Room room) {
        if (room == null) {
            throw new IllegalArgumentException("Room cannot be null");
        }

        room.cleanRoom();
        hotel.checkOut(room);
    }
}
```

Here, the **CheckOutUseCase** is solely responsible for the check-out process. The domain logic for cleaning the room and removing the guest is applied through the **Room** entity, keeping the business rules clean and isolated.

The **CheckInUseCase** orchestrates the check-in process, which includes checking room availability and handling payments through a domain service. This separation of concerns allows the use case to focus solely on the orchestration while delegating domain logic to the appropriate services and entities.

```java
import org.jmolecules.architecture.hexagonal.Application;

@Application
```

```java
public class CheckInUseCase {

    private final Hotel hotel;
    private final PaymentService paymentService;

    public CheckInUseCase(Hotel hotel, PaymentService paymentService) {
        this.hotel = hotel;
        this.paymentService = paymentService;
    }

    public Room checkIn(Guest guest) {
        if (hotel.countBy() >= 100) {
            throw new IllegalStateException("Hotel is full");
        }

        var emptyRoom = hotel.findEmptyRoom().orElseThrow(() -> new
IllegalStateException("No empty room available"));
        paymentService.pay(guest);  // Delegating domain logic to
PaymentService
        emptyRoom.setGuest(guest);
        return hotel.checkIn(emptyRoom);
    }
}
```

TIP: **In this sample, we are using `IllegalStateException`, but here you can explore the creation of the exception hierarchy. For example, `HotelException` that extends `RuntimeException` and `HotelFullException` that extends `HotelException`.**

In this use case, the check-in logic is focused on the business tasks of ensuring that the hotel is not overbooked, finding an available room, and processing payment. The payment business logic is encapsulated within the **`PaymentService`**, maintaining a clear separation between the application and domain layers.

Creating a bridge between the core application and external systems

The next step in combining DDD with Clean Architecture is creating adapters that translate between the domain model and the external systems (ports). In this case, we will use **Data Transfer Objects (DTOs)**, which are responsible for carrying data across system boundaries. These DTOs are simple, immutable objects that hold data without business logic, making them ideal for interaction between the use cases and external interfaces like controllers or APIs.

In the hexagonal architecture, adapters bridge the core application and external systems, translating requests and responses. Adapters can translate inputs from a user interface or an API into commands that are understood by the domain layer. In our case, the **GuestDTO** and **RoomDTO** act as the adapters, converting data to and from the domain objects (e.g., **Guest** and **Room**) and the external systems.

```
import org.jmolecules.architecture.hexagonal.Adapter;


@Adapter
public record GuestDTO(String documentNumber, String name) {
}

@Adapter
public record RoomDTO(int number, GuestDTO guest) {
}
```

These DTOs, annotated with **@Adapter**, represent how data flows between the use cases and the outside world. They convert the internal domain objects (like **Room** and **Guest**) into a more suitable format for external systems (like APIs, web controllers, or other interfaces), and vice versa.

In the hexagonal model, a **port** is what defines the boundary between the application and the outside world. It represents interfaces that the application exposes to external systems, such as controllers, APIs, or other applications. The application interacts with the domain through the use cases, and the ports expose these use cases to the outside world.

In the following example, we use the **HotelController** as a port. This controller is the entry point for user interactions and delegates business logic to the relevant use cases.

```
import expert.os.books.ddd.chapter06.hotels.CheckInUseCase;
import expert.os.books.ddd.chapter06.hotels.CheckOutUseCase;
import expert.os.books.ddd.chapter06.hotels.Room;
import org.jmolecules.architecture.hexagonal.Port;


// Here we have either a controller or a resource to expose the application
services
@Port
public class HotelController {

    private final CheckInUseCase checkInUseCase;
    private final CheckOutUseCase checkOutUseCase;
    private final HotelMapper hotelMapper;
```

```
    public HotelController(CheckInUseCase checkInUseCase, CheckOutUseCase
checkOutUseCase, HotelMapper hotelMapper) {
        this.checkInUseCase = checkInUseCase;
        this.checkOutUseCase = checkOutUseCase;
        this.hotelMapper = hotelMapper;
    }

    public RoomDTO checkInRoom(GuestDTO guestDTO) {
        var guest = hotelMapper.toEntity(guestDTO);
        Room room = checkInUseCase.checkIn(guest);
        return hotelMapper.toDTO(room);
    }

    public void checkOutRoom(RoomDTO roomDTO) {
        var room = hotelMapper.toEntity(roomDTO);
        checkOutUseCase.checkOut(room);
    }
}
```

This design ensures that the domain logic remains untouched, encapsulated in the application layer, while the controllers (ports) manage external interactions without directly involving domain entities or logic.

Thus, the following are all the components we have created to combine DDD with Clean Architecture:

- **Domain layer**:
  - o **Room**: Entity representing a room in the hotel.
  - o **Guest**: Value object representing a guest.
  - o **Hotel**: Repository interface for managing room check-ins, check-outs, and reservations.
- **Application layer**:
  - o **CheckInUseCase**: Handles the check-in logic, ensuring room availability and payment processing.
  - o **CheckOutUseCase**: Handles the check-out logic, including cleaning the room and updating the repository.
- **Adapters**:
  - o **GuestDTO and RoomDTO**: DTOs used to communicate data between the domain and external systems.

- **Port**:

  o **HotelController**: The entry point for user interactions, delegating tasks to the respective use cases, and mapping data between DTOs and domain entities.

This combination of DDD and hexagonal architecture ensures a clean separation of concerns. The core domain logic is insulated from infrastructure concerns, and the system remains flexible for future changes.

The following section will explore *structuring code for maintainability*, discussing strategies to ensure the code remains clean, modular, and scalable as the system evolves. This will help ensure that changes can be implemented with minimal effort, maintaining the architecture's integrity and simplicity.

Structuring code for maintainability

In the previous section, we saw how DDD principles and Clean Architecture impacted the use case layer. The most impactful improvement was the splitting of the service into two distinct use cases, which provided clarity and simplicity. This approach made the application easier to understand and improved its documentation and testability.

However, defining use cases is not always the starting point in software design. While separating responsibilities into individual use cases helps with maintainability, starting with this task is not mandatory in every scenario.

Another possible starting point would be during refactoring, which can be a powerful tool in software development when properly backed by a solid test suite. Refactoring allows us to adapt the code as the system evolves, preventing software erosion (the gradual decline in code quality over time).

The field of software is ever-changing due to shifts in businesses and products, as a reflection of market demands. In this environment, it is crucial to engage in refactoring to uphold code quality and prevent the introduction of unmanageable complexity when making changes. It is essential to steer clear of overengineering, as adding excessive layers or abstractions too soon can result in unnecessary complexity, even when done with good intentions.

Hence, as we previously did, it is often more practical to begin with a simple service that serves as both a service and an application layer, and only introduce additional layers, like use cases, when the responsibilities within the service start to diverge. This approach ensures clarity and maintainability, keeping the codebase clean without overengineering.

Not all scenarios require breaking down into distinct use cases. If a particular business logic has common behavior across multiple actions, it might make more sense to maintain a shared service rather than breaking it down into separate use cases. For example, the **HotelService** could serve as a common service shared by both the **CheckInUseCase** and **CheckOutUseCase**, as shown in the following code snippet:

```java
@Application
public class CheckOutUseCase {

    private final Hotel hotel;
    private final HotelService hotelService;

}

@Application
public class CheckInUseCase {

    private final Hotel hotel;
    private final PaymentService paymentService;
    private final HotelService hotelService;


}
```

In this case, the **HotelService** component can encapsulate common logic shared by both use cases, reducing code duplication and preserving maintainability. To decide whether to use Clean Architecture, DDD, or a combination of both, you need to understand the purpose of each as follows:

- **Clean Architecture**: It focuses on maintaining independence between different system layers (UI, business rules, data access, etc.). It emphasizes decoupling so that the core business logic is isolated from frameworks or external libraries. It is beneficial when you need flexibility and adaptability in the system's structure.

- **DDD**: It is a strategic approach to solving complex business problems. It focuses on creating a model that represents the domain, using building blocks like entities, value objects, aggregates, and repositories. DDD is useful when dealing with a complex domain and needing to integrate business logic deeply with software design.

There are specific situations where using Clean Architecture alone makes sense. It is ideal to ensure flexibility and adaptability when the primary focus is on decoupling different application layers, such as the user interface, data access, and business logic. Clean Architecture is also effective when the business logic is not particularly complex, allowing the system to remain framework-independent. It is well-suited for small to medium-sized applications where domain complexity does not justify the full use of DDD.

On the other hand, using DDD alone is advantageous when the domain complexity is high, requiring a detailed business logic model using entities, value objects, and other rich domain constructs. This approach is beneficial in scenarios where strategic domain modeling is more critical than decoupling the different layers of the system. Additionally, when a system must evolve based on complex business rules that must be reflected directly in the code, DDD offers a structured approach for managing this complexity.

Combining Clean Architecture and DDD provides the most balanced solution for more complex systems. This combination is necessary when decoupling the system's layers is important, but the business logic is also complex. It is particularly effective in large systems with multiple bounded contexts, where the goal is to protect core business logic from external dependencies while still managing application complexity through proper layering. Using both together ensures that maintainability and business logic expressiveness are addressed simultaneously.

Using and combining each approach

We can combine these approaches or let both work alone, while they work better together, and you can, in the continuous evolution of your project, start with DDD only and put layers of Clean Architecture when it does make sense based on the context, as follows:

- Use Clean Architecture when decoupling and flexibility are the primary concerns, and domain complexity is low.

- Use DDD when domain complexity is high and detailed business logic modeling is needed.

- Use both Clean Architecture and DDD when you need to balance decoupling layers while managing complex business logic.

The following table introduces a view of both approaches, when you could try only using one against the other, and finally, the best combination is when you can apply both together:

Aspect	Clean Architecture	DDD	When to use both
Focus	Decoupling system layers (UI, business rules, data access)	Capturing business logic and complexity in domain models	Decoupling of system layers + complex business domains modeling
Core component	application services; Use cases, such as orchestrating business logic.	Entities, value objects, repositories, services	Use cases for logic orchestration, + domain entities for core business complexity
Independence	business logic independent from UI/ databases / external systems	Software model alignment, business domain, and rules	Business logic is independent from external actors, + rich domain model
Complexity	Good for a simple business	Handle complex business rules, bounded contexts, and strategic modeling	Best for large systems that need both separation of concerns and domain modeling.

Aspect	Clean Architecture	DDD	When to use both
Flexibility	High flexibility. Easy to swap frameworks, UI layers, or databases	Low flexibility. Focus on capturing the domain accurately.	Framework flexibility + rich, accurate domain
Testing	Isolated use cases, easier to test	Self-contained domain entities, testable domain logic	Independent testing can be applied both by layer and by functionality, supporting simpler maintenance and greater scalability across the system.
Refactoring	Easy due to decoupled layers	It can be harder to refactor if the domain model becomes tightly coupled with the infrastructure	Easier refactoring of Clean Architecture, protected domain logic from DDD.

Table 6.1: DDD vs. Clean Architecture

There is no one-size-fits-all answer when choosing between Clean Architecture and DDD. The decision depends on the complexity of the domain and the need for system flexibility.

Starting with a simpler architecture and evolving it as the system grows is a pragmatic approach that allows you to balance simplicity with maintainability.

Conclusion

This chapter explored how Clean Architecture and DDD can be combined to structure code for maintainability. We discussed how splitting services into distinct use cases improves clarity, simplifies testing, and supports better documentation. We also compared scenarios where Clean Architecture alone is sufficient, where DDD alone is needed, and how combining both approaches provides a powerful way to handle complex systems. By keeping refactoring in mind and applying layers only when necessary, we can ensure that our software remains adaptable and resilient.

In the next chapter, we will focus on a crucial aspect of DDD data modeling. We will explore in detail how to design models that accurately reflect business logic while maintaining flexibility and simplicity. This will include a comprehensive discussion on aggregates, repositories, and the integration of DDD concepts with database design. We aim to ensure that our data layer aligns with the domain while supporting efficient and scalable operations.

Points to remember

- **Clean Architecture**: Enforces a layered structure where dependencies always point inward, protecting core business logic from external influences.

- **The dependency rule**: Ensures that inner layers remain independent of outer layers, preventing framework-specific details from affecting domain logic.

- **Entities layer**: Contains enterprise-wide business rules and represents the domain model in Clean Architecture.

- **Use cases layer**: Orchestrates application-specific logic without implementing domain rules directly, aligning with application services in DDD.

- **Interface adapters**: Act as a bridge between the core logic and external systems, handling data transformations and communication.

- **Frameworks and drivers layer**: The outermost layer that contains tools like databases, APIs, and UI frameworks, keeping them separate from business logic.

- **DDD and Clean Architecture integration**: Ensures that business logic remains isolated while keeping infrastructure flexible and replaceable.

- **Hexagonal architecture (ports and adapters)**: Naturally aligns with Clean Architecture, supporting modularity and testability.

- **Decoupling business logic**: Allows systems to evolve without major refactoring by separating domain concerns from technical details.

- **Combining Clean Architecture with DDD**: Results in a robust software design that is both expressive and resilient to change.

Multiple choice questions

1. **What is the main principle of Clean Architecture?**

    a. Dependencies should always point outward.

    b. Business logic should depend on external frameworks.

    c. Dependencies should always point inward.

    d. Data formats should always remain the same across layers.

2. **Which of the following is not a typical layer in Clean Architecture?**

    a. Entities

    b. Use cases

    c. Interface adapters

    d. Controllers

3. **Which layer in Clean Architecture contains the system's core business rules?**
   a. Use cases
   b. Entities
   c. Interface adapters
   d. Frameworks and drivers

4. **In Clean Architecture, which layer is responsible for handling communication with external systems?**
   a. Entities
   b. Use cases
   c. Interface adapters
   d. Frameworks and drivers

5. **What is the purpose of the dependency rule in Clean Architecture?**
   a. To ensure that the outer layers depend on the inner layers
   b. To allow inner layers to depend on outer layers
   c. To decouple the UI from the business logic
   d. To keep inner layers from knowing about outer layers

6. **How does Clean Architecture help maintain flexibility in a system?**
   a. By placing all business logic in the outermost layers
   b. By allowing dependencies to flow both inward and outward
   c. By isolating core business logic from implementation details
   d. By coupling business logic with UI and databases

7. **Which concept from DDD aligns most closely with the entities layer in Clean Architecture?**
   a. Repositories
   b. Aggregates
   c. Domain entities
   d. Value objects

8. **How does Clean Architecture ensure that changes in outer layers do not affect the core business logic?**
   a. By maintaining a flat structure with no layers
   b. By using the dependency rule to isolate inner layers from outer layers

    c.   By integrating all frameworks into the core layers

    d.   By allowing shared access to databases and APIs across all layers

9. **What is the key benefit of combining DDD with Clean Architecture?**

    a.   It reduces the need for use cases in the application layer.

    b.   It allows business logic and infrastructure concerns to be tightly coupled.

    c.   It creates systems that are both expressive and resilient to change.

    d.   It eliminates the need for interface adapters.

10. **In a system that uses both DDD and Clean Architecture, where would you expect to find the domain-specific business rules?**

    a.   In the outermost layer of the architecture

    b.   In the use cases layer

    c.   In the interface adapters layer

    d.   In the entities layer

Answers

Question number	Answer option letter
1.	c.
2.	d.
3.	b.
4.	c.
5.	d.
6.	c.
7.	c.
8.	b.
9.	c.
10.	d.

References

1. *Evans, Eric. (2003). Domain-Driven Design: Tackling Complexity in the Heart of Software.*

2. *Newman, Sam. (2020). Should I Use Microservices?*

3. *Martin, Robert C. (2012). The Clean Architecture.* **https://blog.cleancoder.com/uncle-bob/2012/08/13/the-clean-architecture.html**

4. *Cockburn, Alistair. Hexagonal Architecture.*

Join our Discord space

Join our Discord workspace for latest updates, offers, tech happenings around the world, new releases, and sessions with the authors:

https://discord.bpbonline.com

CHAPTER 7
DDD and Data Modeling

Introduction

Achieving an efficient database design while maintaining a meaningful application layer is challenging given the fact that databases and applications usually *speak different languages*, rooted in distinct paradigms. In this chapter, we will address this challenge, guiding you through **domain-driven design** (**DDD**) and database principles that help bridge these differences.

This chapter provides practical insights about data modeling in both SQL and NoSQL environments. By exploring their strengths and trade-offs, you will learn to align database structures with your application's needs.

Structure

In this chapter, we will explore more about the following topics:

- Principles of DDD in data modeling
- Modeling data in SQL databases
- Modeling data in NoSQL databases

Technical requirements

We will use a relational and NoSQL database to use Hibernate and MongoDB drivers to communicate with Java for this sample project. To avoid additional configuration, we will use H2, an in-memory database, and an embedded MongoDB instance. However, this configuration can be changed, and Docker can be used instead to have access to the code repository.

- Java 21

- Git

- Maven

- Any preferred IDE

Objectives

This chapter will equip readers with the knowledge and strategies to design effective data models that align with DDD principles while leveraging SQL and NoSQL databases. By exploring the differences between relational and schema-less data structures, understanding impedance mismatch, and implementing mapping strategies, readers will learn how to create scalable, adaptable systems that maintain a strong connection between business logic and data storage. This chapter uses practical examples to guide the structuring of data models that optimize performance and domain integrity.

Principles of DDD in data modeling

Databases and applications operate under different paradigms, whether using SQL or NoSQL databases. In Java, for example, the code structure differs significantly from the database's. This difference, called **impedance mismatch**, describes the gap between object-oriented languages like Java and both relational and NoSQL databases.

In Java, we establish relationships using pointers, encapsulation, and inheritance. In contrast, SQL databases represent data relationships using tables, foreign keys, and normalization. Understanding these differences is crucial for effective database management and application development.

The following figure illustrates this concept with a simple example: a **Person** class that contains a list of **Address** instances. In Java, this relationship is created through pointers or references, but in SQL, the same relationship is represented using separate tables linked by foreign keys.

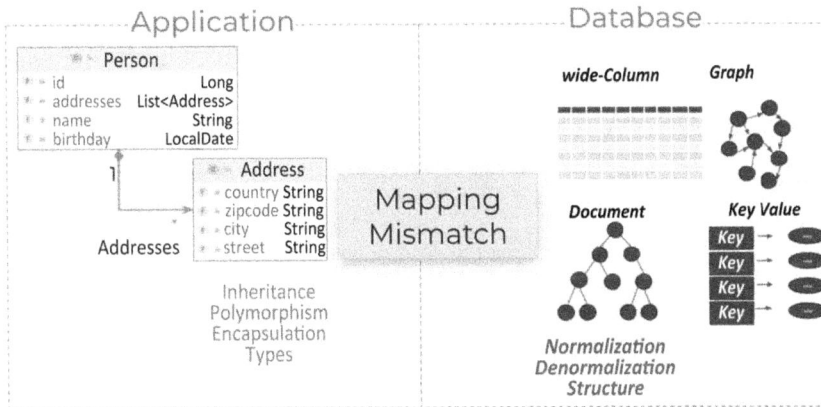

Figure 7.1: Distance between the application and the database

The impedance mismatch of the inherent lack of alignment between Java and database principles can be perceived by the possibility of using abstractions, encapsulation, and inheritance in Java, but having to maintain data in normalized or denormalized on the database structures.

To bridge this gap, we introduce a translator between the two paradigms called a **mapping layer**. This layer mitigates most differences and impacts, to some level, some aspects of the application, such as additional overhead in data translation, potential mismatching behaviors, and lower performance.

In addition to the impedance mismatch, there are other patterns that can help ease the integration between databases and applications. These patterns range between leaning towards the database or the application.

Patterns that are closer to the application side prioritize semantics by encapsulating data and exposing behavior through object-oriented programming.

Patterns that are more data-oriented, and that lean more to the database side, focus on immutability and data exposure.

The following table helps visualize the trade-offs of each approach:

Aspect	Object-oriented programming	Data-oriented programming
Focus	Behavior and encapsulation	Data exposure and immutability
Goal	Hide data details; expose behavior	Expose data details; prioritize immutability
Primary usage	Application-level modeling (e.g., repositories)	Database-level modeling
Trade-offs	Enhanced semantics, the potential for complex abstractions	Simplified data access, potential model limitations
Example	DDD repositories, domain services	SQL tables, NoSQL collections

Table 7.1: Object-oriented vs. data-oriented programming

Let us focus on the aspects surrounding DDD, in particular, let us take a look at the Repository pattern, represented in the following figure. Note that this is a pattern that sits closer to the application side, hence, allowing us to emphasize semantics, abstraction, and object-oriented principles in Java.

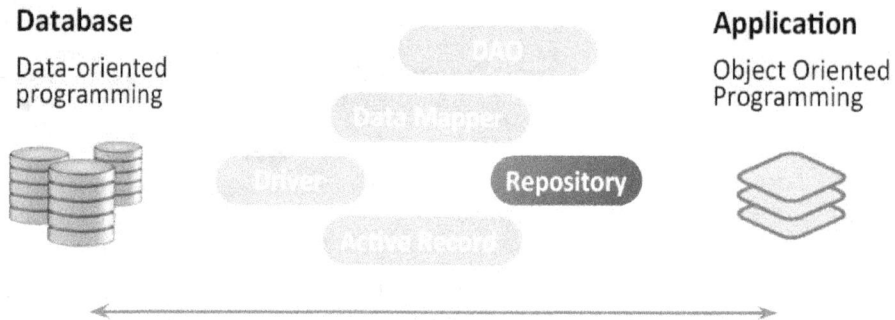

Figure 7.2: Gap and the distance based on the Java data pattern

Considering the impedance mismatch, a common question arises: should we create distinct entity classes to separate the domain and the database, or should we have both under the same class? While the usage of separate classes improves flexibility, it also increases complexity and may raise performance concerns. On the other hand, reusing the same class simplifies the structure but may require adaptations that could impact the domain model, especially if switching between SQL and NoSQL databases. Ultimately, there is no one-size-fits-all answer. A pragmatic approach would be to start with a unique entity for both, then refactor, if necessary, as the model evolves.

In the next section, we will explore *modeling data in SQL databases* and examine approaches to navigating these differences within the structure of SQL.

Modeling data in SQL databases

When we discuss relational databases, maturity is often the first characteristic that comes to mind. This technology has been evolving for over a century, amassing a wealth of knowledge, literature, and practical case studies. Relational (SQL) databases are frequently the go-to choice for new projects, providing stability, community support, and extensive resources. Additionally, it benefits from a standard communication language: SQL, which enables consistent querying across systems. This standardization makes SQL databases compatible with many tools and applications, easing data modeling and retrieval. Moreover, normalization prevents redundant data and preserves data integrity by organizing data into structured, related tables.

In contrast to relational databases' structured and data-driven paradigm, DDD emphasizes domain logic and application semantics. This difference, is also an impedance mismatch, as it requires a mapping layer to translate between database tables and object-oriented domain models.

The following is a summary of the key differences between SQL databases and DDD:

Aspect	SQL databases	DDD
Focus	Data consistency, integrity, and structure	Domain logic and behavior representation
Data relationships	Normalized tables with foreign keys	Encapsulated domain entities and value objects
Access patterns	Data-oriented; optimized for querying	Behavior-oriented; encapsulates operations
Primary purpose	Data storage and retrieval	Business logic representation within applications
Modeling paradigm	Relational, tabular	Object-oriented, behavior-focused

Table 7.2: SQL vs. DDD

Jakarta Persistence in action

To illustrate this integration, let us consider a practical example. In our scenario, we implement a **Hotel**, essentially a collection of **Room** entities, each containing a reference to a **Guest**. For simplicity and to maintain framework independence, we will use Jakarta Persistence (formerly JPA) with Hibernate. By not using frameworks of the Spring or Quarkus ecosystems, your learning focuses solely on the persistence layer and its relationship with the domain layer.

Note: **In this example, we are isolating the persistence layer to focus specifically on these topics. However, in a real-world application, the Hotel class would likely be structured as a repository, as operations like check-in and check-out introduce additional business requirements, such as handling payments. For simplicity, we are not using dependency injection in this example, which would typically simplify handling connection pooling and other infrastructure concerns. In production, not using dependency injection could lead to issues like connection leaks, but for learning purposes, it allows us to focus on persistence mechanics without extra layers of complexity.**

In the following code block, we define two entity classes, **RoomJPA** and **GuestJPA**, representing a hotel room and a guest. The **RoomJPA** class includes a **ManyToOne** relationship with **GuestJPA**, indicating that guests can stay in multiple rooms.

```
@Entity
class RoomJPA {

    @Id
    private Long number;

    @ManyToOne
```

```
    @JoinColumn(name = "guest_id", referencedColumnName = "id")
    private GuestJPA guest;


}

@Entity
class GuestJPA {

    @Id
    @GeneratedValue(strategy = GenerationType.IDENTITY)
    private Long id;

    @Column
    private String documentNumber;

    @Column
    private String name;


}
```

Next, we will employ a mapper to manage the structural differences between the domain and database representations. In this case, we use **MapStruct** to define a **JPAMapper** interface, which handles the conversion between the **Room** and **Guest** domain objects and their JPA representations, **RoomJPA** and **GuestJPA**:

```
@Mapper
interface JPAMapper {

    GuestJPA toEntity(Guest guest);

    Guest toDomain(GuestJPA guestJPA);

    RoomJPA toEntity(Room room);

    Room toDomain(RoomJPA roomJPA);


}
```

By leveraging a mapper, we can encapsulate the translation logic and ensure that the domain layer remains unaware of the database schema.

With the entity definitions and mapper in place, we can now implement **HotelJPA**, which acts as the persistence layer. This class utilizes JPA to interact with SQL data, isolating the domain logic from the specifics of the database framework. Here, we handle check-in and check-out operations, managing room and guest data within the same class. In a real-world application, separate repositories for **Room** and **Guest** would likely be more suitable, but we focus solely on the room operations for simplicity.

```java
public class HotelJPA implements Hotel {

    private final SessionFactory sessionFactory;
    private final JPAMapper mapper;

    public HotelJPA(SessionFactory sessionFactory, JPAMapper mapper) {
        this.sessionFactory = sessionFactory;
        this.mapper = mapper;
    }

    @Override
    public Room checkIn(Room room) {
        try (var session = sessionFactory.openSession()) {
            Transaction transaction = session.beginTransaction();

            RoomJPA roomJPA = session.get(RoomJPA.class, room.getNumber());
            if (roomJPA != null) {
                GuestJPA guestJPA = mapper.toEntity(room.getGuest());

                GuestJPA existingGuest = (GuestJPA) session
                        .createQuery("from GuestJPA where documentNumber =
:documentNumber")
                        .setParameter("documentNumber", guestJPA.
getDocumentNumber())
                        .uniqueResult();

                if (existingGuest == null) {
                    session.save(guestJPA);
                } else {
                    guestJPA = existingGuest;
                }
                roomJPA.setGuest(guestJPA);
                session.saveOrUpdate(roomJPA);
```

```
                transaction.commit();
                return mapper.toDomain(roomJPA);
            }

            transaction.rollback();
            throw new IllegalArgumentException("Room not found");
        }
    }

    @Override
    public void checkOut(Room room) {
        try (Session session = sessionFactory.openSession()) {
            Transaction transaction = session.beginTransaction();
            RoomJPA roomJPA = session.get(RoomJPA.class, room.getNumber());
            if (roomJPA != null) {
                roomJPA.cleanRoom();
                session.saveOrUpdate(roomJPA);
                transaction.commit();
            } else {
                transaction.rollback();
                throw new IllegalArgumentException("Room not found");
            }
        }
    }

    @Override
    public Optional<Room> reservation(String number) {
        try (Session session = sessionFactory.openSession()) {
            RoomJPA roomJPA = session.createQuery("from RoomJPA where number =
:number", RoomJPA.class)
                        .setParameter("number", Long.parseLong(number))
                        .uniqueResult();
            return Optional.ofNullable(roomJPA).map(mapper::toDomain);
        }
    }

    @Override
    public Long countBy() {
        try (Session session = sessionFactory.openSession()) {
```

```
            return session.createQuery("select count(r) from RoomJPA r", Long.
class).uniqueResult();
        }
    }


    @Override
    public Optional<Room> findEmptyRoom() {
        try (Session session = sessionFactory.openSession()) {
            RoomJPA emptyRoom = session.createQuery("from RoomJPA where guest
is null", RoomJPA.class)
                        .setMaxResults(1)
                        .uniqueResult();
            return Optional.ofNullable(emptyRoom).map(mapper::toDomain);
        }
    }
}
```

The structured persistence layer we explored effectively isolates the domain layer from the underlying database and allows the domain model to remain focused on business logic while leaving the database-specific details to the persistence infrastructure.

The impedance mismatch between domain models and relational databases can be managed by isolating the database-specific components within the persistence layer and mapping domain entities to database representations. This example demonstrates how effective data modeling for SQL databases can be achieved by aligning relational structures with domain-driven principles. By focusing on key practices such as normalization, mapping strategies, and encapsulating database-specific details, this approach ensures the application remains adaptable while maintaining a clear separation between domain logic and database structure.

In the next section, *modeling data in NoSQL databases*, we will explore how to adapt DDD principles to NoSQL databases. NoSQL offers flexibility and scalability that may be more appropriate in certain scenarios, and we will examine how these differences influence data modeling and domain alignment.

Modeling data in NoSQL databases

When we talk about NoSQL databases, flexibility is often the defining feature. Unlike SQL databases, which follow a structured schema and well-defined standards, NoSQL databases offer a schema-less structure, prioritizing adaptability and performance over rigid consistency models. This flexibility is reflected in the types of NoSQL databases, including key-value, document, wide-column, graph, and time-series, each with its own approach to data modeling. While both SQL and NoSQL databases share the same fundamental purpose, storing information, NoSQL databases diverge significantly in behavior and design. In contrast to SQL databases' **atomicity, consistency, isolation, and durability (ACID)** compliance, NoSQL databases generally follow the **basically available, soft state, and eventual consistency (BASE)** model, focusing on eventual consistency rather than strict transactional integrity. Additionally, NoSQL databases emphasize denormalization, where data is modeled based on access patterns to optimize read operations, making querying efficient even though data might be duplicated across entries.

When applying DDD principles in a NoSQL context, certain challenges emerge, particularly around encapsulation, abstraction, and consistency. Document-based databases, like *MongoDB*, reduce this gap somewhat, as they can store entities and their related data within a single JSON-like document. It allows for a denormalized data model that can better align with the domain, yet still requires careful consideration for data consistency and updates on logic in scenarios that require multiple entities synchronization.

The following is a comparison table outlining key differences between DDD and NoSQL databases:

Aspect	NoSQL databases	DDD
Structure	Schema-less, flexible	Encapsulated, behavior-driven entities
Consistency model	BASE (eventual consistency)	Focus on integrity and encapsulation
Data modeling	Denormalization, query-optimized	Domain logic and behavior representation
Data relationships	Embedded documents (e.g., subdocuments)	Encapsulated entities, value objects
Access patterns	Optimized for reads based on query design	Encapsulates operations and business logic

Table 7.3: NoSQL vs. DDD

Let us continue with our **Hotel** example. We will use MongoDB, a document-based NoSQL database, to model a **Hotel** with a collection of **Room** entities. Each **Room** will have a **Guest** as a property, stored as a subdocument rather than in a separate table, as would be the case in a relational database. The MongoDB entities are coded as follows:

```java
public class RoomNoSQL {

    @BsonProperty("number")
    private Long number;

    @BsonProperty("guest")
    private GuestNoSQL guest;
```

```
}

public class GuestNoSQL {

    @BsonProperty("documentNumber")
    private String documentNumber;

    @BsonProperty("name")
    private String name;

}
```

Then, we will use a mapping layer similar to our SQL example to maintain consistency in mapping between the domain and database representations. This layer translates **Room** and **Guest** domain objects into **RoomNoSQL** and **GuestNoSQL** entities as follows:

```
@Mapper
interface NoSQLMapper {

    GuestNoSQL toEntity(Guest guest);

    Guest toDomain(GuestNoSQL guestNoSQL);

    RoomNoSQL toEntity(Room room);

    Room toDomain(RoomNoSQL roomNoSQL);

}
```

Finally, we implement the **HotelMongoDB** class using MongoDB to handle operations such as check-in, check-out, and finding empty rooms. Here, we serialize the MongoDB entity classes directly for storage, with MongoDB handling the document format requirements. Still, it requires public classes, a constructor, a getter, and a setter. This setup allows us to maintain a rich domain model while MongoDB handles the storage and retrieval of document-based entities.

```
public class HotelMongoDB implements Hotel {

    private final MongoCollection<RoomNoSQL> roomCollection;
    private final NoSQLMapper mapper;

    public HotelMongoDB(MongoCollection<RoomNoSQL> roomCollection, NoSQLMapper
mapper) {
```

```java
        this.roomCollection = roomCollection;
        this.mapper = mapper;
    }

    @Override
    public Room checkIn(Room room) {
        RoomNoSQL roomNoSQL = mapper.toEntity(room);
        Bson filter = eq("number", room.getNumber());

        roomCollection.updateOne(filter, Updates.set("guest", roomNoSQL.
getGuest()), new UpdateOptions().upsert(true));
        return mapper.toDomain(roomNoSQL);
    }

    @Override
    public void checkOut(Room room) {
        Bson filter = eq("number", room.getNumber());
        roomCollection.updateOne(filter, Updates.unset("guest"));
    }

    @Override
    public Optional<Room> reservation(String number) {
        RoomNoSQL roomNoSQL = roomCollection.find(eq("number", Long.
parseLong(number))).first();
        return Optional.ofNullable(roomNoSQL).map(mapper::toDomain);
    }

    @Override
    public Long countBy() {
        return roomCollection.countDocuments();
    }

    @Override
    public Optional<Room> findEmptyRoom() {
        RoomNoSQL emptyRoom = roomCollection.find(Filters.eq("guest", null)).
first();
        return Optional.ofNullable(emptyRoom).map(mapper::toDomain);
    }
}
```

This example illustrates how MongoDB can store an entire room and guest record in a single document, with **Guest** as a subdocument within **Room**, aligning with NoSQL's denormalized structure, and giving us the ability to optimize read operations by storing all relevant data together. However, it is important to recognize the trade-offs in NoSQL data modeling, as flexibility and speed come at the cost of strict consistency, and maintenance of data integrity might require additional logic in certain scenarios.

Conclusion

This chapter explored data modeling fundamentals using DDD for SQL and NoSQL databases. We examined how SQL's structured, schema-driven design contrasts with DDD, often requiring a mapping layer to resolve the impedance mismatch between domain models and database tables.

We highlighted NoSQL's flexibility and schema-less structure, which can reduce this mismatch but demands careful modeling to maintain data integrity. Through examples with Jakarta Persistence and MongoDB, we illustrated how to align SQL and NoSQL data models with DDD, acknowledging each approach's unique trade-offs.

In the next chapter, we will explore *Enterprise Java with Jakarta EE*, focusing on using this scalable platform to develop enterprise-level applications based on DDD principles. We will look at tools, best practices, and design patterns for building resilient systems that integrate SQL and NoSQL databases, enhancing our understanding of DDD-aligned applications at scale.

Points to remember

- **Impedance mismatch**: The structural and conceptual gap between object-oriented application models and relational database schemas requires a mapping layer to align them.

- **SQL databases follow normalization**: In relational databases, normalization reduces redundancy and ensures data integrity, but it may require joins that impact performance.

- **NoSQL databases prioritize denormalization**: NoSQL databases often favor denormalization to optimize query performance by storing related data together, reducing the need for joins.

- **ACID vs. BASE**: SQL databases follow the ACID model for strong consistency, while NoSQL databases use the BASE model, prioritizing availability and eventual consistency.

- **Data modeling in SQL requires schema definition**: Before storing data, relational databases require predefined schemas, ensuring structure and integrity, but reducing flexibility.

- **NoSQL provides schema flexibility**: Most NoSQL databases allow schema-less data storage, enabling adaptable structures but requiring careful consistency management.

- **Mapping layers bridge application and database models**: Tools like JPA and **Object-Document Mappers (ODMs)** facilitate communication between domain models and databases.

- **Embedding vs. referencing in NoSQL**: Document databases like MongoDB support embedding related data (subdocuments) for faster reads but may require updates across multiple documents.

- **DDD focuses on behavior**: Unlike databases, which focus on data storage, DDD emphasizes encapsulating behavior within domain models to reflect real-world business rules.

- **Database choice is a trade-off**: Selecting SQL or NoSQL depends on factors such as consistency requirements, scalability needs, query complexity, and how closely the database model aligns with the domain.

Multiple choice questions

1. **What is the primary advantage of relational databases in data modeling?**
   a. Flexibility in schema
   b. Support for denormalization
   c. Maturity and established standards
   d. Focus on the BASE consistency model
   e. No need for structured tables

2. **What is the main purpose of normalization in SQL databases?**
   a. Increasing data redundancy
   b. Optimizing data for reads
   c. Avoiding duplicate data and preserving integrity
   d. Storing data as JSON documents
   e. Simplifying complex query design

3. **In DDD, what is the term used to describe the difference in structure between object-oriented and relational models?**
   a. Object mismatch
   b. Schema conflict
   c. Design divergence

    d.   Impedance mismatch

    e.   Mapping gap

4. **Which type of NoSQL database is MongoDB an example of?**

    a.   Key-value store

    b.   Document database

    c.   Graph database

    d.   Time-series database

    e.   Wide-column store

5. **What is a common strategy in NoSQL modeling to optimize data access patterns?**

    a.   Normalization

    b.   Using foreign keys

    c.   Data encapsulation

    d.   Denormalization

    e.   Schema enforcement

6. **Which consistency model is most commonly associated with NoSQL databases?**

    a.   ACID

    b.   CAP

    c.   BASE

    d.   RDBMS

    e.   SQL

7. **In the MongoDB example, what is the purpose of embedding Guest as a subdocument in Room?**

    a.   To reduce the need for joins

    b.   To follow ACID principles strictly

    c.   To support foreign key constraints

    d.   To increase normalization

    e.   To make the schema rigid

8. **Which of the following best describes a difference between SQL and NoSQL databases in the context of DDD?**

    a.   SQL databases are typically denormalized.

    b.   NoSQL databases prioritize query structure over schema.

c. SQL databases do not support BASE consistency.

d. NoSQL databases have strict standards across vendors.

e. DDD cannot be applied to NoSQL databases.

9. **In DDD with NoSQL, why might you use a mapping layer?**

a. To perform joins between tables

b. To create direct relationships without foreign keys

c. To align domain models with document structures

d. To enforce strict SQL compliance

e. To implement triggers and stored procedures

10. **What will the next chapter cover concerning DDD?**

a. Advanced NoSQL indexing

b. Schema design patterns in MongoDB

c. Enterprise Java with Jakarta EE

d. Front-end integration with NoSQL

e. SQL tuning and optimization

Answers

Question number	Answer option letter
1.	c.
2.	c.
3.	d.
4.	b.
5.	d.
6.	c.
7.	a.
8.	b.
9.	c.
10.	c.

CHAPTER 8
Enterprise Java with Jakarta EE

Introduction

After exploring **domain-driven design** (DDD) in a Java-agnostic context in the previous chapter, it is time to see how these principles come to life within a full-featured enterprise platform. This chapter introduces you to Jakarta EE, a robust enterprise platform that can simplify and streamline DDD implementation, making the process more efficient and accessible for Java developers. You will find that the complexities associated with DDD, such as managing dependencies, encapsulating domain logic, and handling persistence, are addressed more intuitively within the platform.

As we walk through applying DDD with Jakarta EE, you will discover how this platform's built-in capabilities can reduce boilerplate code, offer better encapsulation through Jakarta Data, and support seamless integration of DDD into enterprise-level applications. By the end of this chapter, you will have a practical understanding of how Jakarta EE can enhance your DDD practices, helping you build applications that are not only well-structured and maintainable but also aligned with the core concepts of your business domain.

Structure

In this chapter, we will explore more about the following topics:

- Applying DDD with Jakarta EE

- Leveraging Jakarta Data for better encapsulation

- Integrating DDD into enterprise Java applications

Technical requirements

This chapter will explore the **Contexts and Dependency Injection (CDI)** approach using Helidon, which could also be easily applied using Quarkus. In this chapter, we will run an Oracle NoSQL database in Docker. Thus, it is crucial to have a database running; Running the Oracle NoSQL database in various environments, including Oracle Cloud, is possible. However, for this chapter, the assumption is that the instance will be executed locally using Docker.

- Java 21

- Git

- Maven

- Any preferred IDE

- Docker running

- Oracle NoSQL database running using the following Docker command:

  ```
  docker run -d --name oracle-instance -p 8080:8080 ghcr.io/oracle/
  nosql:latest-ce
  ```

Objectives

This chapter aims to demonstrate how Jakarta EE facilitates the implementation of DDD by providing standardized enterprise features that simplify data access, dependency management, and domain encapsulation. Through practical examples, we explore key Jakarta EE specifications such as Jakarta Data, CDI, Bean Validation, Jakarta NoSQL, and **Jakarta API for RESTful Web Services (JAX-RS)**, showing how they enable a clean and maintainable DDD architecture. By the end of this chapter, you will clearly understand how to apply Jakarta EE to build domain-centric applications while reducing boilerplate code and leveraging a robust enterprise Java ecosystem.

Applying DDD with Jakarta EE

Previously known as Java EE, Jakarta EE provides a standardized API that is widely adopted across frameworks, such as *Spring*, *Quarkus*, and *Helidon*. This standardization allows developers to access consistent tools that ease the complexity of enterprise development. Now managed by the *Eclipse Foundation*, Jakarta EE also benefits from integration with the MicroProfile specification, which extends Jakarta EE's capabilities to support microservices architectures. This close relationship between Jakarta EE and MicroProfile is built on essential components like CDI, JSON, and JAX-RS, making Jakarta EE a robust base for implementing DDD in Java projects.

CDI is at the core of DDD in Jakarta EE, a specification that facilitates object creation and lifecycle management. CDI helps manage dependencies within the application, making it easier to construct well-organized domain layers. CDI replaces traditional approaches like service locators and factories, allowing you to build highly testable, reusable, and maintainable applications. This capability is essential in DDD, where domain objects often must live across multiple requests. For example, CDI's producer methods enable centralized management of entity creation and resources, ensuring consistency across the domain. Scoped annotations provide additional lifecycle management for domain objects, while interceptors allow you to handle cross-cutting concerns, like error handling, without polluting domain logic. CDI events further support DDD by enabling asynchronous communication within your application, encouraging modularity, and reducing coupling between components.

In the following table, you can see each CDI feature and how you can take advantage of your DDD code:

CDI feature	Role in DDD
Producer methods	Centralizes creating and managing domain entities and resources, promoting consistency and simplifying testing.
Scoped annotations	Manages lifecycles of domain objects, aiding in modular, layered architectures that align with DDD boundaries.
Interceptors	Handles cross-cutting concerns, like error handling, to keep domain logic isolated and focused.
CDI events	Enables asynchronous communication between domain objects, fostering loose coupling and enhancing modularity.

Table 8.1: CDI features and how to use them on DDD

In addition to CDI, Jakarta Bean Validation is essential in preserving the integrity of domain objects by enforcing constraints throughout the application. Bean Validation allows you to define rules that guarantee the consistency of your data, from incoming requests to persistence layers. These rules ensure that domain constraints are consistently applied across services, controllers, and databases. For instance, a constraint on an email field guarantees that an invalid email will not pass through any application layer. Additionally, Bean Validation supports complex constraints that span multiple fields, ensuring your domain objects align with business rules.

The following table shows more about how you can take advantage of DDD with Bean Validation, mainly where you can explore constraints using an annotation-driven approach:

Bean Validation feature	Role in DDD
Annotation-based constraints	Ensures attributes in domain objects are validated against business rules, e.g., a valid email or a minimum age.
Cross-field constraints	Provides advanced validation logic that spans multiple fields, ensuring holistic integrity of domain objects.
Group constraints	Defines validation groups to apply context-specific rules, supporting context-driven behaviors in domains.

Table 8.2: Bean Validation features and how to use them on DDD

Persistence is another critical element of DDD. **Jakarta Persistence (JPA)** and Jakarta NoSQL facilitate saving and retrieving domain states, allowing you to implement the Repository pattern with minimal effort. While these specifications do not directly represent DDD patterns, they provide the foundational tools needed to encapsulate data and ensure your domain objects can be saved in both relational and NoSQL databases. JPA offers a comprehensive set of features for relational data mapping, while Jakarta NoSQL supports a more flexible model that's especially useful for complex domain objects. The following table shows how to apply those specifications with DDD:

Persistence feature	Role in DDD
JPA	Manages relational mappings and provides an entity-based API, supporting domain state aggregates and persistence.
Jakarta NoSQL	Simplifies interactions with NoSQL stores, ideal for aggregate roots and rich domain models that require flexibility.

Table 8.3: Bean Validation features and how to use them on DDD

Combining these Jakarta EE features with DDD principles allows you to build enterprise applications that reflect core business concepts while reducing boilerplate code and focusing on your domain's integrity. Through these specifications, Jakarta EE empowers you to create clean, maintainable, and business-aligned applications, enhancing the effectiveness of your DDD implementation.

In the next section, we will discuss the new specification that can help you with this integration in DDD with the database Jakarta Data.

Leveraging Jakarta Data for better encapsulation

Jakarta Data introduces an efficient and intuitive way to implement the Repository pattern directly on the Jakarta EE platform. Inspired by DDD, Jakarta Data simplifies the data access layer with a consistent API for various database types, both relational and NoSQL. With Jakarta

Data, developers can create repositories that facilitate seamless data interactions without extensive boilerplate code, bridging domain concepts and database operations in a clean, Jakarta-based programming model. This flexibility makes Jakarta Data particularly powerful in DDD applications, where repositories represent central access points for domain objects.

The Jakarta Data specification classifies repository abstractions into built-in and custom categories. Built-in repository interfaces like **DataRepository**, **CrudRepository**, and **BasicRepository** cover a range of common data operations, establishing a strong foundation for your data layer. For example, extending **BasicRepository**, a **CarRepository** automatically gains CRUD functionality for **Car** entities. In this repository interface, method names drive database operations, following a convention-based query structure that aligns naturally with DDD. For instance, **findByType** in the following code sample retrieves a list of **Car** entities filtered by type, passing the type as a method parameter:

```
@Repository
public interface CarRepository extends BasicRepository<Car, Long> {

  List<Car> findByType(CarType type);

  Optional<Car> findByName(String name);

}
```

If the built-in repository methods do not cover your requirements, Jakarta Data's custom repository interfaces offer more flexibility. Custom repositories allow you to shape queries to fit your domain language, aligning clearly with DDD's Ubiquitous Language. With annotations like **@Insert**, **@Update**, **@Delete**, and **@Save**, you can define domain-specific methods that precisely reflect your application's needs. For instance, in a **Garage** repository, we can use **@Insert** and **@Delete** annotations to manage **Car** entities in a domain-focused way as follows:

```
@Repository
public interface Garage {

  @Insert
  Car park(Car car);

  @Delete
  Car unpark(Car car);

}
```

Jakarta Data introduces pagination options for applications that handle large datasets to improve data handling efficiency. It supports two types of pagination: offset-based and cursor-based. Offset-based pagination calculates pages using a positional offset, while cursor-based pagination uses a pointer (cursor) to navigate data, reducing the risk of missed or duplicated results across pages. The following is an example that demonstrates both pagination types in the **CarRepository**:

```
@Repository
 public interface CarRepository extends BasicRepository<Car, Long> {


 Page<Car> findByTypeOrderByName(CarType type, PageRequest pageRequest);


 @Find
 @OrderBy(_Car.NAME)
 @OrderBy(_Car.VIN)
 CursoredPage<Car> type(CarType type, PageRequest pageRequest);


}
```

Jakarta Data also introduces the **Jakarta Data Query Language** (JDQL), a lightweight query language tailored for repository methods, simplifying complex queries across data stores. As a subset of **Jakarta Persistence Query Language** (JPQL), JDQL supports SQL and NoSQL backends, providing consistency while leveraging JPQL's familiar syntax. Using the **@Query** annotation, developers can create flexible queries that work seamlessly in different storage technologies. In this example, **BookRepository** defines JDQL queries that can run on either SQL or NoSQL databases as follows:

```
@Repository
public interface BookRepository extends BasicRepository<Book, UUID> {

 // Find books with titles matching a specific pattern
 @Query("where title like :titlePattern")
 List<Book> booksMatchingTitle(String titlePattern);

 // Select books by a specific author and sort them by title
 @Query("where author.name = :author order by title")
 List<Book> findByAuthorSortedByTitle(String author);
}
```

As you can see, developers can bring the Repository pattern to life with minimal effort through Jakarta Data, making DDD-inspired data handling straightforward and expressive.

In the following section, we will apply Jakarta EE concepts in a practical code example using a NoSQL database, showing how to leverage Jakarta Data's capabilities for a domain-centered approach to data management.

Integrating DDD into enterprise Java applications

In this section, we will take a practical approach to using Jakarta EE with Helidon and the Oracle NoSQL database by implementing a microservice for hotel management. Building on the hotel sample from earlier chapters, we will expand it into a microservice architecture, utilizing a NoSQL database to store hotel room reservations and guests. Let us dive into the setup and development steps required for this example.

To start, set up the project structure with Helidon's Starter UI, which makes configuration simple and intuitive as follows:

1. Visit the Helidon Starter (**https://helidon.io/starter/4.1.4?step=1**).

2. Choose the Helidon MP flavor and select Quickstart for the application type.

3. Under Media Support, select JSON-B.

4. Define **groupId**, **artifactId**, **version**, and **package name** based on your project needs.

5. Once configured, download the generated project and add the latest version of the Oracle JNoSQL driver for database integration.

With the initial project structure in place, configure the database settings to run the application locally. Update **src/main/resources/META-INF/microprofile-config.properties** with the following properties:

```
jnosql.keyvalue.database=hotel
jnosql.document.database=hotel
jnosql.oracle.nosql.host=http://localhost:8080
```

Using environment variables for production settings, aligned with the Twelve-Factor App methodology, ensures secure management of credentials and makes it easier to switch environments without hard-coded values.

We can move on to defining entities once the Oracle NoSQL database is running, bringing its extensive relational database experience into the NoSQL Realm. Here, we will implement DDD principles by treating **Room** as an entity and **Guest** as a value object. The **Guest** is embedded within the **Room** as a subdocument, streamlining the data model while staying true to our domain-focused approach. Note the use of Jakarta NoSQL annotations, which are similar to Jakarta Persistence annotations:

```
@Entity
public record Room (@Id String number, @Column Guest guest) {
}
```

```
@Embeddable(Embeddable.EmbeddableType.GROUPING)
public record Guest (@Column String documentNumber, @Column String name) {
}
```

With the entities defined, let us move to the repository layer. Here, we implement the **Hotel** repository interface, utilizing annotations like **@Save** and **@Delete** to manage data persistence with minimal boilerplate code. This repository provides methods for check-in, check-out, and room reservation, capturing DDD concepts while leveraging Jakarta EE's repository features as follows:

```
@Repository
public interface Hotel {

    @Save
    Room checkIn(Room room);

    @Delete
    void checkOut(Room room);

    @Find
    Optional<Room> reservation(@By(expert.os.books.ddd.chapter08.hotels._Room.
NUMBER) String number);

    Page<Room> findBy(PageRequest pageRequest);
}
```

Lastly, we should expose these operations through a RESTful API using Helidon's CDI support. Injecting the **Hotel** repository into the **HotelResource** class enables us to create a resource class that performs basic operations on rooms and reservations. This resource layer provides endpoints for actions like retrieving rooms, checking in, and checking out, all made intuitive by Helidon's JAX-RS and CDI integration:

```
@Path("/hotels")
@ApplicationScoped
@Produces(MediaType.APPLICATION_JSON)
@Consumes(MediaType.APPLICATION_JSON)
public class HotelResource {

    private static final Logger LOGGER = Logger.getLogger(HotelResource.class.
getName());
```

```
  private final Hotel hotel;

  @Inject
  public HotelResource(Hotel hotel) {
      this.hotel = hotel;
  }

  public HotelResource() {
      this(null);
  }

  @GET
  public List<Room> rooms(@QueryParam("page") @DefaultValue("1") int page,
                          @QueryParam("size") @DefaultValue("1") int size) {
      LOGGER.info("Finding rooms page: " + page + " size: " + size);
      var pageRequest = PageRequest.ofPage(page).size(size);
      var rooms = hotel.findBy(pageRequest).content();
      LOGGER.info("Found rooms: " + rooms.size());
      return rooms;
  }

  @GET
  @Path("/{number}")
  public Room reservation(@PathParam("number") String number) {
      LOGGER.info("Finding reservation: " + number);
      return hotel.reservation(number)
              .orElseThrow(() -> new WebApplicationException("Room not
found", Response.Status.NOT_FOUND));
  }

  @PUT
  public Room checkIn(Room room) {
      LOGGER.info("Check in: " + room);
      return hotel.checkIn(room);
  }

  @DELETE
  @Path("/{number}")
  public void checkOut(@PathParam("number") String number) {
```

```
        LOGGER.info("Check out: " + number);
        var room = hotel.reservation(number)
                .orElseThrow(() -> new WebApplicationException("Room not
found", Response.Status.NOT_FOUND));
        hotel.checkOut(room);
    }
}
```

With the code and configuration complete, it is time to execute the application locally. Begin by packaging the application and running it with the following commands:

```
mvn package
java -jar target/hotel-reservation.jar
```

Once the application runs, you can interact with it through HTTP requests using **cURL**. The following are a few examples to get you started with the hotel reservation microservice:

- **Check-in a guest**: This command registers a guest to a specific room by sending a JSON payload containing the room number and guest details:

  ```
  curl -X PUT -H "Content-Type: application/json" -d '{"number":"101",
  "guest":{"name":"John    Doe",    "documentNumber":"12345"}}'    http://
  localhost:8181/hotels
  ```

- **Get all rooms**: Retrieve the list of all rooms and their reservation statuses with this **GET** request:

  ```
  curl -X GET http://localhost:8181/hotels
  ```

- **Check out a guest**: To check out a guest from a specific room, use the following **DELETE** request, specifying the room number:

  ```
  curl -X DELETE http://localhost:8181/hotels/101
  ```

These simple commands allow you to manage room check-ins, check-outs, and room listings in your hotel microservice. They demonstrate the seamless interaction that Jakarta EE, Helidon, and Oracle NoSQL can provide within a DDD-aligned architecture.

Through this example, we have illustrated how Jakarta EE, combined with Helidon and Oracle NoSQL, simplifies the creation of DDD-aligned microservices. Following this approach, you can build scalable, flexible, and domain-centered applications that maximize Jakarta EE's capabilities in a microservices environment.

Conclusion

This chapter explored how Jakarta EE supports DDD principles through Jakarta Data, CDI, and Jakarta NoSQL. We implemented a hotel reservation microservice using Helidon and the Oracle NoSQL database, demonstrating Jakarta EE's ability to create domain-focused enterprise applications. This approach offers powerful repository abstractions, effective dependency injection, and seamless database integration, simplifying the development and scalability of DDD-aligned applications.

The next chapter will use Spring for DDD. Spring's flexibility and popularity make it well-suited for applying DDD principles in Java applications, supporting modular architectures and adequate data access. We will explore leveraging Spring for DDD and compare its approach with Jakarta EE to highlight how each platform can enhance development.

Points to remember

- **Jakarta EE is the enterprise standard for Java development**: It provides a consistent API that simplifies the implementation of enterprise applications, independent of the framework being used.

- **Contexts and dependency injection (CDI) enhance modularity**: It helps manage dependencies, object lifecycles, and enables better separation of concerns in DDD applications.

- **Jakarta Data introduces built-in and custom repositories**: It simplifies data access by offering predefined repository interfaces while allowing domain-specific query methods.

- **The Repository pattern is natively supported in Jakarta Data**: It provides a structured way to interact with the database, abstracting persistence logic from business rules.

- **Jakarta Data supports method-based queries**: Developers can define query methods using naming conventions or annotations like `@Insert`, `@Find`, and `@Delete`.

- **Pagination in Jakarta Data can be offset-based or cursor-based**: Offset-based pagination is positional, while cursor-based pagination improves consistency in large datasets.

- **Jakarta Data Query Language (JDQL) is a subset of JPQL**: It provides a flexible and database-independent query mechanism that works with both relational and NoSQL databases.

- **Bean Validation enforces domain constraints**: It ensures that business rules, such as required fields or specific formats, are applied across application layers.

- **Jakarta NoSQL enables flexibility in data modeling**: It simplifies NoSQL database interactions while keeping a structure familiar to Jakarta Persistence users.

- **Jakarta EE integrates seamlessly with Helidon and microservices**: This allows building scalable, cloud-native applications while applying DDD principles efficiently.

Multiple choice questions

1. **What is the primary purpose of Jakarta EE in the context of enterprise applications?**

    a. To create lightweight Java applications

    b. To define a standard API for enterprise application development

    c. To compete with the Spring framework

    d. To provide a Java-only microservices solution

    e. To eliminate the need for databases

2. **Which specification in Jakarta EE is primarily responsible for dependency management and lifecycle handling?**

    a. Jakarta Data

    b. Jakarta NoSQL

    c. Contexts and Dependency Injection

    d. Bean Validation

    e. Jakarta RESTful Web Services

3. **What is Jakarta Data's primary role in a DDD context?**

    a. Managing application security

    b. Providing repository abstractions for data access

    c. Enforcing domain constraints

    d. Handling frontend UI interactions

    e. Managing user authentication

4. **Which of the following Jakarta Data repository types allows developers to define their query methods using annotations like @Insert and @Delete?**

    a. Built-in repository interfaces

    b. Custom repository interfaces

    c. Dynamic repositories

    d. External repository interfaces

    e. Service repositories

5. **What does the @Save annotation in Jakarta Data do?**

    a. It deletes data from the database

    b. It validates data before saving

    c. It checks if data exists, then inserts or updates it accordingly

    d.   It encrypts data

    e.   It performs a soft delete

6.   **What type of pagination does Jakarta Data support for handling large datasets?**

    a.   Page-based and offset-based

    b.   Offset-based and cursor-based

    c.   Cursor-based and dynamic-based

    d.   Page-based and sequence-based

    e.   Sequential-based and offset-based

7.   **Which feature of CDI helps reduce boilerplate code for creating and managing domain entities?**

    a.   Interceptors

    b.   Scoped annotations

    c.   CDI events

    d.   Producer methods

    e.   Transaction management

8.   **What is JDQL, as introduced in Jakarta Data?**

    a.   Jakarta Data Query Language, a subset of JPQL for database queries

    b.   A JSON parser for Jakarta EE applications

    c.   A new framework for managing microservices

    d.   Java Data Query Language for mobile applications

    e.   Java Data Quality Language for data validation

9.   **Which statement best describes the role of the Repository pattern in Jakarta Data?**

    a.   It centralizes all business logic within the data layer

    b.   It serves as a bridge between domain objects and the underlying database, abstracting data access

    c.   It provides complex business logic for CRUD operations

    d.   It handles only transactions in a DDD application

    e.   It validates data across all layers

10. **Which Jakarta EE feature helps enforce data consistency across the application layers by validating constraints?**

    a. CDI

    b. Jakarta NoSQL

    c. Bean Validation

    d. JAX-RS

    e. Jakarta Messaging

Answers

Question number	Answer option letter
1.	b.
2.	c.
3.	b.
4.	b.
5.	c.
6.	b.
7.	d.
8.	a.
9.	b.
10.	c.

Join our Discord space

Join our Discord workspace for latest updates, offers, tech happenings around the world, new releases, and sessions with the authors:

https://discord.bpbonline.com

CHAPTER 9
Enterprise Java with Spring

Introduction

The Spring platform has become a valuable resource for simplifying enterprise Java application development. By offering a modular, lightweight framework and a suite of tools, Spring helps developers address intricate design requirements effectively. This chapter highlights how Spring's abstraction layers and infrastructure support enhance best practices, boost productivity, and enable the delivery of reliable applications.

The chapter also demonstrates one of the main strengths of the Spring ecosystem: its support for **domain-driven design** (**DDD**). We will explore how Spring Boot, with its convention-over-configuration approach, enhances DDD by linking business logic to the underlying infrastructure, allowing you to focus on design while Spring handles the complexities.

Structure

In this chapter, we will explore more about the following topics:

- Overview of Spring Framework with DDD
- Applying DDD with Spring Boot

Technical requirements

For this chapter, we will work with the Spring platform. We will use a database in memory. Thus, it would avoid any complexity and infrastructure, such as Docker or database installation, but, as we are using JPA, other databases can also be used; to achieve this, we need to update the Driver and ensure that the database is running correctly.

- Java 21
- Git
- Maven
- Any preferred IDE

Objectives

This chapter aims to demonstrate how the Spring Framework simplifies the implementation of DDD in enterprise applications by providing powerful abstractions for dependency injection, data persistence, and application-layer exposure. Through practical examples, we explore how Spring's ecosystem, leveraging Spring Boot, Spring Data JPA, and other key components, helps developers focus on business logic while efficiently managing infrastructure concerns. By the end of this chapter, readers will understand how to structure a Spring-based DDD application, integrate persistence, expose domain logic through a RESTful API, and ensure robustness through comprehensive testing.

Overview of Spring Framework with DDD

The Spring Framework is a powerful, modular Java ecosystem platform, simplifying enterprise-level application development. With its lightweight architecture, Spring provides a comprehensive toolkit that aligns seamlessly with DDD, making it ideal for building complex, business-driven applications. Core features, such as dependency injection, transaction management, and data access, allow developers to focus on modeling domain logic without being burdened by infrastructure concerns. Additionally, Spring's extensive use of annotations provides a convenient shorthand for DDD concepts, empowering developers to represent domain services, repositories, and aggregates with precision.

Spring annotations simplify the code and help clarify the domain roles of classes and components. Here are some examples:

- The @Service annotation represents domain services, where business logic and domain actions reside. These services operate at the business logic layer and coordinate actions across aggregates or entities.

- The @Repository annotation encapsulates data storage and retrieval, representing the Repository pattern promoted by DDD. Repositories focus on the persistence layer, storing and retrieving domain objects while abstracting infrastructure concerns.

- Meanwhile, @Entity models domain entities with a unique identity, mapping directly to a database table or document to enable object-relational mapping.

- Finally, @Component is a more general-purpose annotation that can support aggregates or infrastructure concerns, allowing for flexible integration of non-domain-specific components.

As discussed in *Chapter 4, Testing and Validating DDD Applications*, validating code design through tests ensures that applications remain aligned with DDD principles. jMolecules, a powerful design validation tool, introduces design checks through tests on any platform. It goes a step further when used in the Spring ecosystem: its annotations integrate with Spring Data JPA and Spring Data MongoDB, enabling DDD-oriented annotations to influence code structure and persistence behavior. With this integration, Spring links the domain model with infrastructure, reinforcing DDD principles through well-structured code.

The features of Spring naturally support DDD practices, making it simpler to create a well-architected domain model. For example, Spring Data JPA simplifies the Repository pattern and abstract entity persistence, which helps model repositories and manage aggregate roots. Similarly, Spring Data MongoDB enables persistence for aggregate roots in NoSQL databases, providing a natural fit for DDD in non-relational contexts. With its convention-over-configuration approach, Spring Boot streamlines the setup of DDD-based services and promotes a Clean Architecture.

Spring Integration supports domain events and message-driven architectures, essential in event-driven DDD applications. At the same time, Spring **Aspect Oriented Programming (AOP)** manages cross-cutting code concerns like logging and transaction control, keeping domain logic clean and isolated from infrastructure concerns.

The following table introduces Spring and how it can enhance the design using DDD. It is essential to highlight that Spring is a vast technology stack. If using Spring, it is worth checking these elements. The following table introduces a small set of relevant technologies and dependencies:

Spring feature	DDD application
Spring Data JPA	Automates Repository pattern; simplifies entity persistence
Spring Data MongoDB	Enables persistence for aggregate roots in NoSQL; aligns with DDD
Spring Boot	Convention-over-configuration quickly sets up DDD-based services
Spring Integration	Supports domain events and message-driven architecture
Spring AOP	Handles cross-cutting concerns like logging and transaction control

Table 9.1: Apply Spring with DDD

Another essential feature of Spring is its dependency injection framework, which allows objects to be provided automatically to classes where they are needed. The @Autowired annotation is central to this process, simplifying dependency management without manual configuration. Dependency injection can be achieved through either field or constructor injection, although the Spring team recommends constructor injection due to its clarity and the benefits of immutability. The constructor-based injection is particularly valuable in a DDD context, ensuring that all necessary dependencies are available when the object is created. This supports DDD's emphasis on stable, self-contained domain models. While field injection is possible, it is generally discouraged as it reduces visibility and can complicate testing. By enforcing dependencies through constructors, Spring helps create a clean, maintainable, and testable codebase consistent with DDD principles of encapsulation and clear boundaries.

In a DDD application, dependency injection facilitates the separation of concerns by allowing services and repositories to be injected precisely where they are needed without direct dependency management. This approach keeps dependencies explicit, strengthening the boundaries between layers and improving modularity and maintainability.

In the following section, we will move from concepts to practical applications. We will see how to implement DDD with Spring through real-world code examples, including using @ Autowired for constructor injection in services and repositories. This hands-on approach will demonstrate leveraging Spring's features to create a structured, scalable DDD architecture that aligns closely with business needs.

Applying DDD with Spring Boot

To demonstrate how Spring supports DDD, we will build a sample project for a hotel management system using Spring with H2, an in-memory relational database. In real-world applications, other databases, such as PostgreSQL, are used instead; however, for learning purposes, we will rely on the database with a simpler setup, so we can focus on the integration with Spring.

Creating and setting up a new Spring Boot project

Setting up the project is straightforward, thanks to Spring's **Spring Initializr**, which allows you to generate a Spring Boot project quickly. To support our application's needs, we will include the following dependencies: Spring Web to enable RESTful web services, Spring Data JPA to simplify data access, and H2 for the in-memory database.

After creating the project, we configure the H2 database in the **application.properties** file. Following best practices from the Twelve-Factor App principles, Spring allows configurations to be flexible and manageable across environments. For local development, we set database properties directly in **application.properties**, and for production, we can override them with environment variables, ensuring that sensitive credentials remain secure. The following is an example configuration:

```
spring.application.name=chapter-09
spring.datasource.url=jdbc:h2:mem:testdb
spring.datasource.driverClassName=org.h2.Driver
spring.datasource.username=sa
spring.datasource.password=password
spring.jpa.database-platform=org.hibernate.dialect.H2Dialect
spring.jpa.defer-datasource-initialization=true
spring.h2.console.enabled=true
```

This configuration sets up an H2 database with a console interface, making it easy to inspect tables and data as we test our application.

Defining the core domain entities

With the project configured, we can define the core domain entities for the hotel management system: **Guest** and **Room**, using the following code. These entities represent key business concepts and include annotations for persistence. The **Guest** entity has an ID, document number, and name, while the **Room** entity includes a room number and a reference to a guest, reflecting the relationship between rooms and guests.

```
@Entity
public class Guest {

    @Id
    @GeneratedValue(strategy = GenerationType.IDENTITY)
    private Long id;

    @Column
    private String documentNumber;

    @Column
    private String name;

    // Getters and Setters
}
```

In the **Guest** entity, we define basic properties and an autogenerated ID for database identification.

```
@Entity
public class Room {

    @Id
```

```
@GeneratedValue(strategy - GenerationType.IDENTITY)
private Long number;

@ManyToOne
@JoinColumn(name = "guest_id", referencedColumnName = "id")
private Guest guest;

// Getters and Setters
}
```

In the **Room** entity, each room has a unique number and a possible association with a guest, representing a check-in relationship.

Shaping the repository and services

Next, we create repository interfaces for data access. Using the Repository pattern aligns with DDD principles by centralizing data operations, and Spring Data JPA provides built-in support for this pattern. By extending **JpaRepository**, we gain essential CRUD operations and the flexibility to define query methods by convention, which Spring interprets and implements automatically.

```
@Repository
public interface GuestRepository extends JpaRepository<Guest, Long> {

    Optional<Guest> findByDocumentNumber(String documentNumber);
}
```

The **GuestRepository** interface includes a method for finding guests by their document number. Similarly, the **RoomRepository** interface provides methods to check if a room is vacant and retrieve rooms by number.

```
@Repository
public interface RoomRepository extends JpaRepository<Room, Long> {

    Optional<Room> findByGuestIsNull();

    Optional<Room> findByNumber(Long number);
}
```

To coordinate data operations across entities, we implement a **RoomService** class, which acts as the main business service for managing rooms and guests. Spring handles dependency injection through the constructor, simplifying the process of connecting repositories to this service. Here, **@Autowired** on the constructor injects **RoomRepository** and **GuestRepository**, allowing **RoomService** to perform check-in, check-out, and other operations.

```java
@Service
public class RoomService {

    private final RoomRepository roomRepository;
    private final GuestRepository guestRepository;

    public RoomService(RoomRepository roomRepository, GuestRepository
guestRepository) {
        this.roomRepository = roomRepository;
        this.guestRepository = guestRepository;
    }

    public List<Room> findRooms(PageRequest pageRequest) {
        Page<Room> page = roomRepository.findAll(pageRequest);
        return page.getContent();
    }

    @Transactional
    public Room checkIn(Room room) {
        Room roomEntity = roomRepository.findByNumber(room.getNumber())
                .orElseThrow(() -> new EntityNotFoundException("Room not
found, the room number is " + room.getNumber()));

        Guest guest = guestRepository.findByDocumentNumber(room.getGuest().
getDocumentNumber())
                .orElseGet(() -> guestRepository.save(room.getGuest()));

        roomEntity.setGuest(guest);
        return roomRepository.save(roomEntity);
    }

    @Transactional
    public void checkOut(Room room) {
        Room roomEntity = roomRepository.findByNumber(room.getNumber())
                .orElseThrow(() -> new EntityNotFoundException("Room not
found, the room number is " + room.getNumber()));

        roomEntity.setGuest(null);
        roomRepository.save(roomEntity);
```

```
    }

    public Optional<Room> reservation(Long number) {
        return roomRepository.findByNumber(number);
    }

    public Long countBy() {
        return roomRepository.count();
    }

    public Optional<Room> findEmptyRoom() {
        return roomRepository.findByGuestIsNull();
    }
}
```

The **RoomService** class coordinates operations between the two repositories. It includes methods for finding rooms, handling check-in and check-out, and identifying empty rooms. The **checkIn** method finds a room by its number and checks if a guest already exists by their document number. If not, it creates a new **Guest** and associates them with the room. **checkOut** clears the guest assignment for a room, freeing it for future reservations.

In this example, we see how Spring's annotations and dependency injection streamline the development of a DDD-oriented system. By leveraging Spring's Repository pattern, dependency injection, and transaction management, the code remains clean, maintainable, and aligned with the principles of DDD.

Exposing the service through REST endpoints

With the service layer complete, we can now expose it to the application layer through a **HotelController**. This controller acts as an API layer, allowing external systems or front-end clients to interact with our application. It uses HTTP endpoints to handle requests related to room management in our hotel system and serves as a bridge between the client and the **RoomService**.

```
@RestController
@RequestMapping("/hotels")
public class HotelController {

    private static final Logger LOGGER = Logger.getLogger(HotelController.
class.getName());

    private final RoomService roomService;
```

```java
    @Autowired
    public HotelController(RoomService roomService) {
        this.roomService = roomService;
    }

    @GetMapping
    public ResponseEntity<List<Room>> getRooms(@RequestParam(defaultValue =
"0") int page,
                                               @RequestParam(defaultValue =
"10") int size) {
        LOGGER.info("Finding rooms page: " + page + " size: " + size);
        PageRequest pageRequest = PageRequest.of(page, size);
        List<Room> rooms = roomService.findRooms(pageRequest);
        LOGGER.info("Found rooms: " + rooms.size());
        return ResponseEntity.ok(rooms);
    }

    @GetMapping("/{number}")
    public ResponseEntity<Room> getReservation(@PathVariable Long number) {
        LOGGER.info("Finding reservation: " + number);
        var room = roomService.reservation(number)
                .orElseThrow(() -> new EntityNotFoundException("Room not found
with number " + number));
        return ResponseEntity.ok(room);
    }

    @PutMapping
    public ResponseEntity<Room> checkIn(@RequestBody Room room) {
        LOGGER.info("Check in: " + room);
        Room checkedInRoom = roomService.checkIn(room);
        return ResponseEntity.ok(checkedInRoom);
    }

    @DeleteMapping("/{number}")
    public ResponseEntity<Void> checkOut(@PathVariable Long number) {
        LOGGER.info("Check out: " + number);
        Room room = roomService.reservation(number)
                .orElseThrow(() -> new EntityNotFoundException("Room not found
```

```
with number " + number));
      roomService.checkOut(room);
      return ResponseEntity.noContent().build();
   }
}
```

HotelController defines RESTful endpoints corresponding to the application's main actions. The **@RestController** annotation tells Spring to treat this class as a web controller and automatically convert responses to JSON format. We use constructor injection to inject **RoomService** into **HotelController**, adhering to Spring's recommended best practices for dependency management, those resources:

- **GET /hotels**: Retrieves a paginated list of all rooms.
- **GET /hotels/{number}**: Retrieves a specific room reservation by its room number.
- **PUT /hotels**: Handles check-in for a guest by assigning them to a room.
- **DELETE /hotels/{number}**: Handles check-out, clearing the guest from a room.

Polishing error handling

To handle errors like a room not being found, we will implement a custom exception handler to convert these exceptions into meaningful HTTP responses. In our case, we will use **EntityNotFoundException** to represent missing records and map this to a **404 Not Found** HTTP status.

```
@ControllerAdvice
public class CustomExceptionHandler {

   @ExceptionHandler(EntityNotFoundException.class)
   @ResponseStatus(HttpStatus.NOT_FOUND)
   public ErrorResponse handleEntityNotFoundException(EntityNotFoundException
ex) {
      return new ErrorResponse("Entity not found", ex.getMessage());
   }

   public static class ErrorResponse {
      private String error;
      private String message;

      public ErrorResponse(String error, String message) {
         this.error = error;
         this.message = message;
```

```
        }

        public String getError() {
            return error;
        }

        public String getMessage() {
            return message;
        }
    }
}
```

The **CustomExceptionHandler** class uses **@ControllerAdvice** to apply globally across the application. Here, we define an **@ExceptionHandler** for **EntityNotFoundException** that returns a **404** status with a custom error message. This approach provides a consistent way of handling exceptions and ensures clear communication with API clients.

Ensuring code behavior with unit tests

Testing is one of Spring's standout features, making it easy to test each layer in isolation or combination. We will start with repository tests to verify custom queries and JPA functionality, followed by service tests to check business logic, and finally, controller tests to simulate HTTP requests and validate the API endpoints.

Testing the repository layer involves verifying that database operations, especially custom queries, work as expected. Using **@DataJpaTest** and **H2**, we can test database interactions with minimal setup.

```
@DataJpaTest
class GuestRepositoryTest {

    @Autowired
    private GuestRepository guestRepository;

    @BeforeEach
    void setUp() {
        guestRepository.deleteAll();
    }

    @Test
    void shouldSaveAndRetrieveGuestByDocumentNumber() {
        Guest guest = new Guest("123456789", "John Doe");
```

```
        guestRepository.save(guest);

        Optional<Guest> retrievedGuest = guestRepository.
findByDocumentNumber("123456789");
        assertThat(retrievedGuest).isPresent()
                                .get().extracting(Guest::getName)
                                .isEqualTo("John Doe");
    }

    @Test
    void shouldReturnEmptyWhenGuestNotFoundByDocumentNumber() {
        Optional<Guest> retrievedGuest = guestRepository.
findByDocumentNumber("999999999");
        assertThat(retrievedGuest).isNotPresent();
    }
}
```

Service layer tests allow us to validate business logic, including coordination between repositories. With **@SpringBootTest** and **H2**, we can run integration tests on the service.

```
@SpringBootTest
@Transactional
class RoomServiceTest {

    @Autowired
    private RoomService roomService;

    @Autowired
    private RoomRepository roomRepository;

    @Autowired
    private GuestRepository guestRepository;

    @BeforeEach
    void setUp() {
        roomRepository.deleteAll();
        guestRepository.deleteAll();
    }

    @Test
```

```
    void shouldCheckInGuestWhenGuestExists() {
        Guest guest = guestRepository.save(new Guest("123456789", "John
Doe"));
        Room room = roomRepository.save(new Room(6L, null));
        room.setGuest(guest);

        Room checkedInRoom = roomService.checkIn(room);
        assertThat(checkedInRoom.getGuest()).isEqualTo(guest);
    }

    @Test
    void shouldThrowExceptionWhenRoomNotFoundForCheckIn() {
        Room room = new Room();
        room.setNumber(3L);

        assertThatThrownBy(() -> roomService.checkIn(room))
                .isInstanceOf(EntityNotFoundException.class);
    }
}
```

Controller tests simulate HTTP requests and validate responses. With **@SpringBootTest** and **MockMvc**, we can verify that **HotelController** handles requests as expected.

```
@SpringBootTest
@AutoConfigureMockMvc
class HotelControllerTest {

    @Autowired
    private MockMvc mockMvc;

    @Autowired
    private RoomRepository roomRepository;

    @Autowired
    private GuestRepository guestRepository;

    @BeforeEach
    void setUp() {
        roomRepository.deleteAll();
        guestRepository.deleteAll();
```

```
    }

    @Test
    void shouldReturnPagedRooms() throws Exception {
        Room room = roomRepository.save(new Room());
        mockMvc.perform(get("/hotels?page=0&size=1")
                .contentType(MediaType.APPLICATION_JSON))
                .andExpect(status().isOk())
                .andExpect(jsonPath("$", hasSize(1)))
                .andExpect(jsonPath("$[0].number", is(room.getNumber().
intValue()))));
    }

    @Test
    void shouldCheckInGuest() throws Exception {
        Room room = roomRepository.save(new Room());
        String checkInJson = """
                {
                    "number": %d,
                    "guest": {
                        "documentNumber": "123456789",
                        "name": "John Doe"
                    }
                }
                """.formatted(room.getNumber());

        mockMvc.perform(put("/hotels")
                .contentType(MediaType.APPLICATION_JSON)
                .content(checkInJson))
                .andExpect(status().isOk())
                .andExpect(jsonPath("$.guest.documentNumber", is
("123456789")))
                .andExpect(jsonPath("$.guest.name", is("John Doe")));
    }
}
```

These tests verify that each layer works as intended and supports DDD principles. By providing practical testing tools, Spring ensures confidence in the behavior and reliability of each part of our application. While this example covers core concepts, Spring's features extend to security, advanced validation, and caching, which can enhance the application even further. Through Spring, we have seen how DDD can be implemented in a structured, maintainable way, aligning our code with business objectives while maintaining flexibility for future growth.

This section examined how Spring's toolkit effectively supports a DDD approach. We learned about defining entities, managing persistence, and exposing services through a clean API while ensuring thorough testing. We created a structured and maintainable application aligned with DDD principles by leveraging Spring Data JPA, dependency injection, and extensive testing support.

This example highlights Spring's seamless integration across all application layers, allowing developers to concentrate on business logic while the framework manages infrastructure concerns. Ultimately, Spring's flexibility and robust ecosystem make it an excellent choice for delivering scalable, business-aligned software solutions in today's enterprise environment.

Conclusion

This chapter examined Spring's strengths as a platform for building enterprise applications using DDD. By utilizing Spring's ecosystem, such as Spring Data JPA, dependency injection, and testing tools, we demonstrated its ability to simplify the development of complex applications. Our hotel management example separated concerns and aligned with DDD principles.

In the next chapter, we will discuss tools that can be applied to DDD, this time, Eclipse MicroProfile.

Points to remember

- **Spring simplifies DDD implementation**: By providing tools for dependency injection, data persistence, and RESTful APIs, Spring makes it easier to focus on business logic.

- **Spring annotations align with DDD principles**: Annotations like @Service, @Repository, and @Entity help clearly define domain layers.

- **Constructor injection is recommended**: Using constructor injection ensures immutability, improves testability, and makes dependencies explicit.

- **Spring Data JPA simplifies persistence**: The Repository pattern in Spring Data JPA enables easy data access and integration with relational databases.

- **Spring supports environment-based configuration**: Application properties can be overridden with environment variables, following the Twelve-Factor App methodology.

- **Exception handling can be centralized**: The @ControllerAdvice annotation allows global exception handling, making error responses more consistent.

- **Testing is a major strength of Spring**: Spring's test framework supports integration testing with H2, service-level testing, and controller testing using MockMvc.

- **Spring promotes separation of concerns**: By structuring applications into repositories, services, and controllers, Spring enforces a clean and maintainable architecture.

- **Spring Boot accelerates setup and development**: Convention-over-configuration allows developers to focus on features rather than boilerplate code.

- **Spring's flexibility allows easy database switching**: While this chapter used H2, applications can be easily configured to use databases like PostgreSQL, MySQL, or MongoDB.

Multiple choice questions

1. **What is the primary purpose of using Spring's @Service annotation in a DDD application?**
   a. To map domain entities to database tables
   b. To represent business logic services
   c. To define database repository interfaces
   d. To manage cross-cutting concerns like logging
   e. To handle exception processing

2. **Which dependency is used to create RESTful web services in Spring?**
   a. Spring Boot Actuator
   b. Spring Security
   c. Spring Web
   d. Spring Data JPA
   e. Spring Cloud

3. **What type of injection is generally recommended by the Spring team for managing dependencies?**
   a. Field injection
   b. Setter injection
   c. Constructor injection
   d. Static injection
   e. Interface injection

4. **Which annotation is used in Spring to define a custom exception handler across the application?**

   a. @ExceptionHandler

   b. @ControllerAdvice

   c. @RestController

   d. @ResponseStatus

   e. @EnableWebMvc

5. **What does the @DataJpaTest annotation in Spring primarily support?**

   a. Testing web endpoints

   b. Testing the entire application context

   c. Unit testing of the service layer

   d. Testing JPA-based repository interactions

   e. Testing controller logic

6. **Which of the following is a benefit of using constructor injection in Spring?**

   a. Simplifies dependency management by hiding dependencies

   b. Ensures that required dependencies are available at object creation

   c. Allows dependencies to be added dynamically during runtime

   d. Hides dependencies, making the code more secure

   e. Reduces boilerplate by eliminating constructors

7. **How does the @Autowired annotation function within a service class in Spring?**

   a. It directly manages entity instances

   b. It injects dependencies automatically through the constructor

   c. It configures the database properties

   d. It enables caching within the service

   e. It maps endpoints to service methods

8. **What is the role of @Repository in a Spring DDD application?**

   a. To store entities in a database and provide data access methods

   b. To manage business logic across services

   c. To expose the service layer to external systems

   d. To define endpoints for HTTP requests

   e. To manage cross-cutting concerns like logging

Answers

Question number	Answer option letter
1.	b.
2.	c.
3.	c.
4.	b.
5.	d.
6.	b.
7.	b.
8.	a.

Join our Discord space

Join our Discord workspace for latest updates, offers, tech happenings around the world, new releases, and sessions with the authors:

https://discord.bpbonline.com

CHAPTER 10
Eclipse MicroProfile and Domain-driven Design

Introduction

Eclipse MicroProfile is a lightweight framework designed to enhance Java microservices by providing a set of specifications tailored for cloud-native applications. It extends Jakarta EE's capabilities with features like configuration management, health checks, metrics, and distributed tracing. These capabilities align well with **domain-driven design (DDD)** principles, allowing developers to optimize the domain model while delivering on essential enterprise needs, such as low resource consumption (cost reduction), high scalability, and resiliency.

This chapter explores how MicroProfile can be used to structure microservices-based applications that adhere to DDD principles. We will demonstrate how MicroProfile Config can decouple infrastructure concerns from business logic and how best practices for structuring applications in a way that keeps the domain model at the core of the architecture. By leveraging these features, developers can balance domain purity and pragmatic cloud-native implementation.

Structure

In this chapter, we will explore more about the following topics:

- Understanding Eclipse MicroProfile and its purpose

- Integrating Eclipse MicroProfile with DDD

- Practical microservices example

Technical requirements

This chapter will explore the usage of CDI with Helidon. The same concepts could be implemented using Quarkus. In this chapter, we will need Docker to run a MongoDB database.

- Java 21

- Git

- Maven

- Any preferred IDE

- Docker

- MongoDB NoSQL database

    o To kickstart a new instance of MongoDB, you can use Docker CLI and the following command:

    ```
    docker run -d --name mongodb-instance -p 27017:27017 mongo
    ```

Objectives

This chapter explores how Eclipse MicroProfile enhances the development of cloud-native Java microservices while maintaining a strong DDD approach. The objective is to demonstrate how MicroProfile's lightweight and modular specifications, such as Config, OpenAPI, and Jakarta NoSQL, help developers build scalable, flexible, and well-structured microservices. By the end of this chapter, readers will understand how to integrate these technologies effectively to create resilient, maintainable, and loosely coupled services that align with business needs.

Understanding Eclipse MicroProfile and its purpose

Eclipse MicroProfile is a lightweight specification designed to enhance Java microservices by providing a set of specifications tailored for cloud-native applications. MicroProfile contains Jakarta EE's capabilities and uses features like configuration management, health checks, metrics, and distributed tracing. However, the opposite is not true; Jakarta EE does not depend on MicroProfile.

At first glance, it is natural to compare Eclipse MicroProfile to Jakarta EE, as both are used to build enterprise Java solutions, and are two projects under the umbrella of the Eclipse Foundation.

Clarifying Jakarta EE and MicroProfile similarities

They have several similarities, such as the organizations that collaborate with the Eclipse Foundation on the evolution of the project and their licenses. However, as of 2025, both these projects stand as distinct and separate projects.

Consider exploring both MicroProfile and Jakarta EE, especially when working together, for a better understanding of the architectural enhancements derived from their integration. One way to look at Jakarta EE is by considering it as the minimal requirements of the Eclipse MicroProfile; for example, the Jakarta EE Core Profile, which includes CDI, is the core of the MicroProfile. Indeed, the first version of Eclipse MicroProfile was based on three Jakarta EE specifications: CDI, JSON-P, and JAX-RS. Jakarta EE does not, and cannot, depend on the MicroProfile projects. The dependency between both projects resulted in a long discussion about the project Jakarta Config, as it is ultimately targeting the same problems on both MicroProfile and Jakarta EE, and to some extent, it even has the same code under different package names[1]. It is unpleasant to see duplicated code as a user, and as a committer on both projects, it feels even worse.

Note: **Code duplication between specifications, such as Jakarta Config and MicroProfile Config, is not ideal. While the goal is consistency across the Jakarta EE and MicroProfile ecosystems, current limitations lead to duplicated code with different package names. This situation is suboptimal from both a committer's and a user's perspective, and should be improved in the future to enhance cohesion and usability.**

Eclipse MicroProfile architecture and specifications

The following figure illustrates the architecture and specifications of Eclipse MicroProfile version 7. It showcases how various specifications interact within the MicroProfile ecosystem, highlighting the dependencies on Jakarta EE Core Profile and standalone MicroProfile specifications. This visual representation helps developers understand how the framework is structured and how different specifications tackle different requirements of cloud-native Java applications.

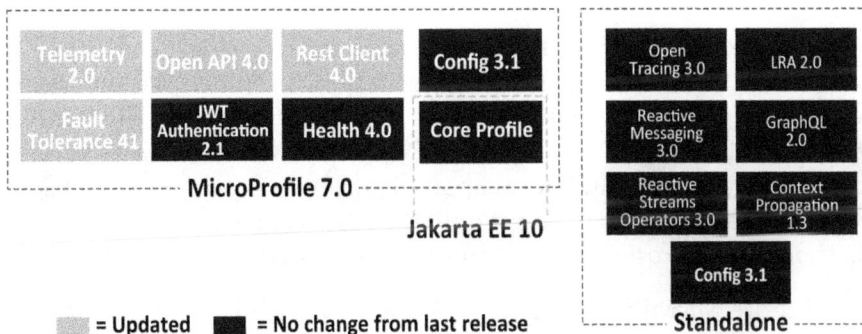

Figure 10.1: Eclipse MicroProfile version 7

In addition to the Jakarta EE core profile, Eclipse MicroProfile contains other vital projects that mainly focus on the architecture and behaviors of distributed systems (e.g., microservices). One of the most impactful is Eclipse MicroProfile Config, which allows dynamic configuration management and externalization of configuration variables (as proposed in the twelve-factor app[2] methodology). In addition to Config, it is also worth exploring the Metrics project, as it unlocks out-of-the-box insights about the application performance and health, as well as offering a straightforward way to define and expose new metrics of that application.

To better understand the capabilities of Eclipse MicroProfile, let us explore its key specifications, each designed to address different aspects of building and maintaining cloud-native microservices:

- **MicroProfile Config**: Enables externalized configuration for applications, following the Twelve-Factor App methodology.

- **MicroProfile Fault Tolerance**: Provides resilience mechanisms such as retries, bulkheads, and circuit breakers.

- **MicroProfile Health**: Defines health checks to ensure service availability.

- **MicroProfile Metrics**: Enables application monitoring through standardized metrics.

- **MicroProfile OpenAPI**: Facilitates API documentation using the OpenAPI specification.

- **MicroProfile OpenTracing**: Provides distributed tracing capabilities for microservices.

- **MicroProfile JWT Authentication**: Enables JSON Web Token-based authentication.

- **MicroProfile Rest Client**: Simplifies HTTP-based communication between microservices.

- **MicroProfile Reactive Messaging**: Supports event-driven communication using messaging systems.

- **MicroProfile GraphQL**: Adds support for GraphQL APIs within MicroProfile applications.

A key feature of MicroProfile is its support for standalone specifications. While many of its capabilities are based on Jakarta EE, several specifications can be used independently. This allows developers to utilize only what they need without adopting the entire Jakarta EE stack. For example, MicroProfile Config, MicroProfile Metrics, and MicroProfile Health can be integrated into various Java runtimes without requiring components from Jakarta EE. This modular approach enables teams to adopt only the essential parts of MicroProfile, making it an adaptable choice for microservices and other lightweight deployments.

As we explore Eclipse MicroProfile further, we will explore how each project contributes to building efficient, scalable, and maintainable microservices architectures.

Integrating Eclipse MicroProfile with DDD

Modern software development demands scalable and maintainable architectures while keeping business logic at the forefront. DDD provides a methodology for structuring applications around business domains, ensuring clarity and long-term adaptability. When combined with Eclipse MicroProfile, developers gain powerful tools to implement DDD principles in distributed, cloud-native environments.

Eclipse MicroProfile extends Jakarta EE by offering lightweight specifications that address microservices-specific concerns, such as externalized configuration, observability, and resilience. These capabilities enable teams to design services focused on business logic and equipped to handle the complexities of modern distributed architectures. MicroProfile provides a flexible foundation for implementing DDD patterns, ensuring that technical concerns do not overshadow the core domain model.

While DDD emphasizes keeping the domain model central, real-world implementations often require additional infrastructure to support scalability, fault tolerance, and monitoring. MicroProfile bridges this gap with key specifications that complement DDD principles as follows:

- **Contexts and Dependency Injection (CDI)**: A core part of MicroProfile, CDI enables Clean Code design, enforces separation of concerns, and promotes modularity, which is essential for organizing domain logic efficiently.

- **MicroProfile Config**: It externalizes configuration, keeping domain models clean and allowing business logic to be unaffected by environment-specific settings.

- **MicroProfile Fault Tolerance**: This feature protects critical domain operations from failures using retries, circuit breakers, and bulkheads, ensuring domain integrity in distributed environments.

- **MicroProfile Metrics and Health**: It supports observability by providing visibility into domain service behavior. It helps teams monitor performance and detect anomalies before they affect business processes.

- **MicroProfile OpenTracing**: Enables distributed tracing across services, making debugging interactions between domain-driven services easier.

- **MicroProfile Reactive Messaging**: It supports event-driven DDD implementations by allowing services to communicate asynchronously, aligning with domain events, and ensuring consistency.

The following table illustrates how Eclipse MicroProfile specifications contribute to implementing DDD in a microservices context. Each specification is critical in maintaining a clean domain model while ensuring that infrastructure concerns like configuration, resilience, and communication are handled effectively. By integrating these capabilities, MicroProfile enables developers to focus on the business domain without being overwhelmed by technical complexities.

MicroProfile specification	DDD benefit
MicroProfile Config	Separates domain logic from infrastructure by externalizing configuration.
MicroProfile Fault Tolerance	Ensures resilience in domain services, preventing failures from propagating.
MicroProfile Health	Monitors the health of domain services, ensuring system reliability.
MicroProfile Metrics	Provides insights into domain service behavior, improving maintainability.
MicroProfile OpenTracing	Enables tracing of domain interactions across multiple microservices.
MicroProfile JWT Authentication	Secures domain services with role-based access control.
MicroProfile Rest Client	Simplifies communication between bounded contexts in a microservices setup.
MicroProfile Reactive Messaging	Supports domain event propagation, enabling eventual consistency.
MicroProfile GraphQL	Enhances querying capabilities for domain aggregates.

Table 10.1: Eclipse MicroProfile components

By leveraging Eclipse MicroProfile, developers can apply DDD principles effectively in modern, cloud-native applications. The combination of a strong domain model and well-integrated microservices infrastructure ensures that business concerns remain the focal point while benefiting from the flexibility and resilience of distributed systems.

The following section will explore how to apply these concepts in practice. We will use concrete examples demonstrating how MicroProfile's capabilities, such as Config, can be leveraged to build robust, domain-centric microservices. We will see how MicroProfile enhances DDD principles in real-world applications through hands-on implementations.

Practical microservices example

We will build a microservice that manages product entities to demonstrate how Eclipse MicroProfile can be applied effectively using a DDD approach. Helidon is a runtime that offers support to Eclipse MicroProfile. Although it supports multiple Jakarta EE specifications, it is not considered a full Jakarta EE implementation like *GlassFish* or *Open Liberty*. This implementation will follow a structured design, separating concerns across domain, infrastructure, and application layers while leveraging MicroProfile's capabilities, such as OpenAPI, Config, and Fault Tolerance.

For persistence, we will use MongoDB as our database, integrate it via Jakarta NoSQL and Jakarta Data, and utilize the Eclipse JNoSQL implementation. The primary difference in configuration compared to *Chapter 8, Enterprise Java with Jakarta EE*, is that we will replace Oracle with MongoDB by modifying the driver dependency, as shown in the following code:

```
<dependency>
    <groupId>org.eclipse.jnosql.databases</groupId>
    <artifactId>jnosql-mongodb</artifactId>
    <version>${jnosql.version}</version>
</dependency>
```

Our microservice will follow a well-defined structure that enforces the separation of concerns to ensure a modular and maintainable architecture. This approach allows the system to remain scalable, testable, and aligned with DDD principles while effectively leveraging MicroProfile's capabilities on the multiple layers:

- **Domain layer**: Contains the core business logic and domain entities.

- **Infrastructure layer**: Manages database interactions, external dependencies, and configurations.

- **Application layer**: Exposes RESTful endpoints and handles HTTP requests using MicroProfile features.

After setting up the MongoDB driver, we also need to update the configuration to define our database connection as follows:

```
jnosql.mongodb.url=mongodb://localhost:27017
# mandatory define the database name
jnosql.document.database=products
```

This is where we encountered our first MicroProfile specification: MicroProfile Config. It allows us to define configurations that can be easily modified across different environments. For example, while running the application locally, authentication might not be required, but we can configure secure credentials without modifying the application code in production. MicroProfile Config ensures flexibility and maintainability by enabling external configuration and environment-specific overrides.

With the configuration in place, the next step is to define the domain model. We introduce each class and explain its role in the domain package in the following section.

The **Product** class represents the primary entity in our domain. Note the annotation **@Entity**, which makes this class a Jakarta NoSQL document entity that will be persisted in MongoDB:

```
@Entity
public class Product {

    @Id
```

```
@Convert(ObjectIdConverter.class)
private String id;

@Column
private String name;

@Column
private Manufacturer manufacturer;

@Column
private List<String> tags;

@Column
private Set<Category> categories;

// Getters, equals, hashCode, and toString methods
}
```

This class defines a product with an ID, name, manufacturer, associated tags, and categories. It follows DDD principles by incorporating composition, where the **Manufacturer** and **Category** classes are modeled as embedded objects rather than separate entities.

The **Manufacturer** class represents a value object, meaning it does not have a unique identity and is part of the **Product** document.

```
@Embeddable(Embeddable.EmbeddableType.GROUPING)
public record Manufacturer(@Column String name, @Column String address, @
Column String contactNumber) {
}
```

By embedding manufacturer details, we avoid unnecessary relationships and maintain a self-contained product entity. The **@Embeddable(Embeddable.EmbeddableType.GROUPING)** annotation ensures that the **Manufacturer** object is stored as a subdocument inside the **Product** document, keeping related information together. This differs from relational databases, where embeddable objects are usually flattened into the same table. If **EmbeddableType.FLAT** was used instead; the fields of **Manufacturer** would be merged directly into the **Product** document instead of being grouped into a subdocument.

Similarly, the **Category** class is also a value object, classifying a product under multiple categories.

It is marked with **@Embeddable(Embeddable.EmbeddableType.GROUPING)**, meaning its attributes will be stored as a subdocument within the **Product** document in MongoDB. If

EmbeddableType.FLAT used, its attributes would be stored as part of the leading **Product** document instead of a nested structure.

```
@Embeddable(Embeddable.EmbeddableType.GROUPING)
public record Category(@Column String name, @Column String description) {
}
```

The **ProductRepository** interface handles data persistence. It is part of the Jakarta Data specification, which provides a standardized way to define repositories for Jakarta applications. Extending **BasicRepository** enables automatic CRUD functionality without requiring explicit implementation, allowing for a clean and declarative approach to data access.

```
@Repository
public interface ProductRepository extends BasicRepository<Product, String> {
}
```

With our domain model and repository in place, the next step is to implement the application layer. This layer exposes RESTful endpoints using MicroProfile features like *OpenAPI* and *Fault Tolerance*.

As the next step, we focus on the application layer, exposing the domain model while ensuring it remains isolated from external concerns. The goal is to provide a clean interface without contaminating the domain logic with outside dependencies. We use **Data Transfer Objects** (**DTOs**) to separate the domain model from the application layer to achieve this. In our example, we leverage MapStruct to automatically convert between entities and DTOs, reducing manual mapping effort and keeping the code concise.

Maintaining fewer lines of code simplifies development and improves maintainability, a crucial principle to consider when designing Clean Architectures.

Another key aspect of this isolation is defining OpenAPI documentation separately from our domain model. Instead of directly annotating domain entities, potentially exposing unnecessary or sensitive information, we use DTOs to control precisely what is shared externally.

We use DTOs inside both **Request** and **Response** objects to ensure consistency. There is no strict industry standard for how to handle this, and developers take different approaches, including the following:

- Using the same DTO class for both requests and responses.

- Creating separate **ProductRequest** and **ProductResponse** classes that wrap a **ProductDTO** inside a data field.

- Duplicating fields across distinct **ProductRequest** and **ProductResponse** classes.

The last option, duplicating fields, is not recommended, as it increases maintenance overhead without adding value.

The **CategoryDTO** class represents the category of a product and ensures that only relevant information is exposed via the API as follows:

```
@Schema(description = "Represents a category for a product.")
@JsonbVisibility(FieldVisibilityStrategy.class)
public class CategoryDTO {

    @Schema(description = "Name of the category.")
    private String name;

    @Schema(description = "Description of the category.")
    private String description;

    // Getters, setters, equals, hashCode, and toString methods
}
```

The **ManufacturerDTO** class encapsulates manufacturer information while ensuring only necessary details are shared through the API. Using this DTO, we keep the domain model clean and prevent unintended exposure of domain-related logic to the application layer. This approach enhances maintainability and security by decoupling external representation from internal business logic.

```
@Schema(description = "Represents the manufacturer of a product.")
@JsonbVisibility(FieldVisibilityStrategy.class)
public class ManufacturerDTO {

    @Schema(description = "Name of the manufacturer.")
    private String name;

    @Schema(description = "Address of the manufacturer.")
    private String address;

    @Schema(description = "Contact number of the manufacturer.")
    private String contactNumber;

    // Getters, setters, equals, hashCode, and toString methods
}
```

The **ProductDTO** class serves as a DTO for products, ensuring that only necessary information is exposed through the API while keeping the internal domain model clean. Using this DTO, we decouple the domain logic from external representations, preventing unwanted dependencies and reducing the risk of exposing implementation details. This structured approach allows flexibility when modifying the external contract without affecting the core business logic.

```java
@Schema(description = "Represents a product.")
@JsonbVisibility(FieldVisibilityStrategy.class)
public class ProductDTO {

    @Schema(description = "Unique identifier for the product.")
    private String id;

    @Schema(description = "Name of the product.")
    private String name;

    @Schema(description = "Manufacturer details of the product.")
    private ManufacturerDTO manufacturer;

    @Schema(description = "Tags associated with the product.")
    private List<String> tags;

    @Schema(description = "Categories the product belongs to.")
    private Set<CategoryDTO> categories;

    // Getters, setters, equals, hashCode, and toString methods
}
```

Converting between domain entities and DTOs can be tedious and error-prone, leading to unnecessary boilerplate code. We use **MapStruct**, a code-generation tool that automatically produces mapping logic at compile time to streamline this process. This approach reduces manual effort and ensures that the mapping remains consistent and maintainable across different application layers.

```java
@Mapper(componentModel = MappingConstants.ComponentModel.JAKARTA_CDI)
public interface ProductMapper {
    ProductDTO toDTO(Product product);
    Product toEntity(ProductDTO productDTO);
    ManufacturerDTO toDTO(Manufacturer manufacturer);
    Manufacturer toEntity(ManufacturerDTO manufacturerDTO);
    CategoryDTO toDTO(Category category);
    Category toEntity(CategoryDTO categoryDTO);
}
```

The **ProductService** class bridges the domain layer and the API, ensuring that business logic is executed correctly while remaining independent of HTTP-specific concerns. This service maintains a clean separation of responsibilities by encapsulating operations like querying, saving, and deleting products, preventing the REST layer from directly interacting with the persistence layer. This design promotes maintainability, reusability, and testability, making it easier to adapt and extend the system in the future.

```java
@ApplicationScoped
public class ProductService {

    private final ProductRepository repository;
    private final ProductMapper mapper;

    @Inject
    public ProductService(ProductRepository repository, ProductMapper mapper)
{
        this.repository = repository;
        this.mapper = mapper;
    }

    public List<ProductDTO> findAll(PageRequest request, Order<Product> order)
{
        return repository.findAll(request, order).content().stream()
                .map(mapper::toDTO)
                .toList();
    }

    public ProductDTO save(ProductDTO product) {
        return mapper.toDTO(repository.save(mapper.toEntity(product)));
    }

    public void deleteById(String id) {
        repository.deleteById(id);
    }

    public Optional<ProductDTO> findById(String id) {
        return repository.findById(id).map(mapper::toDTO);
    }
}
```

The **ProductResource** class serves as the exposure layer of the application, making the product domain accessible through RESTful endpoints. It ensures that interactions with the system occur via well-defined HTTP operations while keeping the internal business logic isolated. This layer transforms incoming JSON requests into domain operations and returns structured JSON responses.

We simplify handling HTTP requests and responses by leveraging Jakarta RESTful Web Services (Jakarta REST API). This API eliminates the complexity traditionally associated with building RESTful services, enabling a clean and declarative way to define resources. Additionally, MicroProfile OpenAPI annotations provide automatic API documentation, ensuring that endpoints are clearly defined and easily discoverable by consumers.

```
@ApplicationScoped
@Path("/products")
@Tag(name = "Products", description = "Operations related to product
management")
public class ProductResource {

    private final ProductService service;

    @Inject
    public ProductResource(ProductService service) {
        this.service = service;
    }

    @GET
    @Operation(summary = "Retrieve a paginated list of products")
    public List<ProductDTO> get(@QueryParam("page") @DefaultValue("1") int
page,
                                 @QueryParam("size") @DefaultValue("10") int
size) {
        return service.findAll(PageRequest.ofPage(page).size(size), Order.
by(Sort.asc("name")));
    }

    @POST
    @Operation(summary = "Create a new product")
    public ProductDTO insert(ProductDTO product) {
        return service.save(product);
    }
```

```
@DELETE
@Path("{id}")
@Operation(summary = "Delete a product by ID")
public void delete(@PathParam("id") String id) {
    service.deleteById(id);
}

@GET
@Path("{id}")
@Operation(summary = "Find a product by ID")
public ProductDTO findById(@PathParam("id") String id) {
    return service.findById(id)
            .orElseThrow(() -> new WebApplicationException("Product not
found", Response.Status.NOT_FOUND));
    }
}
```

Before testing the API, ensure that the MongoDB database is running so that the application can connect and persist data.

To compile and execute the application, run the following command:

mvn clean package && java -jar target/chapter-10.jar

Once the application is running, developers can access the OpenAPI UI to visualize and interact with the available endpoints through an intuitive web interface. By navigating to:

http://localhost:8181/openapi/ui/index.html users can explore the API documentation, test endpoints, and verify request/response structures without needing external tools. The following figure shows the Swagger of our OpenAPI generated by the Schema annotations:

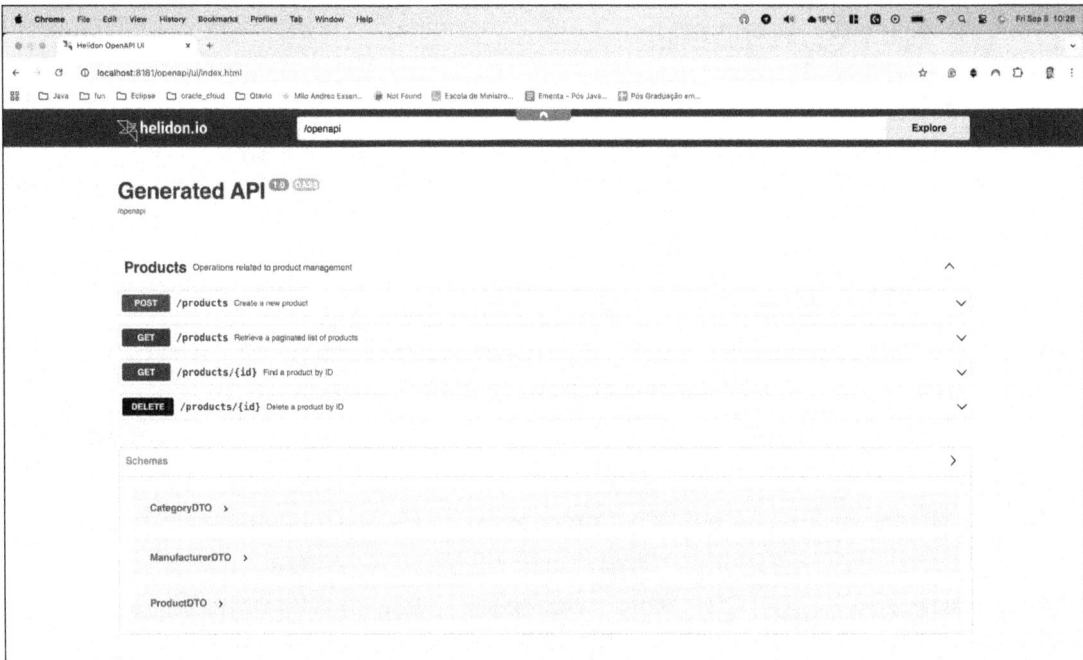

Figure 10.2: Helidon Open API generated

By applying Eclipse MicroProfile in our application layer, we have successfully designed a structured and maintainable approach to expose domain logic while keeping it decoupled from external concerns. Using DTOs, Jakarta REST API, and OpenAPI, we ensured that the microservices remained clean, flexible, and easily testable.

Conclusion

Eclipse MicroProfile provides essential tools for developing resilient and observable microservices. By integrating fault tolerance, health checks, and metrics, we ensure that our services can recover from failures, provide real-time insights, and optimize performance. These capabilities are critical for building robust applications that withstand unpredictable conditions in distributed environments.

We will explore DDD with Quarkus as we move forward. Quarkus is a robust framework that enhances MicroProfile while optimizing performance for cloud-native applications. In the next chapter, we will see how Quarkus enables faster development, improves startup times, and integrates seamlessly with DDD principles to build efficient and scalable microservices.

Points to remember

- **Eclipse MicroProfile**: A lightweight framework designed to enhance cloud-native Java microservices by extending Jakarta EE with microservices-specific capabilities.

- **MicroProfile Config**: Allows externalized configuration, enabling runtime flexibility without modifying application code.

- **Jakarta NoSQL**: Provides a standardized API for integrating NoSQL databases like MongoDB, ensuring seamless database interactions.

- **MicroProfile OpenAPI**: Automatically generates API documentation, making RESTful services more accessible and improving interoperability.

- **DTOs**: Help separate domain logic from external representations, preventing direct exposure of domain models.

- **MapStruct**: Automates object mapping between DTOs and domain entities, reducing boilerplate code and improving maintainability.

- **Jakarta Data Repositories**: Simplify database interactions by providing a declarative approach to CRUD operations without requiring boilerplate code.

- **MicroProfile Rest Client**: Facilitates communication between microservices by simplifying HTTP client implementations.

- **Application layer isolation**: Keeping the domain model clean by ensuring business logic is not coupled with infrastructure concerns.

- **Next Step—Quarkus**: The next chapter explores how Quarkus enhances MicroProfile, improving startup times and optimizing microservices for cloud-native environments.

Multiple choice questions

1. **What is the primary purpose of Eclipse MicroProfile?**
   a. To replace Java EE with a new framework
   b. To provide lightweight, cloud-native capabilities for Java microservices
   c. To enforce a strict monolithic architecture
   d. To manage relational database connections more efficiently
   e. To improve front-end application performance

2. **Which Jakarta EE specification is included in Eclipse MicroProfile and helps with dependency injection?**
   a. Jakarta Persistence
   b. Jakarta Faces

    c. Contexts and Dependency Injection

    d. Jakarta Transactions

    e. Jakarta Batch

3. **How does MicroProfile Config improve application flexibility?**

    a. By storing application data in a relational database

    b. By allowing configuration properties to be externalized and overridden at runtime

    c. By enforcing strict compile-time checks on environment variables

    d. By reducing the need for any configuration files

    e. By automatically encrypting all application settings

4. **What is the role of Jakarta NoSQL in a MicroProfile-based application?**

    a. It provides a standard API for interacting with NoSQL databases

    b. It forces developers to avoid using relational databases

    c. It automatically optimizes SQL queries for performance

    d. It acts as a caching mechanism for high-speed data access

    e. It replaces Jakarta Persistence entirely

5. **What is the main benefit of using OpenAPI in a MicroProfile-based microservice?**

    a. It generates API documentation automatically and improves interoperability

    b. It enhances security by encrypting HTTP requests

    c. It reduces the need for dependency injection

    d. It replaces the need for RESTful endpoints

    e. It limits API access based on user roles

6. **How does the use of DTOs benefit a MicroProfile application?**

    a. DTOs replace the need for a domain model

    b. DTOs expose the domain model directly to the API consumers

    c. DTOs help isolate the domain model from the application layer

    d. DTOs eliminate the need for serialization and deserialization

    e. DTOs ensure that all data is stored in an embedded database

7. **What is the purpose of the @Repository annotation in Jakarta Data?**

    a. To define a RESTful API endpoint

    b. To indicate that a class should act as a NoSQL database entity

c. To provide an interface for interacting with the database without writing boilerplate queries

d. To enforce caching at the repository level

e. To secure database queries with role-based access

8. **Which of the following best describes the role of MapStruct in a MicroProfile application?**

a. It automatically generates mapping code between domain entities and DTOs

b. It replaces CDI as the default dependency injection mechanism

c. It enhances database queries by optimizing entity relationships

d. It forces all classes to be immutable

e. It provides a NoSQL query language for MongoDB integration

9. **What is the correct way to access the OpenAPI UI in a MicroProfile application?**

a. **http://localhost:8181/api/docs**

b. **http://localhost:8181/swagger-ui/index.html**

c. **http://localhost:8181/openapi/ui/index.html**

d. **http://localhost:8181/q/admin**

e. **http://localhost:8181/open-tracing/visualizer**

10. **What is the next step after learning about MicroProfile and its integration with DDD?**

a. Exploring how Quarkus enhances MicroProfile's capabilities

b. Replacing all MicroProfile configurations with YAML files

c. Moving from NoSQL to a relational database model

d. Implementing microservices without CDI support

e. Removing Jakarta NoSQL in favor of direct database connections

Answers

Question number	Answer option letter
1.	b.
2.	c.
3.	b.
4.	a.
5.	a.

6.	c.
7.	c.
8.	a.
9.	c.
10.	a.

References

1. *Evans, Eric. (2003). Domain-Driven Design: Tackling Complexity in the Heart of Software.*

2. *Newman, Sam. (2020). Should I Use Microservices?*

3. *Eclipse Foundation. (2023). Jakarta Config Discussion – Configuration and Lifecycle.***https://www.eclipse.org/lists/config-dev/msg00203.html**

4. *Heroku. (2011). The Twelve-Factor App.* **https://12factor.net/**

5. *Martin, Robert C. (2012). The Clean Architecture.* **https://blog.cleancoder.com/uncle-bob/2012/08/13/the-clean-architecture.html**

6. *Cockburn, Alistair. Hexagonal Architecture.* **http://alistair.cockburn.us/Hexagonal+architecture**

Join our Discord space

Join our Discord workspace for latest updates, offers, tech happenings around the world, new releases, and sessions with the authors:

https://discord.bpbonline.com

CHAPTER 11
Quarkus and Domain-driven Design

Introduction

Quarkus has redefined enterprise Java by combining high performance, low resource consumption, fast start-up times, and a developer-friendly experience. Its adoption has been increasing, and it has proven to be an ideal runtime for building modern, cloud-native applications. For developers embracing **domain-driven design** (**DDD**), Quarkus provides a robust ecosystem that supports domain modeling while ensuring responsiveness and scalability.

This chapter explores how Quarkus enhances DDD practices by leveraging its extension-based architecture, reactive capabilities, and efficient dependency injection with CDI. By integrating these features, developers can create lightweight microservices that maintain a rich domain model. From structuring clean domain layers to optimizing persistence with Panache, we will examine how Quarkus simplifies the development of business-driven applications without sacrificing performance.

Structure

In this chapter, we will explore more about the following topics:

- Quarkus, Jakarta EE, and MicroProfile integration
- Quarkus in action

Technical requirements

This chapter will explore CDI using Quarkus. While it is possible to run the database using external services such as **database-as-a-service** (**DBaaS**), for this chapter, the relational database will be executed in-memory using H2.

- Java 21

- Git

- Maven

- Any preferred IDE

Objectives

This chapter demonstrates how Quarkus Panache simplifies database interactions while aligning with DDD principles. By exploring three different approaches: PanacheEntityResource, Active Record with PanacheEntity, and Repository pattern with PanacheRepository, developers clearly understand how to balance productivity, encapsulation, and maintainability. This chapter provides practical insights into choosing the right approach based on project complexity, ensuring that persistence logic remains efficient, scalable, and well-structured within a DDD architecture.

Quarkus, Jakarta EE, and MicroProfile integration

Quarkus is closely connected to Jakarta EE and MicroProfile, offering extensive support for their specifications while optimizing them for modern cloud-native environments. In previous chapters, we explored how Jakarta EE provides a strong foundation for enterprise Java applications, featuring well-established APIs for dependency injection, transaction management, security, and more. We also discussed how MicroProfile enhances Java development by introducing APIs tailored for microservices, such as configuration, fault tolerance, health checks, and metrics. All the information about these specifications applies seamlessly to Quarkus, further enhancing its capabilities by optimizing them for high performance, fast startup, and efficient resource utilization.

At its core, Quarkus supports a wide range of Jakarta EE APIs, ensuring a smooth transition for developers who are familiar with standards like **Contexts and Dependency Injection (CDI)**, **Jakarta Persistence API (JPA)**, **Jakarta RESTful Web Services (JAX-RS)**, and Jakarta **JSON Binding (JSON-B)**. Unlike traditional enterprise application runtimes and frameworks, which rely heavily on reflection at runtime, Quarkus moves much of the processing to build time. This shift reduces memory overhead and improves execution speed, and is especially beneficial in containerized and serverless environments, where quick startup times and low resource consumption are essential.

MicroProfile, designed to enhance Jakarta EE for microservices, is also fully embraced by Quarkus. It includes key specifications such as MicroProfile Config, which allows externalized and dynamic configuration, and MicroProfile Health, which enables built-in readiness and liveness probes for cloud-native deployments. Quarkus enhances these capabilities with its unified configuration model, providing a repeatable and consistent approach to configuring the application, which streamlines configuration management across environments. MicroProfile's observability features, such as metrics and tracing, integrate seamlessly with Quarkus, making monitoring and optimizing distributed applications easier.

Beyond compatibility, Quarkus actively contributes to the evolution of enterprise Java. Features like CDI Lite, which was inspired mainly by Quarkus' efficient dependency injection model, demonstrate its impact on the broader ecosystem. By leveraging GraalVM for native compilation and optimizing Jakarta EE and MicroProfile APIs for the cloud, Quarkus modernizes enterprise Java while retaining its core strengths. Developers can continue to rely on well-known Jakarta EE and MicroProfile patterns while benefiting from Quarkus' efficiency, flexibility, and cloud-native capabilities.

Quarkus does not replace Jakarta EE or MicroProfile; it enhances them. It provides the best of both worlds: the stability and maturity of enterprise Java specifications and the speed and lightweight nature of cloud-native development. Whether building traditional applications, microservices, or serverless functions, Quarkus enables developers to leverage familiar technologies while taking full advantage of modern optimizations.

Built on a solid foundation of Jakarta EE and MicroProfile, Quarkus enables developers to create enterprise applications using familiar technologies while taking advantage of performance optimizations. Let us move beyond the theoretical aspects and see Quarkus in action. We will explore how its streamlined development model allows for the creation of efficient, lightweight applications with minimal boilerplate code and maximum productivity.

Quarkus in action

Now that we have explored Quarkus' foundation and its connection to Jakarta EE and MicroProfile, it is time to put these concepts into practice.

As a software developer, Quarkus is known to streamline development and significantly enhance developer productivity. Its deep integrations allow for an effortless setup, much like the seamless experience of Apple's ecosystem, where starting a task on an iPhone and continuing on a Mac feels natural. Similarly, Quarkus simplifies database connections. If you add PostgreSQL as a dependency, Quarkus can automatically spin up a Docker-based instance, reducing the configuration burden. This level of automation creates an intuitive development experience, enabling developers to focus on business logic rather than infrastructure concerns.

To simplify our integration with the database, we will use Panache, a Quarkus-specific library designed to simplify the development of the persistence layer. Panache simplifies data access in Quarkus by reducing boilerplate code while maintaining a clean domain model, making it an excellent choice for a DDD approach.

In our example, we will define three semantically synonymous entities: developer, programmer, and software engineer. While they represent the same role conceptually, we will use them to demonstrate different ways to structure resources with Quarkus. Exploring multiple approaches will highlight how Quarkus supports flexibility while keeping development concise and efficient.

Creating and setting up a new project

The first step is to create a Quarkus project. You can quickly generate one using the Quarkus website, which provides an interactive interface for selecting dependencies. For this example, we will include the following components:

- **quarkus-rest**: Enables RESTful APIs in Quarkus.

- **quarkus-rest-jsonb**: Provides JSON serialization and deserialization.

- **quarkus-jdbc-h2**: Configures an in-memory H2 database for easy testing.

- **quarkus-hibernate-orm-rest-data-panache**: Simplifies data access with Hibernate ORM and Panache.

With the project set up, we are ready to explore the implementation. In the next section, we will define our entities and explore the different ways Quarkus allows us to expose them as resources.

Configuring the database integration

With our dependencies in place, the next step is to configure the application properties to ensure Quarkus correctly sets up the database and ORM layer. Since we are using H2 as an in-memory relational database, we define the following settings in **application.properties**:

```
quarkus.datasource.db-kind=h2
quarkus.datasource.jdbc.url=jdbc:h2:file:../src/main/resources/data/
database;AUTO_SERVER=true;DB_CLOSE_DELAY=-1
quarkus.hibernate-orm.dialect=org.hibernate.dialect.H2Dialect
quarkus.hibernate-orm.database.generation=drop-and-create
quarkus.hibernate-orm.log.sql=true
```

These configurations ensure that Quarkus initializes an H2 database instance, applies Hibernate ORM for entity persistence, and logs SQL statements for better visibility. The drop-and-create strategy resets the database on each startup, making it ideal for development and testing environments.

Panache entity and resource code generation

Let us move to the first and most straightforward approach to exposing a resource using Quarkus. We can create a fully functional RESTful API without writing additional logic with just two classes: one entity and one interface.

We start by creating the **Developer** entity using Jakarta Persistence annotations. This entity extends **PanacheEntity**, a feature from Quarkus Panache that simplifies entity management by providing built-in CRUD operations.

```
import io.quarkus.hibernate.orm.panache.PanacheEntity;
import jakarta.persistence.Column;
import jakarta.persistence.Entity;


@Entity
public class Developer extends PanacheEntity {

    @Column
    public String name;

    @Column
    public String email;

    @Column
    public String language;

    @Column
    public String city;
}
```

Since **PanacheEntity** already includes an ID field with autogenerated values, we do not need to define it explicitly. The entity's fields represent the basic attributes of a developer, making it a straightforward yet practical example for our demonstration.

In Quarkus, we can expose this entity as a REST resource using **PanacheEntityResource**, eliminating the need to implement REST endpoints manually.

All we need to do is create an interface like the following:

```
import io.quarkus.hibernate.orm.rest.data.panache.PanacheEntityResource;

public interface DevelopersResource extends PanacheEntityResource<Developer,
Long> {
}
```

After defining the developer entity and exposing it as a resource using **PanacheEntityResource**, we can explore how to interact with this API.

Validating the application's behavior

Since Quarkus automatically generates the necessary RESTful endpoints, we can perform operations without writing additional code.

By sending a **POST** request with the required data, we can add a new developer to the system. Using `curl`, we can execute the following command to create a new developer entry:

```
curl -X POST "http://localhost:8080/developers" \
    -H "Content-Type: application/json" \
    -d '{
        "name": "Alice",
        "email": "alice@example.com",
        "language": "Java",
        "city": "San Francisco"
    }'
```

Once the request is processed, Quarkus will persist the new developer in the H2 database. To verify that the data was correctly stored, we can retrieve all registered developers using a **GET** request:

```
curl -X GET "http://localhost:8080/developers" -H "Accept: application/json"
```

If we need to retrieve a specific developer by ID, we can modify the **GET** request by appending the developer's identifier. Assuming that the developer we created was assigned ID 1, we can retrieve their details using the following command:

```
curl -X GET "http://localhost:8080/developers/1" -H "Accept: application/json"
```

Updating an existing developer follows a similar approach. If Alice decides to change her preferred programming language or move to a new city, we can send a **PUT** request with the updated data while keeping the same ID:

```
curl -X PUT "http://localhost:8080/developers/1" \
    -H "Content-Type: application/json" \
    -d '{
        "name": "Alice",
        "email": "alice.new@example.com",
        "language": "Kotlin",
        "city": "New York"
    }'
```

Quarkus will update the existing record while maintaining consistency within the database. Lastly, we can issue a **DELETE** request to remove a developer from the system. For example, to delete the developer with ID 1:

```
curl -X DELETE http://localhost:8080/developers/1
```

This command will remove the corresponding entry from the database, ensuring that it is no longer available when querying the resource. These simple commands demonstrate how Quarkus enables an intuitive and efficient approach to working with RESTful APIs. It requires minimal setup while maintaining a clean and structured development flow. Now that we have explored the most straightforward approach to exposing resources, we can move forward to alternative implementations that provide more control and flexibility while leveraging Quarkus' efficiency.

Using Active Record with Panache

Continuing from the previous example, where we explored the simplest way to expose an entity as a REST resource using PanacheEntityResource, we now move to the following approach: using the Active Record pattern with PanacheEntity.

Note: For readers who are not familiar with the Active Record pattern, it is a design approach in which domain objects are responsible for their persistence[2]. It is a design pattern where an object represents a row in a database table, encapsulating the database access logic while allowing domain logic to be embedded directly into the entity. The concept is well-documented by Martin Fowler and widely adopted in frameworks that aim to simplify persistence management.

In this example, we will follow the same structure as before but introduce an additional class to manually define the resource, providing more control over the behavior of our endpoints. While we still leverage Quarkus Panache, this approach demonstrates how developers can build a more explicit and customizable API while maintaining a clean domain model.

The first step is defining the **SoftwareEngineer** entity. Like the previous example, this entity extends **PanacheEntity**, inheriting built-in persistence methods. It means we do not need to specify an ID field or CRUD operations manually. However, unlike the previous **Developer** example, we will now rely on **PanacheEntity**'s static methods for querying and persisting data.

```
import io.quarkus.hibernate.orm.panache.PanacheEntity;
import jakarta.persistence.Column;
import jakarta.persistence.Entity;

@Entity
public class SoftwareEngineer extends PanacheEntity {

    @Column
    public String name;

    @Column
```

```
    public String email;

    @Column
    public String language;

    @Column
    public String city;
}
```

With the entity in place, we now define the resource class, **SoftwareEngineerResource**, to expose the service. Instead of using an interface like before, we explicitly implement the REST endpoints. The key difference here is that all CRUD operations interact directly with the **SoftwareEngineer** entity using Panache's built-in methods, such as **findById()**, **listAll()**, and **persist()**.

```
import io.quarkus.panache.common.Sort;
import jakarta.enterprise.context.ApplicationScoped;
import jakarta.transaction.Transactional;
import jakarta.ws.rs.*;
import jakarta.ws.rs.core.MediaType;
import jakarta.ws.rs.core.Response;

import java.util.List;

@ApplicationScoped
@Path("software-engineers")
@Consumes(MediaType.APPLICATION_JSON)
@Produces(MediaType.APPLICATION_JSON)
public class SoftwareEngineerResource {

    @GET
    @Path("{id}")
    public SoftwareEngineer get(@PathParam("id") Long id) {
        SoftwareEngineer softwareEngineer = SoftwareEngineer.findById(id);
        if (softwareEngineer == null) {
            throw new WebApplicationException(404);
        }
        return softwareEngineer;
    }
```

```java
    @GET
    public Response list() {
        List<SoftwareEngineer> softwareEngineers = SoftwareEngineer.
listAll(Sort.by("name"));
        return Response.ok(softwareEngineers).build();
    }


    @GET
    @Path("/count")
    public long count() {
        return SoftwareEngineer.count();
    }


    @Transactional
    @POST
    public Response add(SoftwareEngineer softwareEngineer) {
        SoftwareEngineer.persist(softwareEngineer);
        return Response.ok(softwareEngineer).build();
    }


    @Transactional
    @PUT
    @Path("{id}")
    public Response update(@PathParam("id") Long id, SoftwareEngineer
softwareEngineer) {
        if (SoftwareEngineer.findById(id) == null) {
            SoftwareEngineer.persist(softwareEngineer);
            return Response.status(Response.Status.CREATED).build();
        }
        SoftwareEngineer.persist(softwareEngineer);
        return Response.ok.build();
    }


    @Transactional
    @DELETE
    @Path("{id}")
    public void delete(@PathParam("id") Long id) {
        if (!SoftwareEngineer.deleteById(id)) {
            throw new WebApplicationException(Response.Status.NOT_FOUND);
```

```
                    }
            }
    }
```

TIP: **Note that the PUT endpoint is designed to be idempotent, meaning that repeated identical requests will produce the same result without side effects, aligning with REST best practices. In other words, if the entity with that ID exists, it is updated; if not, a new one is created. In production, it is essential to verify that strict idempotency meets the requirements. If so, non-existent updates would be rejected with a 404 error.**

This resource class explicitly maps REST endpoints to entity operations, providing greater flexibility while still benefiting from Panache's simplified data access. **SoftwareEngineer**'s static methods execute all database operations, such as fetching, counting, creating, updating, and deleting records.

We can use curl commands similar to the previous example to test this API. Creating a new software engineer entry can be done with the following **POST** request:

```
curl -X POST "http://localhost:8080/software-engineers" \
    -H "Content-Type: application/json" \
    -d '{
            "name": "Bob",
            "email": "bob@example.com",
            "language": "Python",
            "city": "Berlin"
        }'
```

For retrieving, updating, or deleting a **SoftwareEngineer**, the principle remains the same as in the previous example, with only the resource name changing from **developers** to **software-engineers**. The **GET**, **PUT**, and **DELETE** requests follow the same structure, interacting with the **/software-engineers** endpoint instead.

This implementation demonstrates how the Active Record approach simplifies data access by directly allowing entity classes to handle persistence logic. While this method provides a quick and effective way to manage database interactions, some applications require a more structured separation of concerns. In the next step, we will explore another approach, leveraging repositories to decouple persistence logic from the domain model further, while benefiting from Quarkus Panache's capabilities.

Using the Repository pattern with Panache

The third and final approach to exploring Quarkus Panache is the Repository pattern using **PanacheRepository**. Unlike the previous methods, where persistence logic is embedded within the entity itself, this approach explicitly separates database operations into a dedicated repository class. This method aligns more closely with traditional DDD principles by keeping business logic within the domain layer and managing persistence concerns in a separate repository.

To demonstrate this approach, we introduce the **Programmer** entity. Structurally, it remains the same as our previous entities, but will now delegate persistence operations to a repository as follows:

```
import io.quarkus.hibernate.orm.panache.PanacheEntity;
import jakarta.persistence.Column;
import jakarta.persistence.Entity;

@Entity
public class Programmer extends PanacheEntity {

    @Column
    public String name;

    @Column
    public String email;

    @Column
    public String language;

    @Column
    public String city;
}
```

In contrast to the previous implementations, where we either used **PanacheEntity**'s built-in methods or relied on **PanacheEntityResource**, this time we introduce a dedicated repository class. The **ProgrammerRepository** extends **PanacheRepository<Programmer>**, encapsulating all database operations separately from the domain model:

```
import io.quarkus.hibernate.orm.panache.PanacheRepository;
import jakarta.enterprise.context.ApplicationScoped;

@ApplicationScoped
public class ProgrammerRepository implements PanacheRepository<Programmer> {
}
```

With the repository in place, we now implement the resource class that exposes the CRUD operations via a REST API. Unlike the **SoftwareEngineerResource**, which relied on static methods, this resource injects the **ProgrammerRepository** and delegates database operations to it:

```java
import io.quarkus.panache.common.Sort;
import jakarta.enterprise.context.ApplicationScoped;
import jakarta.inject.Inject;
import jakarta.transaction.Transactional;
import jakarta.ws.rs.*;
import jakarta.ws.rs.core.MediaType;
import jakarta.ws.rs.core.Response;

import java.util.List;

@ApplicationScoped
@Path("programmers")
@Consumes(MediaType.APPLICATION_JSON)
@Produces(MediaType.APPLICATION_JSON)
public class ProgrammerResource {

    @Inject
    ProgrammerRepository repository;

    @GET
    @Path("{id}")
    @Produces("application/json")
    public Programmer get(@PathParam("id") Long id) {
        Programmer programmer = repository.findById(id);
        if (programmer == null) {
            throw new WebApplicationException(404);
        }
        return programmer;
    }

    @GET
    @Produces("application/json")
    public Response list() {
        List<Programmer> people = repository.listAll(Sort.by("name"));
        return Response.ok(people).build();
    }
```

```java
@GET
@Path("/count")
public long count() {
    return repository.count();
}

@Transactional
@POST
@Consumes("application/json")
@Produces("application/json")
public Response add(Programmer programmer) {
    repository.persist(programmer);
    return Response.ok(programmer).build();
}

@Transactional
@PUT
@Path("{id}")
@Consumes("application/json")
@Produces("application/json")
public Response update(@PathParam("id") Long id, Programmer programmer) {
    if (repository.findById(id) == null) {
        repository.persist(programmer);
        return Response.status(204).build();
    }
    repository.persist(programmer);
    return Response.status(201).build();
}

@Transactional
@DELETE
@Path("{id}")
public void delete(@PathParam("id") Long id) {
    if (!repository.deleteById(id)) {
        throw new WebApplicationException(404);
    }
}
}
```

With this approach, all database interactions go through the **ProgrammerRepository**, making it easier to customize and extend persistence logic without modifying the domain entity itself. The repository-based approach is particularly useful in complex applications where database operations require custom queries or business-specific logic that does not belong in the domain model.

To create a new programmer entry, we can send the following **POST** request:

```
curl -X POST "http://localhost:8080/programmers" \
    -H "Content-Type: application/json" \
    -d '{
        "name": "Charlie",
        "email": "charlie@example.com",
        "language": "C++",
        "city": "London"
      }'
```

The remaining operations for retrieving, updating, and deleting programmers follow the same principles as the previous examples. The only change is the resource name, which has been changed from developers or software engineers to programmers.

This final approach demonstrates how the Repository pattern in Quarkus Panache provides a structured and scalable way to manage data persistence. Decoupling database operations from the domain model offers greater flexibility while benefiting from Quarkus' lightweight persistence framework. With this, we have explored three different ways to integrate Quarkus Panache with a relational database, each offering a different balance between simplicity, flexibility, and architectural control.

Throughout this section, we explored the following three ways to integrate Quarkus Panache with a relational database, each offering a unique balance between simplicity, flexibility, and maintainability:

- The first approach, **PanacheEntityResource**, was the simplest and most declarative. With just an interface, Quarkus automatically generates all necessary CRUD operations, making it the most productive option with minimal effort. However, it tightly coupled the API to the entity model, limiting encapsulation and control.

- The second approach, Active Record with **PanacheEntity**, provided more flexibility while keeping the code minimal. In this model, the entity itself was responsible for database operations using static methods such as **findById()**, **listAll()**, and **persist()**. This structure is robust for small to mid-size applications. Still, it introduces a concern where domain logic and persistence concerns mix, making it less aligned with DDD principles.

- The final approach, the Repository pattern with **PanacheRepository**, introduced a dedicated repository class to handle persistence. Decoupling persistence logic from the entity aligned well with DDD, allowing the domain model to remain pure while keeping database operations separate. Although this method required more code than the previous approaches, it provided the best long-term maintainability and scalability, making it ideal for complex applications.

Using Panache from a DDD perspective

To illustrate the trade-offs between the Active Record and Repository patterns when using Panache, consider the following contrast:

- In the Active Record approach (using `PanacheEntity`), persistence methods are embedded directly in the entity class. This simplifies development for straightforward CRUD but mixes domain logic with persistence, potentially violating DDD's separation of concerns.

- Repository pattern (using `PanacheRepository`) delegates these operations to a separate class, improving maintainability in complex domains by keeping entities pure.

The following table compares each approach's strengths and trade-offs based on key factors such as productivity, encapsulation, performance, and alignment with DDD principles. This comparison highlights how each method balances simplicity and maintainability, helping developers choose the most suitable approach based on their project's complexity and long-term goals.

Approach	Productivity	Encapsulation	Customization capability (new resources, DTOs, layer separation)	DDD alignment
PanacheEntityResource	Very high (fully automated)	Low (exposes entities directly)	Very limited (tightly coupled to the entity)	Low (not aligned with rich domain models)
Active Record (PanacheEntity)	High (simple to use)	Moderate (mixes persistence with domain logic)	Moderate (allows some customization but is still coupled)	Moderate (embedded persistence may lead to domain pollution)
Repository pattern (PanacheRepository)	Moderate (more code required)	High (clear separation of concerns)	Very high (flexible for DTOs, layered architecture, and custom queries)	High (aligns well with rich domain models)

Table 11.1: Analysis of Quarkus approaches

Each approach serves a different purpose depending on the application's complexity and goals. PanacheEntityResource is ideal for rapid prototyping and simple CRUD applications where encapsulation is not a significant concern. The Active Record approach offers more flexibility while maintaining simplicity, making it an excellent option for applications needing lightweight persistence logic. Though requiring more effort, the Repository pattern provides the best structure for maintainable, scalable, and domain-driven applications.

Ultimately, the choice depends on the project requirements. PanacheEntityResource or PanacheEntity can be helpful for simple and fast development. However, for applications following DDD, the Repository pattern with PanacheRepository is the recommended approach. This pattern keeps persistence logic separate from the domain, making the system more adaptable to change while maintaining a clear business-oriented structure.

Conclusion

This chapter explored how Quarkus Panache simplifies persistence in DDD applications, presenting three approaches with different levels of flexibility and maintainability. We started with PanacheEntityResource, the most automated option, which requires minimal effort but tightly couples the API with the domain model. We then examined the Active Record approach, where entities manage their persistence, offering more control but blending domain logic with database operations. Finally, we implemented the Repository pattern, which fully decouples persistence from the domain, providing the best structure for maintainability and scalability in DDD applications.

Each approach serves different needs, from quick prototyping to structured, long-term development. While PanacheEntityResource and Active Record are excellent for simplicity, the Repository pattern offers the best balance for maintainable, business-driven applications. With this foundation in place, the next chapter will focus on Java best practices to refine DDD implementations, providing strategies to enhance maintainability, enforce domain boundaries, and improve overall software design.

Points to remember

- **Panache simplifies persistence**: It reduces boilerplate code and provides built-in methods for CRUD operations.

- **Three approaches to persistence**: Quarkus supports PanacheEntityResource, PanacheEntity (Active Record), and PanacheRepository (Repository pattern).

- **PanacheEntityResource is the easiest**: It automatically generates REST endpoints but tightly couples the API to the entity.

- **Active Record (PanacheEntity) balances simplicity and flexibility**: Entities handle their persistence, reducing the need for repositories but mixing domain and persistence logic.

- **Repository pattern (PanacheRepository) ensures separation of concerns**: It keeps domain logic independent from persistence, making it the best choice for DDD-aligned applications.

- **Customization is best with the Repository pattern**: It allows the use of DTOs, custom queries, and layered architectures.

- **Encapsulation improves from PanacheEntityResource to PanacheRepository**: The more structured the approach, the better the domain model is protected from persistence concerns.

- **Performance remains high across all approaches**: Quarkus optimizes data access efficiently, but architectural choices impact maintainability more than raw performance.

- **Choose the right approach based on project complexity**: Simple CRUD applications benefit from PanacheEntityResource or PanacheEntity, while complex applications should use PanacheRepository.

- **DDD principles favor the Repository pattern**: If long-term maintainability and scalability are key, separating persistence logic into repositories is the best strategy.

Multiple choice questions

1. **What is the primary advantage of using PanacheEntityResource in Quarkus?**
   a. It fully automates CRUD operations with minimal effort
   b. It allows fine-grained control over database queries
   c. It enforces a strict separation between the domain and persistence layers
   d. It requires additional configurations for proper functioning
   e. It prevents direct exposure of the entity model

2. **How does the Active Record pattern work with Quarkus Panache?**
   a. It decouples domain logic from persistence concerns completely
   b. It embeds persistence logic inside the entity using static methods
   c. It relies on external repositories to manage database access
   d. It prevents developers from writing any persistence code
   e. It is only useful for NoSQL databases

3. **What is the main benefit of using PanacheRepository over PanacheEntity?**
   a. It removes the need to define an entity class
   b. It ensures complete encapsulation of persistence logic
   c. It speeds up database queries compared to PanacheEntity
   d. It limits the flexibility of defining custom queries
   e. It automatically generates API endpoints without additional coding

4. **Which approach provides the best encapsulation of business logic in a DDD application?**

    a. PanacheEntityResource

    b. Active Record with PanacheEntity

    c. Repository pattern with PanacheRepository

    d. Mixing PanacheEntity and PanacheRepository

    e. Using plain JPA without Quarkus Panache

5. **What is a key drawback of PanacheEntityResource?**

    a. It requires manual implementation of CRUD operations

    b. It has performance issues when handling large datasets

    c. It tightly couples the API to the entity model

    d. It forces the use of SQL queries instead of ORM

    e. It does not support relational databases

6. **Which of the following best describes PanacheEntity in Quarkus?**

    a. A class that provides automatic database transactions

    b. An alternative to JPA that does not require annotations

    c. A built-in repository that manages entity lifecycle

    d. A base class that simplifies entity persistence with CRUD operations

    e. A framework for implementing microservices

7. **Why is the Repository pattern preferred in complex applications?**

    a. It eliminates the need for a persistence layer

    b. It provides better separation of concerns and flexibility

    c. It requires fewer classes compared to the Active Record approach

    d. It makes the application independent of relational databases

    e. It reduces memory consumption by removing unused dependencies

8. **Which of the following is not a characteristic of Quarkus Panache?**

    a. Simplifies database interactions with minimal code

    b. Allows automatic API generation with PanacheEntityResource

    c. Requires manual SQL query creation for all database operations

    d. Supports both Active Record and Repository patterns

    e. Provides built-in methods for common CRUD operations

9. **What is a major trade-off when using the Active Record approach with PanacheEntity?**

    a. It completely prevents the use of repositories

    b. It introduces a mix of domain and persistence logic in the entity

    c. It requires extensive manual query writing

    d. It cannot be used with relational databases

    e. It is only compatible with NoSQL databases

10. **When should PanacheEntityResource be considered over the other approaches?**

    a. When fine-grained control over database operations is needed

    b. When rapidly prototyping an application with minimal effort

    c. When strict adherence to DDD principles is required

    d. When implementing complex transaction management

    e. When designing a system with multiple bounded contexts

Answers

Question number	Answer option letter
1.	a.
2.	b.
3.	b.
4.	c.
5.	c.
6.	d.
7.	b.
8.	c.
9.	b.
10.	b.

References

1. *Commonhaus Foundation. (n.d.). Quarkus Project Generator. Retrieved from* **https://code.quarkus.io/**

2. *Fowler, M. (2003). Patterns of Enterprise Application Architecture: Active Record. Retrieved from* **https://www.martinfowler.com/eaaCatalog/activeRecord.html**

Join our Discord space

Join our Discord workspace for latest updates, offers, tech happenings around the world, new releases, and sessions with the authors:

https://discord.bpbonline.com

CHAPTER 12

Code Design and Best Practices for DDD

Introduction

Building a maintainable and scalable system requires careful code design that aligns with **domain-driven design** (**DDD**) principles, as well-crafted domain models are crafted to be expressive, encapsulated, and resistant to unintended misuse. However, developers fall into the trap of creating an anemic model, where domain objects are reduced to mere data carriers with minimal behavior. In this case, the result is a design that lacks cohesion and fails to reflect the business domain's true nature accurately.

This chapter explores essential design techniques to ensure your domain model remains rich, encapsulated, and adaptable. We start by examining the pitfalls of the anemic model and how to embrace a rich domain model that effectively encapsulates behavior. Next, we explore powerful design patterns such as the Builder pattern and fluent API, which can enhance the readability and maintainability of your code. Additionally, we discuss best practices for handling exceptions and logging effectively, ensuring that your system remains reliable and easy to debug over time.

Long-term maintainability is critical to any software system. Without careful attention to code quality, even the most well-intentioned design can degrade over time. This chapter covers strategies for keeping your codebase clean, scalable, and adaptable. We will focus on refactoring techniques that reinforce domain integrity while minimizing technical debt. By the end of this chapter, you will have a solid understanding of how to write robust, expressive, and maintainable domain-centric code that can stand the test of time.

Structure

In this chapter, we will explore topics such as:

- Anemic model vs. rich model
- Fluent API vs. Builder pattern in DDD
- Exception handling and logging in DDD
- Long-term code quality and sustainability

Objectives

This chapter explores essential code design principles that enhance the maintainability and scalability of domain-driven applications. By understanding the differences between anemic and rich models, leveraging fluent APIs and the Builder pattern for better expressiveness, handling exceptions effectively, implementing robust logging strategies, and ensuring long-term code quality through testing and documentation, developers can build resilient software that evolves smoothly over time. This chapter provides practical insights and techniques to help developers make thoughtful design choices that align with DDD principles while maintaining simplicity and adaptability in real-world projects.

Anemic model vs. rich model

In his blog[1], *Robert C. Martin*, the author of *Clean Code*, discusses the concept of anemic objects, referring to them as mere *data structures*. He highlights the fundamental difference between data structures and objects by stating: *Classes make functions visible while keeping data implied. Data structures make data visible while keeping functions implied.* This distinction is crucial in designing a domain model that genuinely represents business logic rather than acting as a mere container for data.

A rich domain model encapsulates state and behavior, exposing only the operations relevant to the domain, while an anemic model merely holds data and delegates logic to external services. The lack of encapsulation in an anemic model scatters business rules across multiple layers, leading to duplication, increased complexity, and a higher risk of inconsistency. Consider an example where we model a simple tennis game.

In an anemic model, the **Player** class is nothing more than a structure that holds data. It provides getters and setters, allowing external services to modify their state directly. The game logic does not reside within the **Player** class itself but is handled externally by another component, such as the **TennisGame** class.

```
class Player {
    private String name;
    private int score;
```

```
    public Player(String name) {
        this.name = name;
        this.score = 0;
    }

    public String getName() {
        return name;
    }

    public int getScore() {
        return score;
    }

    public void setScore(int score) {
        this.score = score;
    }
}

class TennisGame {
    private Player playerOne;
    private Player playerTwo;

    public TennisGame(Player playerOne, Player playerTwo) {
        this.playerOne = playerOne;
        this.playerTwo = playerTwo;
    }

    public void playerScores(Player player) {
        player.setScore(player.getScore() + 1);
    }

    public String getScore() {
        return playerOne.getScore() + " - " + playerTwo.getScore();
    }
}
```

While this approach might seem straightforward, it introduces several design issues. The **Player** class acts merely as a data container without any responsibility for managing its state.

The **TennisGame** class takes on the burden of modifying player scores, which creates a tight coupling between game logic and data manipulation. If another part of the system wants to update a player's score, it must follow the same external pattern, increasing the likelihood of duplicated logic across services.

A rich domain model approaches the problem differently:

- Instead of exposing raw data, the **Player** class encapsulates its state and provides behavior for updating it.

- Instead of allowing unrestricted modifications, the model dictates how the score should be updated, keeping the logic close to where it belongs.

The revised implementation ensures that the **Player** is responsible for scoring, leading to a more cohesive design, as follows:

```java
class Player {
    private final String name;
    private int score;

    public Player(String name) {
        this.name = name;
        this.score = 0;
    }

    public String getName() {
        return name;
    }

    public int getScore() {
        return score;
    }

    public void scorePoint() {
        this.score++;
    }
}

class TennisGame {
    private final Player playerOne;
    private final Player playerTwo;
```

```
    public TennisGame(Player playerOne, Player playerTwo) {
        this.playerOne = playerOne;
        this.playerTwo = playerTwo;
    }

    public void playerScores(Player player) {
        player.scorePoint();
    }

    public String getScore() {
        return playerOne.getScore() + " - " + playerTwo.getScore();
    }
}
```

This approach provides multiple benefits. First, the state is encapsulated, ensuring the **Player** is responsible for modifying its score. External components do not need to manipulate the state directly, reducing the risk of inconsistent updates. Second, this design enhances cohesion by grouping related behavior within the entity that owns the data. The **TennisGame** class no longer needs to modify the **Player** directly; it simply delegates the scoring action to the player.

Another common issue in anemic models is excessive reliance on getters and setters, leading to tight coupling and unnecessary data exposure. When objects expose their internal state, other components become dependent on their structure, making it difficult to evolve the model without breaking existing code. The rich model approach avoids this by providing only the operations that make sense within the domain context, minimizing dependencies and improving maintainability.

A well-designed rich domain model also simplifies the use-case implementation. By encapsulating logic within the domain, service classes focus on orchestration rather than handling business rules directly. If new game rules, such as a tie-break system, need to be introduced, they can be implemented within the **Player** without affecting the rest of the application. This reduces the complexity of service layers and makes the domain more expressive and adaptable.

While transitioning from anemic to rich models, it is essential to balance encapsulation with clarity. Not every method belongs inside an entity. Generally, only logic directly related to the entity itself should be included. Use-case-specific behavior should still be handled at the service level to maintain separation of concerns.

The following table summarizes the key differences between anemic and rich models and their impact on DDD:

Feature	Anemic model	Rich model
Encapsulation	Lacks encapsulation; exposes data via getters/setters	Encapsulates state; exposes behavior instead
Business logic	Business rules reside in external services	Business rules reside within domain entities
Cohesion	Low cohesion; logic is scattered	High cohesion; logic is localized within objects
Coupling	High coupling: multiple services manipulate data	Low coupling: each entity manages its state
Maintainability	Hard to maintain due to duplicated logic	Easier to maintain and evolve
Flexibility	Hard to modify without affecting multiple components	Changes are localized within entities
Alignment with DDD	Weak alignment acts as a procedural design	Strong alignment; models domain behavior naturally

Table 12.1: Anemic vs. rich model

Encapsulation and strong domain modeling are key factors in designing a maintainable system. Moving from an anemic to rich models significantly improves code organization, makes objects more autonomous, and allows business rules to be enforced closer to the entities they belong to.

By designing our domain model focusing on behavior rather than just data, we ensure that our system remains resilient to change and expressive in representing the business logic. However, designing such a model requires thoughtful design techniques, especially when dealing with complex object creation. To address these challenges, we can leverage patterns like the Builder pattern and fluent API, which we will explore next.

Fluent API vs. Builder pattern in DDD

Writing clean and readable code is a top priority for software developers, as it makes maintenance and collaboration more manageable and enhances the codebase's overall value. A fluent API is a powerful design approach that promotes clean and expressive code. By allowing method chaining in a way that reads like a sentence, fluent APIs ensure that business logic remains intuitive and aligned with the domain model.

In 2025, aiming to increase code readability, the concept of **domain-specific language (DSL)** was created by *Eric Evans* and *Martin Fowler* when they introduced the concept of fluent API. Unlike traditional approaches, where method calls are scattered and require developers' great effort in memorizing or searching for them, a fluent API enables a guided, natural flow of method invocations. This design provides an experience similar to selecting a meal in a restaurant; each choice determines the available next steps, ensuring consistency and correctness throughout the process.

Several frameworks in the Java ecosystem leverage fluent API design. JOOQ, a framework led by *Lukas Eder*, enables type-safe SQL query construction using method chaining, eliminating the need for verbose string-based SQL statements. Similarly, Jakarta NoSQL provides a fluent interface for interacting with NoSQL databases, ensuring smooth integration between Java applications and various persistence layers.

The Builder pattern is often compared to the fluent APIs, as both rely on method chaining. However, it is important to understand that they serve distinct purposes:

- The Builder pattern focuses on constructing complex objects step-by-step, usually deferring validation until the final **build()** method is called.

- In contrast, a fluent API enforces a structured flow, preventing invalid states.

A comparison between the two is shown in the following table:

Feature	Builder pattern	Fluent API
Primary use case	Constructing complex objects step-by-step	Providing an intuitive and domain-specific interface
Ease of implementation	Easier to implement	Requires thoughtful DSL design and validation
Method sequence	Methods can be invoked in any order	Enforces a logical sequence of method calls
Error handling	Relies on validation in the **build()** method	Uses immediate validation to prevent invalid states
Flexibility	May allow partially constructed objects	Ensures a valid object state at every step

Table 12.2: Builder vs. fluent API patterns

To illustrate the difference, consider a *Hotel Booking System*. Using the Builder pattern, an instance of a **HotelBooking** object is constructed step by step, only validated when **build()** is called.

```
class HotelBooking {
    private final String guestName;
    private final int nights;
    private final boolean breakfastIncluded;
```

```java
    private HotelBooking(Builder builder) {
        this.guestName = builder.guestName;
        this.nights = builder.nights;
        this.breakfastIncluded = builder.breakfastIncluded;
    }

    public static class Builder {
        private String guestName;
        private int nights;
        private boolean breakfastIncluded;

        public Builder guestName(String guestName) {
            this.guestName = guestName;
            return this;
        }

        public Builder nights(int nights) {
            this.nights = nights;
            return this;
        }

        public Builder includeBreakfast(boolean breakfastIncluded) {
            this.breakfastIncluded = breakfastIncluded;
            return this;
        }

        public HotelBooking build() {
            return new HotelBooking(this);
        }
    }

    @Override
    public String toString() {
        return guestName + " booked for " + nights + " nights. Breakfast: " +
(breakfastIncluded ? "Yes" : "No");
    }
}
```

A client using this pattern would write the following:

```java
HotelBooking booking = new HotelBooking.builder()
    .guestName("Alice")
    .nights(3)
    .includeBreakfast(true)
    .build();

System.out.println(booking);
```

Note that the Builder pattern does not enforce a logical sequence. On the other hand, fluent API can ensure that method calls follow a valid flow. The following shows how it can be structured:

```java
class HotelBookingFluent {
    private String guestName;
    private int nights;
    private boolean breakfastIncluded;

    private HotelBookingFluent(String guestName) {
        this.guestName = guestName;
    }

    public static HotelBookingFluent bookFor(String guestName) {
        return new HotelBookingFluent(guestName);
    }

    public HotelBookingFluent nights(int nights) {
        this.nights = nights;
        return this;
    }

    public HotelBookingFluent withBreakfast() {
        this.breakfastIncluded = true;
        return this;
    }

    public String confirm() {
        return guestName + " booked for " + nights + " nights. Breakfast: " +
(breakfastIncluded ? "Yes" : "No");
    }
}
```

With this approach, a booking can be made as follows:

```
String confirmation = HotelBookingFluent.bookFor("Alice")
    .nights(3)
    .withBreakfast()
    .confirm();


System.out.println(confirmation);
```

A well-designed fluent API can prevent invalid method sequences. For instance, enforcing that a booking cannot be confirmed without specifying the number of nights makes the API self-explanatory and eliminates the need for additional developer documentation.

The choice between the Builder pattern and a fluent API depends on the use case. The Builder pattern is well-suited for constructing objects with optional parameters, while a fluent API is ideal for creating expressive, guided interactions that enforce correct domain logic. In a DDD context, a fluent API aligns naturally with Ubiquitous Language principles, ensuring that domain operations are readable and constrained by business rules.

By leveraging fluent APIs where appropriate, developers create interfaces that reduce cognitive load, improve maintainability, and make domain logic more intuitive. The next step in designing robust and maintainable systems is understanding exception handling and logging, ensuring that domain models remain resilient and traceable in production environments.

Exception handling and logging in DDD

Properly handling exceptions is fundamental to writing maintainable and reliable applications. Exceptions are crucial for identifying when something goes wrong during execution and are essential for managing data inconsistency, enforcing business rules, and improving system resilience. In a DDD context, well-structured exceptions help trace issues to specific domain concerns, making debugging and troubleshooting more effective.

Three key aspects must be considered to create effective exceptions:

- Defining a proper exception hierarchy.
- Ensuring meaningful and trackable messages.
- Avoiding security risks when exposing exception details.

Defining the exceptions hierarchy

The first step in designing exceptions is establishing a clear hierarchy that aligns with the domain model. Instead of scattering exceptions across the codebase, a structured approach ensures that errors can be categorized and traced back to specific business concerns. According to DDD principles, exceptions should be named in a meaningful way for the domain. For instance, exceptions can range from a generic company-wide exception to more specific domain-related errors in a credit card processing system.

```java
public class MyCompanyException extends RuntimeException {
    public MyCompanyException(String message) {
        super(message);
    }

    public MyCompanyException(String message, Throwable cause) {
        super(message, cause);
    }
}

public class CreditCardException extends MyCompanyException {
    public CreditCardException(String message) {
        super(message);
    }

    public CreditCardException(String message, Throwable cause) {
        super(message, cause);
    }
}

public class CreditCardNotFoundException extends CreditCardException {
    public CreditCardNotFoundException(String message) {
        super(message);
    }

    public CreditCardNotFoundException(String message, Throwable cause) {
        super(message, cause);
    }
}
```

This hierarchy ensures that if an exception is thrown, it is immediately identifiable as part of the credit card domain, which belongs to the broader business exception framework, simplifying the handling of exceptions at different levels, whether within a specific service, the application layer, or globally across the system.

Creating trackable exception messages

Beyond structuring exceptions, it is crucial to provide trackable exception messages. A well-designed exception message should indicate that an error occurred and provide enough context to diagnose the issue efficiently. For example, in a credit card payment service, including the credit card ID in an exception message can help pinpoint exactly which transaction failed.

```java
public void pay(UUID creditCardId, Product product) {
    LOGGER.info("Paying with credit card: " + creditCardId);
    LOGGER.fine("Paying for product: " + product);

    findById(creditCardId).orElseThrow(() ->
        new CreditCardNotFoundException("Credit card not found with the id: "
+ creditCardId)
    );
}
```

With this approach, when a **CreditCardNotFoundException** is thrown, it will include the specific credit card ID, making it easier to understand why the failure happened and investigate further. However, while providing useful details is important, security considerations must also be taken into account.

Handling exceptions and logs securely

One of the most overlooked aspects of exception handling is security. Exposing sensitive information in error messages can lead to data leaks and security vulnerabilities. Logging detailed error information while returning a more generic exception message to the client helps strike a balance between traceability and security, as follows:

```java
public void pay(UUID creditCardId, Product product) {
    LOGGER.info("Paying with credit card: " + creditCardId);
    LOGGER.fine("Paying for product: " + product);

    findById(creditCardId).orElseThrow(() -> {
        LOGGER.severe("Credit card not found with id: " + creditCardId); //
Detailed log
        return new CreditCardNotFoundException("Credit card not found"); //
Generic message
    });
}
```

Here, the detailed error log includes the credit card ID for internal debugging, but the exception message returned externally does not disclose sensitive details. This prevents potential attackers from gathering information about system internals while still allowing developers to investigate failures effectively.

Logging is another critical aspect of software development, particularly in production environments. Proper logging provides valuable insights into application behavior, helps diagnose issues, and ensures that the system runs smoothly. A well-structured logging strategy considers three key principles: logging relevant information, ensuring trackability, and preventing security risks.

When logging information, it is important to use appropriate log levels to distinguish between different types of messages. Java's logging API provides multiple levels, each serving a specific purpose as follows:

- **SEVERE**: Used for critical failures that require immediate attention.

- **WARNING**: Indicates potential problems, such as deprecated API usage or performance bottlenecks.

- **INFO**: Provides general operational details, such as when a payment is initiated or completed.

- **FINE**: Used for detailed debugging information, such as request payloads and execution details.

Consider a logging implementation for a credit card service as follows:

```java
public class CreditCardService {
    private static final Logger LOGGER = Logger.getLogger(CreditCardService.
class.getName());

    public void pay(CreditCard creditCard, Product product) {
        try {
            LOGGER.info("Paying with credit card: " + creditCard.getId());
            LOGGER.fine("Paying for product: " + product);
        } catch (Exception e) {
            LOGGER.log(Level.SEVERE, "Payment failed: " + e.getMessage(), e);
        }
    }

    @Deprecated
    public void deprecated(CreditCard creditCard, Product product) {
        LOGGER.warning("Deprecated method is called, use pay() instead. It
will be removed in the next release. The id: " + creditCard.getId());
    }
}
```

By using appropriate log levels, developers can filter logs based on severity, making it easier to identify critical errors without being overwhelmed by excessive debug information.

Logs should also be trackable, particularly in systems handling high transaction volumes. Including unique identifiers such as request IDs or entity IDs ensures that specific events can be traced back to their origin.

```java
public void pay(CreditCard creditCard, Product product) {
    try {
        LOGGER.info("Paying with credit card: " + creditCard.getId());
        LOGGER.fine("Paying for product: " + product);
    } catch (Exception e) {
        String errorMessage = String.format(
            "Payment failed: card id: %s and product id: %s. Error message: %s",
            creditCard.getId(), product.getId(), e.getMessage()
        );
        LOGGER.log(Level.SEVERE, errorMessage, e);
    }
}
```

Here, the log message includes both the credit card ID and product ID, ensuring that failures can be traced to specific transactions. However, security remains a major concern in logging as well. Exposing sensitive data in logs, such as credit card numbers or user passwords, can lead to security breaches. Masking sensitive data ensures compliance with security standards, such as the **Payment Card Industry Data Security Standard (PCI DSS)**.

```java
public class CreditCard {
    private UUID id;
    private String number; // Only store the last four digits
    private String password;

    public UUID getId() {
        return id;
    }

    @Override
    public String toString() {
        return "CreditCard{" +
                "id=" + id +
                ", number='" + number + '\'' +
                ", password= *****" +
                '}';
    }
}
```

By overriding the **toString()** method to mask the password, logs remain useful for debugging without exposing sensitive information. This practice ensures that logs comply with security standards and prevent unauthorized access to critical data.

Properly handling exceptions and logs in a DDD context ensures the system remains robust, traceable, and secure. By structuring exception hierarchies, providing meaningful messages, and effectively leveraging logs, developers can build applications that are not only maintainable but also resilient in production environments. Logging and exception handling go hand-in-hand in creating transparent software for debugging and security against threats. The following section will explore maintaining long-term code quality and enforcing best practices to sustain a scalable and maintainable domain model.

Long-term code quality and sustainability

One of the biggest obstacles in software development is managing complexity. As systems evolve, they inevitably become more intricate, but a significant challenge comes from *complexity bias*, the assumption that complex solutions are inherently better. Many developers and architects fall into this trap, believing that an elaborate design with multiple layers, abstract factories, and intricate patterns will future-proof the system. In reality, overengineering introduces unnecessary indirection, makes systems more complicated to understand, and increases long-term maintenance costs.

While designing scalable architectures and anticipating future changes is essential, simplicity must always be prioritized. An overcomplicated codebase becomes a liability, making even minor modifications risky and expensive. This is a recurring problem in long-term projects: technical decisions made today must be maintainable by a team that may not include the original developers years later.

Yet, when discussing long-term sustainability, most literature focuses on writing Clean Code and designing scalable systems. Few resources explore what happens years into a project's lifecycle. A team should handle the incremental updates of core technologies, such as the JVM and database, in a structured and proactive manner. An architect should ensure the system remains adaptable without requiring constant refactoring. These challenges extend beyond writing good code; they involve ongoing maintenance, knowledge retention, and structured decision-making.

A long-term sustainable codebase is not just about choosing the best patterns or frameworks at the start; it is about ensuring the system remains easy to evolve without unnecessary friction. Beyond choosing the right abstractions, testing, and documentation play crucial roles in maintaining code quality over time.

A well-tested codebase provides confidence for future changes. Without tests, every modification becomes a gamble: Will this introduce regressions or compromise existing functionality? As a project grows, refactoring becomes unavoidable, and without tests, developers may hesitate to improve the system out of fear of introducing bugs. In long-term projects, tests serve as an evolutionary safeguard, ensuring that existing behavior remains intact while allowing for new capabilities to be introduced. Well-structured tests make it safer to refactor, optimize, and modernize different parts of the system without risking regressions.

However, not all tests are equally valuable. The biggest mistake teams make is writing tests that tightly couple themselves to implementation details rather than business behavior. Over time, such tests become a maintenance burden, breaking with every minor code refactoring, even when no functionality has changed. To ensure tests remain valuable over time, they should focus on validating critical business rules. Tests should minimize complex setups to improve maintainability and ensure fast, reliable execution, especially in CI/CD pipelines where consistency is essential.

In well-maintained projects, tests are not just about catching bugs; they enable the system to grow safely. Without them, fear-driven development takes over, where every change is delayed or rejected because the risks outweigh the benefits.

Documentation is often a common source of frustration among developers. It is often seen as an afterthought, a tedious task that takes time away from writing actual code. However, in long-term projects, documentation is one of a team's most valuable assets. Without proper documentation, every new team member must rely on word-of-mouth knowledge transfer, often leading to misunderstandings, lost historical context, and costly mistakes.

Code may explain how something is implemented, but it rarely captures why decisions are made. Over time, requirements change, and technical decisions that seemed logical at one point may no longer make sense. If documentation is missing, future developers will not see past trade-offs. They will likely spend hours or even days trying to reverse-engineer the reasoning behind certain implementations.

Unlike common belief, documentation does not mean explaining every line of code. Instead, adequate documentation should focus on the motivations behind architectural decisions, capture the project's historical evolution, and facilitate new developers' onboarding. When developers join the team, they should not have to reverse-engineer why a particular design pattern was chosen or why a seemingly redundant piece of logic exists.

Documentation is most effective when it is close to and evolves alongside the code. When treated as a separate task, it quickly becomes outdated and irrelevant. The best approach is to integrate documentation into the development workflow, ensuring that it is maintained organically rather than retroactively.

A practical documentation strategy includes:

- A README file, which acts as the project's entry point, summarizing its purpose, principal components, and how to get started.

- A CHANGELOG, which tracks modifications, clarifying what has changed, when, and why.

- C4 model diagrams, which provide a high-level view of the system's architecture and allow developers to quickly understand its structure without diving into the code.

By keeping documentation lightweight and directly tied to the codebase, teams can maintain clarity without excessive overhead. Instead of extensive text-heavy manuals, simple yet meaningful documentation allows future developers to quickly grasp the intent behind decisions rather than just their implementation.

Long-term code quality is not about achieving perfection but about ensuring sustainability. A successful system must remain adaptable, understandable, and scalable without unnecessary complexity. To achieve this, teams must balance simplicity with longevity and ensure that their choices do not create technical debt in the future.

A sustainable software system does not just survive over time; it adapts and thrives. Developers can build long-lasting and resilient applications by focusing on maintainability, avoiding unnecessary complexity, and embedding testing and documentation as core practices.

Long-term success in software is not just about writing great code today. It is about ensuring the code remains great tomorrow, next year, and beyond. With these principles in mind, you have the right toolset to ensure the code is not only functional but also sustainable.

Conclusion

Building a maintainable and scalable system requires more than just following good coding practices; it demands thoughtful design choices that align with DDD principles. From structuring a rich domain model to using fluent APIs for expressive and intuitive interfaces, ensuring robust exception handling, leveraging logging for observability, and maintaining long-term code quality, each aspect is critical in keeping a system resilient over time. Avoiding complexity bias and focusing on simplicity, testing, and meaningful documentation ensures that software remains adaptable, easy to evolve, and aligned with business needs.

We reflect on the broader lessons learned as we reach the final chapter. Designing software is about writing code and making decisions that impact long-term maintainability, developer experience, and business agility. In the next chapter, we will explore the final considerations, discussing the mindset required to apply these principles effectively and sustain a culture of well-crafted software in real-world projects.

Points to remember

- **Anemic models lead to scattered business logic**: They expose data without encapsulating behavior, making the system harder to maintain and increasing duplication.

- **Rich models encapsulate state and behavior**: They align with DDD principles by keeping domain logic close to the entities that own it.

- **Fluent APIs improve readability**: They enable method chaining and a natural flow of operations, making code more intuitive and self-explanatory.

- **Builder patterns help construct complex objects**: They provide a step-by-step approach for object creation while ensuring immutability and clarity.

- **Exception hierarchies improve traceability**: Structuring exceptions according to the domain helps in categorizing errors and simplifies debugging.

- **Secure exception handling prevents data leaks**: Logging detailed error messages internally while exposing generic messages externally protects sensitive information.

- **Logging is crucial for system observability**: Proper log levels help track issues, improve monitoring, and provide insights into system behavior.

- **Automated tests enable safe refactoring**: Well-structured tests validate business logic, ensuring the system remains reliable as it evolves.

- **Documentation preserves historical context**: Writing down motivations and architectural decisions helps new developers onboard quickly and prevents knowledge loss.

- **Simplicity ensures long-term maintainability**: Avoiding complexity bias and overengineering makes the codebase adaptable and easier to evolve.

Multiple choice questions

1. **What is the primary issue with an anemic model in DDD?**
   a. It encapsulates too much business logic, making the model inflexible
   b. It leads to scattered business logic across services, increasing maintenance complexity
   c. It forces all domain logic into the database, making it hard to scale
   d. It eliminates the need for repositories, simplifying data access
   e. It ensures better performance by keeping models lightweight

2. **How does a rich model differ from an anemic model?**
   a. A rich model exposes all its attributes through getters and setters
   b. A rich model delegates business logic to external services
   c. A rich model encapsulates state and behavior, reducing duplication
   d. A rich model avoids encapsulation to simplify data access
   e. A rich model is mainly used for logging and exception handling

3. **What is a key advantage of using a fluent API?**
   a. It eliminates the need for method chaining
   b. It reduces the need for domain logic encapsulation
   c. It makes APIs more readable and self-explanatory

  d. It enforces strict method ordering, reducing flexibility

  e. It is only useful for query-building frameworks like JOOQ

4. **How does the Builder pattern differ from a fluent API?**

  a. A Builder pattern enforces a strict method sequence, while fluent APIs do not

  b. A Builder pattern focuses on constructing complex objects, while fluent APIs provide a domain-specific interaction

  c. A fluent API is only used in enterprise applications, whereas the Builder pattern is not

  d. The Builder pattern avoids encapsulation, while fluent APIs enforce it

  e. Fluent APIs always use factories, whereas the Builder pattern does not

5. **Why is it important to structure exception hierarchies in long-term projects?**

  a. To keep exceptions generic and avoid unnecessary detail

  b. To ensure that all exceptions are caught in a single global handler

  c. To categorize errors meaningfully, making debugging and maintenance easier

  d. To prevent the need for logging errors, as structured exceptions provide all necessary information

  e. To make exceptions more difficult to understand, forcing developers to improve their debugging skills

6. **What is the best practice for handling exceptions in a secure manner?**

  a. Display detailed stack traces to users for better troubleshooting

  b. Log detailed error messages but expose only generic messages externally

  c. Always use checked exceptions to force explicit handling

  d. Avoid logging exceptions to prevent performance overhead

  e. Store exceptions in a database for long-term analysis instead of logging them

7. **Why is logging essential in long-term software projects?**

  a. It helps identify issues by providing visibility into system behavior

  b. It replaces the need for documentation, as logs contain all necessary details

  c. It slows down execution, ensuring better performance monitoring

  d. It should only be used in production environments, not during development

  e. It eliminates the need for debugging tools

8. **What is the primary role of automated tests in maintaining long-term code quality?**

  a. They eliminate the need for manual code reviews

  b. They prevent all runtime errors from occurring

    c.   They enable safe refactoring and evolution of the codebase

    d.   They replace documentation by describing system behavior in code

    e.   They are only useful in short-term projects, not long-term maintenance

9. **Why is documentation critical in a long-term software project?**

    a.   It replaces the need for testing by explaining expected behaviors

    b.   It ensures that developers never have to read the code to understand the system

    c.   It captures historical decisions and helps onboard new developers

    d.   It should focus solely on syntax explanations rather than business context

    e.   It is primarily useful for non-technical stakeholders rather than developers

10. **How can documentation remain useful and up to date?**

    a.   By writing extensive documentation manuals separate from the code

    b.   By using documentation-as-code practices, integrating README, changelogs, and architectural diagrams

    c.   By relying on word-of-mouth explanations instead of written documents

    d.   By only documenting major releases and ignoring smaller changes

    e.   By focusing only on API documentation and skipping business logic explanations

Answers

Question number	Answer option letter
1.	b.
2.	c.
3.	c.
4.	b.
5.	c.
6.	b.
7.	a.
8.	c.
9.	c.
10.	b.

References

1. *Martin, Robert C. (2019). Objects and Data Structures.* **https://blog.cleancoder.com/ uncle-bob/2019/06/16/ObjectsAndDataStructures.html**

CHAPTER 13

Final Considerations

Introduction

This final chapter summarizes key insights and looks ahead as we wrap up our exploration of **domain-driven design** (**DDD**) with Java. We will discuss *domain storytelling*, a technique that captures business processes through engaging conversations with domain experts. This approach helps us understand real needs and priorities, enabling us to develop effective software solutions.

Additionally, this chapter addresses key security considerations and practical recommendations, thereby complementing the DDD toolkit with essential guidance for developing well-structured, robust, and secure applications. The content presented herein is intended to support the continued professional development of software engineers, equipping them to apply DDD principles effectively in real-world scenarios.

Structure

In this chapter, we will explore more about the following topics:

- Introduction to domain storytelling
- Further reading and continued exploration

Technical requirements

For the last chapter, we can see some examples with domain storytelling, as follows:

- Java 21
- Git
- Maven
- Any preferred IDE

Objectives

This chapter aims to bridge the gap between theory and practice in DDD by demonstrating how to apply strategic and tactical DDD concepts using Java. Through the lens of domain storytelling, this chapter aims to show how to extract business knowledge, align with the Ubiquitous Language, define bounded contexts, and transition from strategic thinking to concrete implementations. By walking through domain modeling, repository design, and service orchestration, the goal is to equip you with practical tools to structure software that genuinely reflects the domain it serves, ensuring clarity and adaptability as business needs evolve.

Introduction to domain storytelling

In our exploration of DDD, we have emphasized that while tactics bring us close to the code, true mastery comes from understanding the strategic side of the domain. As developers advance to roles like Senior, Staff, and beyond, we realize that writing code is often the more straightforward part. The real challenge lies in understanding *why* we write the code and how it solves complex, real-world problems. It is easy to be drawn to tactical DDD, where we work directly with entities, aggregates, and code structures; however, ignoring strategic DDD can lead to costly misalignment with business objectives. Domain storytelling provides a solution to bridge this gap.

Storytelling has been central to human communication for millennia, enabling societies to share knowledge, history, and values before the advent of writing. Just as storytelling preserved the thoughts of *Socrates* and the myths of *Ancient Greece*, it also has the power to clarify complex business processes. In the book *Nexus: A Brief History of Information Networks from the Stone Age to AI*, historian *Yuval Noah Harari* describes how information networks began through oral stories, creating a shared understanding within communities. Domain storytelling applies this ancient tool to modern software design, leveraging storytelling to bridge the knowledge gap between domain experts and developers.

Domain storytelling is about capturing the essence of a domain by narrating the processes, roles, and tasks involved. By visually mapping these stories with domain experts, we create a shared understanding that clarifies goals, identifies key entities, and defines meaningful boundaries within the system. Through the lens of storytelling, domain experts can quickly confirm whether the development team grasps their story. This process minimizes misunderstandings, aligns perspectives, and paves the way for clearer, more effective software solutions.

Purpose and benefits of domain storytelling

Domain storytelling offers more than just a technique for requirement gathering; it is a versatile tool that enables us to:

- **Understand the domain**: Team members develop a shared understanding of the domain's core concepts and workflows by narrating and visualizing processes.

- **Establish a shared language**: It bridges communication gaps, fostering a common vocabulary between technical and non-technical participants.

- **Align stakeholders**: Domain storytelling aligns all participants: developers, product owners, and domain experts, ensuring everyone has a cohesive view of the goals.

- **Define domain boundaries**: This helps draw clear boundaries that organize the domain into cohesive parts, supporting team structure and software architecture.

- **Design realistic business processes**: The technique enables the design of software-supported processes that are viable and aligned with business realities.

- **Embed requirements into agile workflows**: Through storytelling, domain knowledge naturally translates into requirements that fit seamlessly within agile processes.

- **Optimize IT landscapes**: Domain storytelling reveals the interactions and dependencies in a domain, providing visibility into existing processes and aiding in consolidation and optimization.

In DDD, grasping the strategic context is essential, and domain storytelling is a powerful method to capture it effectively. This approach prioritizes translating complex business narratives into a shared understanding among technical and non-technical stakeholders rather than hastily diving into the code. While agile methodologies often lean on quick brainstorming, domain storytelling takes a structured and systematic approach that enhances clarity and collaboration. This section firmly establishes the advantages of domain storytelling, particularly when paired with tools like **Egon.io**, and decisively contrasts it with agile brainstorming in the framework of strategic DDD.

One of the primary benefits of domain storytelling is its ability to establish a reliable, version-controlled source of domain knowledge. Tools like **Egon.io**, for instance, facilitate domain storytelling sessions by enabling teams to visualize and structure domain narratives in real time, collaboratively. **Egon.io** is lightweight, requires no account or tracking, and works directly in the browser, allowing teams to export files in JSON format (**.egn** files). These exports can be stored and versioned in Git, aligning with GitOps practices and serving as a single source of truth. This approach is invaluable for teams working in fast-evolving domains, as it allows them to adapt to business changes while keeping a historical record of domain knowledge.

Differences between domain storytelling and agile brainstorming

Domain storytelling and agile brainstorming each have their strengths, and understanding when to use each can be pivotal for DDD practitioners. While agile brainstorming is often used to spark ideas and prioritize tasks quickly, domain storytelling is intended to explore the domain's intricacies more deliberately, identifying relationships, processes, and key entities that inform design decisions. The following table highlights the differences between domain storytelling and agile brainstorming:

Aspect	Domain storytelling	Agile brainstorming
Purpose	Deeply understand domain processes and relationships	Generate and prioritize ideas quickly
Approach	Narrative and visual mapping with domain experts	Free-form idea generation and discussion
Output	Structured stories and visual diagrams	List of prioritized ideas or tasks
Stakeholder involvement	Heavy involvement of domain experts, IT, and business stakeholders	Primarily, team members, possibly product owners
Focus	Detailing real-world workflows and interactions	High-level ideation with limited detail
Tooling	Tools like **Egon.io** for versioned, Git-compatible storytelling	Whiteboards, sticky notes, digital boards
Revision and versioning	Supports version control via JSON files (**.egn** format)	Typically lacks built-in version control
Agility in updates	Easy to update and version as the domain evolves	Harder to maintain or track over time
Use case fit	Best for extracting and documenting complex domain knowledge	Ideal for sprint planning, backlog refinement
Collaboration style	Collaborative storytelling with verification from domain experts	Fast-paced ideation within development teams

Table 13.1: Domain storytelling vs. agile brainstorming

Domain storytelling's structured approach offers the added advantage of creating persistent documentation that reflects the domain's real-world intricacies. With tools like **Egon.io**, development teams can iteratively update these narratives as the business grows and evolves.

Storing storytelling outputs as Git-compatible JSON files makes domain knowledge easily accessible and updatable, establishing a strong foundation for ongoing project alignment.

In contrast, agile brainstorming sessions are generally suited for short-term alignment within development sprints. They focus on immediate, high-priority ideas without needing to capture exhaustive details. This fast-paced method is great for prioritizing tasks or refining backlogs, but lacks the depth and long-term perspective that domain storytelling offers.

Exploring domain storytelling

Domain storytelling is, therefore, particularly valuable in strategic DDD, where aligning business processes with software design requires both detail and adaptability. Using domain storytelling alongside agile brainstorming allows teams to balance immediate tactical needs with long-term strategic clarity, ensuring that every project iteration aligns with the evolving domain.

The illustration from Egon brings domain storytelling to life, showing the collaborative process in action: a domain expert narrates the story, a developer captures it in a visual sequence, and the expert reviews and corrects it. This cyclical workflow highlights the importance of shared understanding in DDD. By following this structured storytelling approach, teams leverage the Ubiquitous Language and domain context, which makes translating these concepts into code natural. Refer to the following figure:

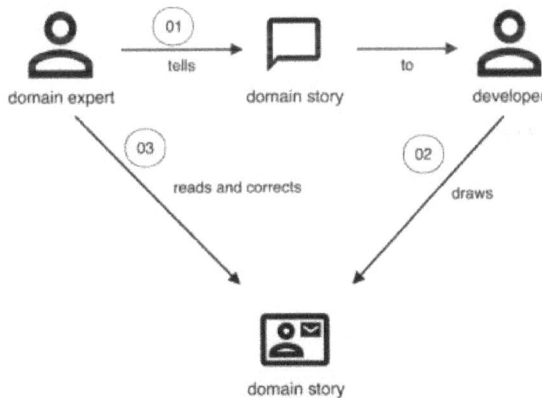

Figure 13.1: A first sample of domain storytelling using Egon

This figure of domain storytelling offers valuable insights into the Java entities needed to model such a process. Within this visual narrative, we can see several strategic DDD elements that underpin the story's structure and flow. For instance, context mapping becomes evident as each role and action is contextualized within the broader domain, establishing boundaries that help us understand where specific interactions begin and end. It helps define bounded contexts, distinct areas within the domain where concepts and behaviors have specific meanings. Additionally, Ubiquitous Language emerges naturally, as domain experts and developers consistently use shared terms and definitions to describe actions and entities. Through domain storytelling, we can observe how these strategic elements form a common understanding of the domain's structure, ensuring all stakeholders align on core concepts before diving into code.

On the tactical side of DDD, we can take this shared understanding and translate it directly into Java entities like **DomainStory**, **DomainExpert**, and **Developer**. Each entity represents the actors and stages shown in the Egon illustration, while repositories ensure the persistent storage and lifecycle management of these evolving stories. Services then act as intermediaries, managing interactions and updates as the domain story progresses through various stages such as *draft, reviewed,* and *approved*. Refer to the following code:

```
@Entity
public class Developer {

    @Identity
    private final UUID id;

    private final String name;

    @Association
    private List<DomainStory> domainStories;

    public Developer(UUID id, String name) {
        this.id = id;
        this.name = name;
    }
...
}

@Entity
public class DomainExpert {

    @Identity
    private final UUID id;

    private final String name;

    @Association
    private List<DomainStory> domainStories;
```

```
    public DomainExpert(UUID id, String name) {
        this.id = id;
        this.name = name;
    }
...
}

@AggregateRoot
public class DomainStory {

    @Identity
    private final UUID id;

    private final String title;

    private StoryStatus status;

    @Association
    private final DomainExpert domainExpert;

    @Association
    private final Developer developer;

    public DomainStory(UUID id, String title, DomainExpert domainExpert,
Developer developer) {
        this.id = id;
        this.title = title;
        this.status = StoryStatus.DRAFT;
        this.domainExpert = domainExpert;
        this.developer = developer;
    }

    public void setStatus(StoryStatus storyStatus) {
        this.status = storyStatus;
    }
    ...
}

@ValueObject
```

```
public enum StoryStatus {
    DRAFT,
    REVIEWED,
    APPROVED
}
```

The **DomainStoryRepository** plays a central role in maintaining this framework's lifecycle of domain stories. The repository supports the domain storytelling process shown in the illustration by defining methods for creating, retrieving, updating, and deleting **DomainStory** entities. The design of this repository ensures that access to domain stories remains abstracted from the technical specifics of storage, allowing developers to focus on managing the flow of domain stories rather than the complexities of persistence.

```
@Repository
public interface DomainStoryRepository {

    DomainStory save(DomainStory domainStory);

    Optional<DomainStory> findById(UUID id);

    List<DomainStory> findAll();

    void deleteById(UUID id);

    List<DomainStory> findByStatus(StoryStatus status);
}
```

The **DomainStoryService** acts as the intermediary between the repository and the rest of the application, orchestrating the lifecycle of **DomainStory** entities and validating business rules. It provides methods that facilitate interactions with domain stories, managing their transitions through various stages, such as *draft*, *reviewed*, and *approved*. This service layer also ensures that each action taken on a domain story aligns with the strategic goals captured in the storytelling process, preserving the Ubiquitous Language and maintaining consistency across the application. By encapsulating the logic for managing domain stories, **DomainStoryService** allows developers to focus on implementing the business's storytelling workflow without directly handling the intricacies of data persistence, as follows:

```
@Service
public class DomainStoryService {

    private final DomainStoryRepository domainStoryRepository;
```

```java
    public DomainStoryService(DomainStoryRepository domainStoryRepository) {
        this.domainStoryRepository = domainStoryRepository;
    }


    public DomainStory createDomainStory(DomainStory story) {
        story.setStatus(StoryStatus.DRAFT);
        return domainStoryRepository.save(story);
    }


    public DomainStory updateDomainStoryStatus(UUID storyId, StoryStatus
newStatus) {
        DomainStory story = domainStoryRepository.findById(storyId)
                .orElseThrow(() -> new RuntimeException("DomainStory not
found"));
        story.setStatus(newStatus);
        return domainStoryRepository.save(story);
    }
}
```

With the **DomainStoryRepository** and **DomainStoryService** in place, we have established the foundations for implementing domain storytelling within a Java-based DDD application. This setup aligns with strategic DDD principles like context mapping and Ubiquitous Language and supports tactical DDD by translating these concepts into entities, repositories, and services.

As we wrap up this book, this foundational knowledge of domain storytelling and its application in DDD positions you to further explore and master the art of strategic software design. Embracing these techniques allows you to extend DDD beyond coding tactics, ultimately fostering software that genuinely resonates with its domain.

Further reading and continued exploration

This book concludes with an invitation to reflect on the broader context of DDD and its application in Java-based systems. This work does not replace or diminish the value of established literature on the subject; rather, it complements it by offering a practical and implementation-focused perspective tailored for Java developers. As emphasized, particularly in the initial chapters, the content draws heavily from foundational works and respected references in the field. These sources remain essential, and readers are strongly encouraged to consult them for a more comprehensive and multidimensional understanding of DDD. A well-rounded software engineer builds upon the knowledge of others, an idea encapsulated in the principle of standing on the shoulders of giants.

Λ critical insight reiterated throughout this book is the importance of understanding what to build before considering how to build it. This remains one of the most persistent challenges in software development. While coding is an integral aspect of software engineering, the ability to align solutions with business objectives through strategic thinking is what separates proficient developers from impactful engineers. For this reason, the book emphasizes the rationale behind DDD and the role of strategic design before progressing to tactical implementations. Maintaining this mindset is essential for creating software that is not only functional but also meaningful, sustainable, and aligned with the real-world problems it seeks to solve.

Conclusion

In this final chapter, we examined the practical application of DDD through domain storytelling. We highlighted the significance of aligning the Ubiquitous Language, understanding context boundaries, and structuring the domain as foundational principles for creating clear and meaningful software.

By analyzing examples of repositories and services, we showed how strategic insight combined with tactical implementation allows developers to build systems that reflect business needs and adapt over time. This approach ensures that our code and architecture remain relevant as the business evolves.

We aimed to bridge the gap between theory and practice, making DDD accessible to Java developers with hands-on examples. Each section equipped you with practical tools for defining entities and repositories and managing services, all within a broader domain context. This toolkit prepares you to implement domain storytelling and DDD principles in your projects. Remember that DDD is a continuous learning process that will help you create adaptable applications in Java and beyond.

Points to remember

- **Understanding before coding**: The biggest mistake in software development is jumping into coding without fully understanding the problem. Strategic DDD helps mitigate this by focusing on the why before the how.

- **Domain storytelling as a bridge**: Domain storytelling connects domain experts and developers, ensuring that knowledge is accurately captured and transformed into software design.

- **Ubiquitous Language is key**: A shared vocabulary between business and development teams prevents misunderstandings and keeps the model aligned with real-world needs.

- **Bounded contexts define clear boundaries**: Each context has its own language and business logic, ensuring clarity and minimizing unnecessary complexity in large systems.

- **Repositories handle persistence, not business logic**: The Repository pattern abstracts data access, allowing business rules to remain in the domain layer.

- **Services orchestrate domain behavior**: Services manage domain workflows, ensuring that entities and value objects interact in a structured manner.

- **Adaptability is crucial**: DDD is an evolving process, domains change, and software must be designed to accommodate growth and transformation.

- **Learn from multiple sources**: No single book or reference can provide the full picture; continuing to explore different perspectives strengthens your understanding of DDD.

- **DDD is not just about code**: It is about building a deep understanding of the domain to create software that solves real business problems effectively.

References

1. *Nexus: A Brief History of Information Networks from the Stone Age to AI.*

Join our Discord space

Join our Discord workspace for latest updates, offers, tech happenings around the world, new releases, and sessions with the authors:

https://discord.bpbonline.com

Index

www.ingramcontent.com/pod-product-compliance
Lightning Source LLC
Chambersburg PA
CBHW061809210326
41599CB00034B/6939